Collected Poems Volume 3
(1992-96)

Other Bill Griffiths titles:

Poetry:

A Book of Spilt Cities (Etruscan Books, 1999)
The Ushabtis (Talus Books, 2001)
Durham & Other Sequences (West House Books, 2002)
The Mud Fort (Salt Publishing, 2004)
A Tour of the Fairground (Etruscan Books, 2007)
The Lion Man & Others (Veer Books, 2008)
Collected Earlier Poems (1966-80) (Reality Street, 2010)
Collected Poems & Sequences (1981-91) (Reality Street, 2014)

Edited/compiled by Bill Griffiths:

A Dictionary of North East Dialect
    (Northumbria University Press, 2005)
Pitmatic: The Talk of the North East Coalfield
    (Northumbria University Press, 2007)
Stotty'n'Spice Cake: The Story of North East Cooking
    (Northumbria University Press, 2007)

About Bill Griffiths:

The Salt Companion to Bill Griffiths (Salt Publishing, 2007)
Journal of British and Irish Innovative Poetry 6.1:
    Bill Griffiths Special Issue (Gylphi, 2014)

Collected Poems
Volume 3
(1992-96)

Bill Griffiths

Edited by Alan Halsey

REALITY STREET

Published by
REALITY STREET
63 All Saints Street, Hastings, East Sussex TN34 3BN
www.realitystreet.co.uk

First edition 2016
All rights remain with the estate of Bill Griffiths
Additional material copyright © Alan Halsey, 2016
Typesetting & book design by Ken Edwards
Cover image: *Sedulous*, hand-coloured drawing by Bill Griffiths

A catalogue record for this book is available from the British Library

ISBN: 978-1-874400-71-4

Preface

Although this third volume of Bill Griffiths' collected poems only extends from 1992 to 1996 it presents a period of his work which even by his own standards was remarkably prolific. Settled in Seaham, County Durham, and granted some modest funding for his new Amra imprint, he produced during these five years twenty-four poetry pamphlets, mostly of recent composition. Alongside the poems appeared thirty other pamphlets including two performance texts in collaboration with Clive Fencott, editions of the North East poets Alexander Barrass and Edward Chicken and of the Newcastle Mystery Play *Noah's Ark*, essays on local history, government and sociopolitical philosophy, Anglo-Saxon studies, dialect readers and word-lists. The latter were the seeds of the work which would culminate in his major studies *Dictionary of North East English, A Dictionary of North East Dialect, Stotty'n'Spice Cake* and *Pitmatic: The Talk of the North East Coalfield*, all published by Northumbria University Press.

In some respects the appearance of North East dialect and 'folk' verse forms such as ballads in Griffiths' poetry of the 1990s will seem the most significant departure from his earlier work. The surprise, perhaps, is partly that a southron should so wholeheartedly embrace the North East as in the fullest possible sense his home and be accepted as a local with reciprocal affection. But once that fact is understood the adoption of dialect follows in Griffiths' case quite naturally: he had been in a possibly uncommon sense a 'dialect poet' from the start. The sheer verve of *Cycles* derives in great part from his use of, and ear for, an irregular form of English heard only in the street diction of his native London. It seems entirely arbitrary that the word 'dialect' should be applied only and pejoratively to non-metropolitan usage, and inevitable that a poet with such an acute awareness of speech patterns should adopt the usage of his newfound homeland. We hear in all his writing the living language of, as he said, 'the world about'.

We also find in the work of this period a return to themes such as biker culture and more especially prisons and imprisonment, a feature of Griffiths' earliest poetry but less evident during the 1980s. His own experience of prison was slight – by reliable account a few hours – but his ability to inhabit the experience of others, particularly society's outcasts, to reframe their fractured narratives in the first person, always alert to the variables of vocabulary and vernacular, lends his prison writings an entirely convincing authority and authenticity. Nevertheless we see a shift in perspective in these later poems: whereas in *Cycle Three: H.M. Prison Brixton*, for example, the speaker or persona is unidentified and thus easily mistaken for the poet himself we find in a poem such as *Star Fish Jail* a clear distinction between the prisoner Delvan MacIntosh and Griffiths as empathetic audience and transcriber. Griffiths states in fact that this poem is 'a two-author work' although its style, tone and organisation are unmistakeably his own. As is the underlying argument: for Griffiths prisons give the ultimate lie to the dominant rhetoric of 'democracy'; they are the places from which democracy is withheld and thus emblematic of a more widespread and insidious disenfranchisement and dispossession. If Griffiths fails to address the issue of criminality itself we may reflect that the legal profession is guilty of the same avoidance. In the twenty years since these poems were written politicians, often lawyers by trade, have identified ever-broadening categories of illegality, creating a huge but only grudgingly acknowledged increase in the prison population which is perhaps proportional to the increase in citizens oppressed and impoverished by measures masquerading as 'austerity'. Meanwhile allegations of police corruption, racism and brutality, anecdotal in so many Griffiths poems, have been substantiated even by the formerly complicit Westminster establishment and a compliant mass media. That Griffiths looks beyond the incidental facts to their sociopolitical and philosophical roots and implications has been the subject of recent studies by William Rowe and Ian Davidson.

The structure of the present volume follows that of its immediate predecessor with the majority of the poems arranged as they appeared in successive pamphlets; previously uncollected or unpublished poems are gathered chronologically in the final section. All but a few of the original pamphlets carried the Amra imprint and were issued in editions with usually unspecified but certainly limited print-runs – probably less than 100 in most cases. The single-poem Amra pamphlets of 1996 have been collected together. Griffiths' digital files show that the poems in *The Cuddy Anthem* were selected from a considerably larger series of dialect poems, many unpublished and here restored. The poems 'The Alien', 'Work World' and 'Pharmacopoeia' were originally published separately but appear in the files as a three-part sequence under the general title *The Alien* and this too has been respected.

The three Reality Street volumes now cover the period 1966-96, thirty years and over 1200 pages of Griffiths' poems which had previously been dispersed and to a large extent unavailable or excerpted in retrospective collections. The majority appeared in fugitive booklets and magazines which rarely show up in booksellers' catalogues. Griffiths' publishing fortunes improved in 1996 when Invisible Books issued *Rousseau and the Wicked* in a substantial edition. From that point on, beginning with *Nomad Sense* in 1998, his collections appeared in commercial or semi-commercial paperbacks from Talus Editions, Etruscan Books, West House Books, Salt Publishing and Veer Books. These are either still in print or easily located. Reality Street's editor Ken Edwards and I have therefore decided to bring this series to a halt – temporarily, at least, since it seems certain that in another decade a further volume or two will be needed and another enterprising publisher and a sprightlier editor will take up the baton. In the files Griffiths left at his death there are late uncollected and some otherwise unrecorded poems which may be published in the interim. Several contributors to the 2014 special issue of the *Journal of British and Irish Innovative Poetry* reflect on the need for a comprehensive edition of his prose. In our gathering of the poems and sequences we have offered just a few pertinent examples of his visual work. We have also only included those translations which have seemed transformations into 'original poems' or are embedded in longer pieces; these do not by any means represent the full range of Griffiths' translations – there are many more, of considerable diversity, the most significant extending the notion of 'translation' beyond conventional bounds.

Once more we thank Joanne Harman for her permission to publish this volume. In the preceding books I have thanked all those who have assisted me with difficult editorial decisions and tracked down elusive poems on my behalf. My thanks to them again but with particular mention for the help and support throughout this endeavour of Geraldine Monk, Michael Mann and Steve Clews.

Alan Halsey
Nether Edge, June 2015

Contents

Calendar Contents 13
    Elements, 15
    Rain-Time, 16
    Rain-Time (2), 17
    Valentine's Day, 17
    Work-Song, 17
    Moon-Time, 18
    St Cecilia's Day, 19
    Moon-Time (2), 19
    On St Benet's Day, 21
    All Saints: MFV Golden Arrow, 21
    Carol, 22
    Work-Song (2), 23
    Night-Rings, 24
    St Valentine's Day (2), 24
    Sunday, 25
    Palm Sunday, 26
    Quotidians, 27
    Maxims for St Swithin's Day, 28
    Palm Sunday (2), 29
    Sandwiches, 29

The Great North Forest 31

Mid North Sea High 49

Quotidiana 67
    On the Sun, 69
    Kurt in Context, 70
    [Untitled] 'Chucking the / carpet in the tip', 71
    [Untitled] 'Shit! / A pub-full of myrmidons', 72
    [Untitled] 'Quiz-miss', 72
    [Untitled] 'House-breakers …', 73
    [Untitled] 'Sanger the showman worked like this', 74
    The Haswell Change-Over, 75
    Starting Up With Doves, 79
    [Untitled] 'What does the Gym do?', 82
    [Untitled] 'It's Sylvester's Day', 83

Review of Brian Greenaway & Notes from Delvan MacIntosh......85

Scaffold Hill..105

Dialect Poems *incorporating*
The Cuddy Anthem: a mini dialect anthology.................................121
   'Nows in the g'eat hwelve', 123
   'It'z a puzzle OK', 123
   'If yi dinna pay yor poll-tax ower', 124
   The Emergency, 125
   'We are upaheet, upaheet, upaheet', 127
   'There sartenly is some canny mysteries', 128
   'Looksthanaw', 130
   'Ye can keep Pensher', 132
   'Lookanaw! Aa dreamt this g'eat mammy-church', 133
   The Tilcon Quarry, 134
   The Parlous Chyase (after Lewis Carroll), 137
   Jetty Song, 138
   On the Tyne, 139
   The Coggly, 140
   In the Neet, 141
   'Did 'oo heer that hinney?', 142
   On Vane Tempest Provisionally Shut, 23 October,
   in the Afternoon, 1992, 144

Delvan's Book 149
   Account, 151
   Reverie, 152
   Terzetto, 153
   Delvan in the SW London Magistrates Court, 153
   Wandsworth, 156
   Letter (1), 157
   Letter (2), 158
   Conan in Trouble, 159
   Medical Report, 160
   Hanuman, 161

Satires 167
   Winchester, 169
   On TV, 173
   The Tories, 174

    On Christianity, 176
    Alphabet of Tories, 183
    Paladin Try To Get Payment To Me Split Into Two Cheques, 188
    Settling Accounts, 189

Star Fish Jail 190

Liam's Song 211

The Secret Commonwealth 221

The Alien 230

The Coal World: Murton Tales Reworked as Dialect Verse 263
    The Trapper Boy Starts Work, 265
    Tom, 266
    The Move, 267
    The Box-Eggs, 268
    Hoo the Rabbits Wor Horribly Thret, 270
    The Strike, 272

The Lion Man or Four Poems in One 275

Amra Pamphlets 1996 305
    On the Abuse of Drugs, 307
    The Genesis of Iron, 311
    Histories, 313
    Hungary, 316
    The Labyrinth, 320
    On the Platform at Stockton, 322

Baldur's Lacrimosa 325

Rousseau and the Wicked 341

Other Poems 387
    On the Bridge, 389
    Marquisisms, 390
    Notes, 390
    Picture, 392

The Ace & Other Scenes, 393
Harley, 396
More Bike (Perpetual Motion), 397
Work, 398
In Rufinum (after Claudian), 399
At the Nevsky Promenade, 405
Verses in Awe, 405
Sextet, 408
Quest, 410
Alliterations, 411
Vampire, 412
Name, 412
Rat to Boat-Master, 413
Spare Stanzas, 415
Retraction, 416
'Petimusque Damusque', 417
Poem ('Lazarus'), 418
Found Potato Poem, 419
Poem ('The force that thru …'), 419
'Dragons', 420
Gang Poem, 427
Introduction to a Library, 435
Poem ('this / is work to'), 435
Contribution to Kelvin's Project, 437
The City of Egypt, 437
Perpetuum Mobile, 441
The Owl, 442
Starting the Fight, 445
In Church, 447
New Year, 448
On Show, 451
Wimbledon Court, 452
Fish, 454
Jingle, 454
Claudian on Transport, 455
The Hog, 456
The Borrowers Aloft, 457
Birds & Wind, 458
On the Beach, 460
Detective Notes, 461

Anti-Sound Poems, 463
How Highpoint is Better than Wandsworth, 465
The Best Jigsaw, 472
Two Poems for Bob Cobbing in One Style, 475
Reveries, 478
Umbro, 489
Quad, 491
The Fire, 494
Paul's Survival Tips, 495
Media Studies, 498
Musical Note, 499
Ride
Thirteen Thoughts as though Woken in Caravan Town …, 501
[Untitled] 'In the brick middle ovens', 508
The Durham Coal-Field, 509

Notes 511

Index of Titles 519

Calendar Contents

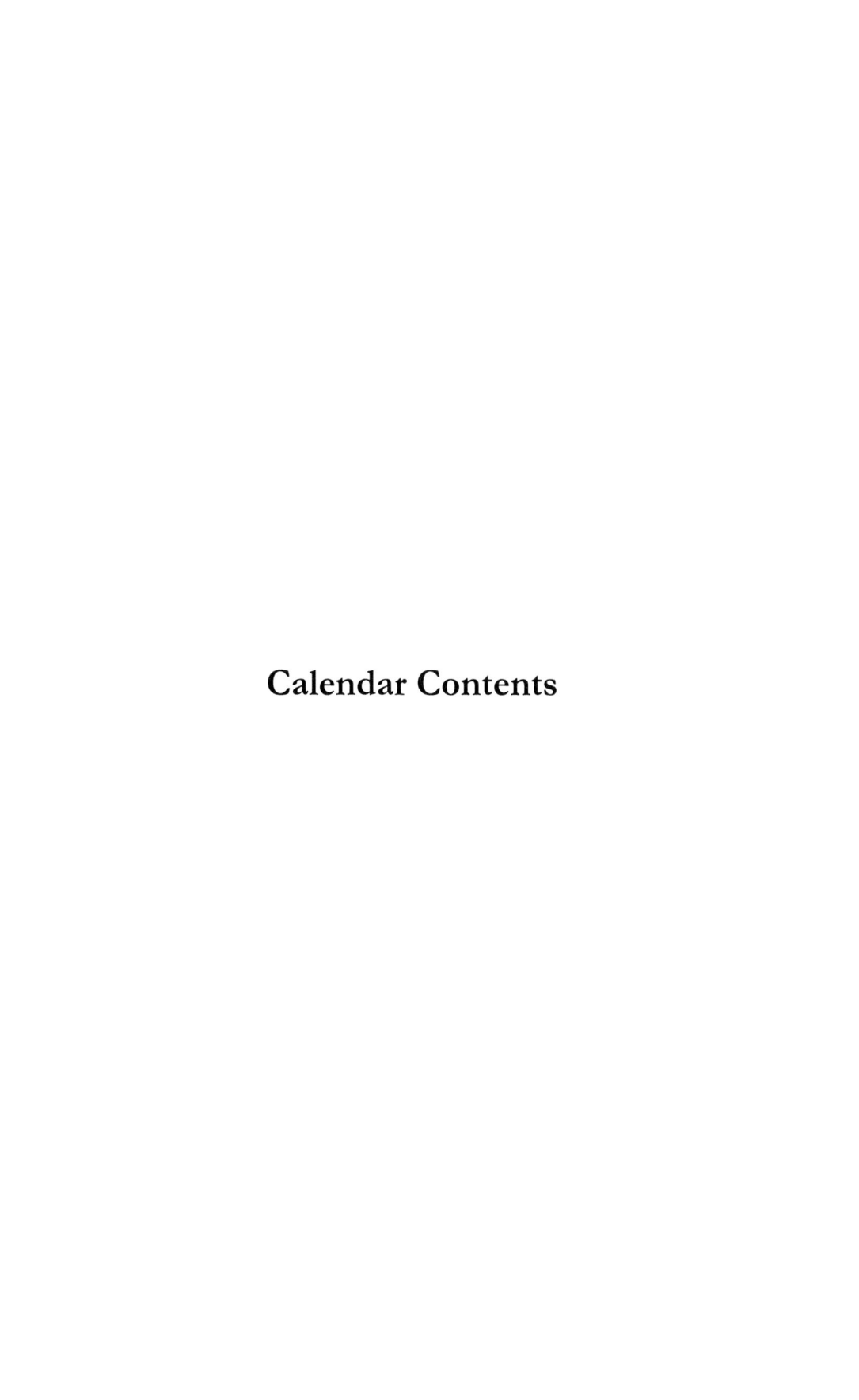

Elements

elemental night.
screw-fire of flower licks into show
and blue, under-bright,
plays shapes w/ things, runs its salt-lick
over the humps, the un-words,
the half-things.
Matter to ghost-marvels.

Untie.
Mispivot.
Heelless, the sailor.
The scamp sea.
He looks into, looks and looks,
and there is never ground / end / bottom.
But indi-curls (slick/thick/brisk)
end-over-hull –
intuplification – opaque –
quisslitude – metábasis – fathomless fun.

Mitra,
will-wind,
rest-lacking
marvel-mix, the one force
to cut a hill, temple-out the cave-top,
tree-cripple, dwarfer, dwindler,
candle-carved ridge AND
makes all to sing in wind WIRES
playing thrumming tuba-choir PILE.

loose-stones, loess,
pitted shingle, grit, the fraying
earth.
The journey, moving
sighing, platitude of a ground,
its sands, lime-lays, clays, pages-shale, flint-balls, little attritted of
    granites, shine & wash,
wetting away.

What's solid floats.

Fire.
Fire & day.
Felicity.
More, more warmth,
no never-to-it false / false passions,
prides in causes, mind-dew
slippers off oh of the Sun
to monkey-gong,
all thesis
to a miss.

Nor harmony nor un-hope.
Heroes of carbon!
It is not possible.

Rain-Time

Outside of the doors of the house
itoz raining
harbouring
People-who-find-life-interesting:
Suspects of
people-who-find-life-uninteresting
and
The brave dan·ly-seed
landed
on the pool-fil·n

Rain-Time (2)

Waiting for a space in the rain
'For the bus can be terribly prompt'
Myself, a robin, six doves, a neighbour kestrel, and the oak-trees.

The rehearsal of doves is exact: it is a knack.
I hear milkers, a crow, low thunder & the rumble of ancient weather,
Egged on by a hammer.

Valentine's Day

Words, I bet you, are alive
Are the body itself.
A heaving acid-work, kangaroo-ferment,
racing strainily to the –
settling gently in the –
cupping, a warmth, round them
(selves) heart
and LIIVE
and a second sight.

Work-Song

So it is:
sharp flowers, boulder-coloured,
bright, practise the pins, it
is this fit.

The sudden clamp of steel,
chewn rubber, start;
what engine moves
makes sounds for/to me.

jars limb and limb
slides fibre
as sponge/apricot
make a melt.

The tune is long enough.

Moon-Time

The halo
up (agate!) and around
the moon
harbingers GHOSTS

things of long tuck
and weazle-wing

chain us
like railings as grave-rivets

the humble bunsen-in-a-fog
shakes gleam,
goes

and each asseveration of the day
along of it
filtered (out)

the dust-steel core
maybe corrodes, then, completely
at its out-of-context (nox)

no magical man

no mysterious woman

nothing but incapacity –
bald lightless zones
we cannot go about

the sworded self rebels
boils

large lemons load

St Cecilia's Day

Mr Noah comes out
stirred at the bracing weather;
Mrs Noah, indoors,
has delicately-expressed, confessional emotions
formless thoughts.

Mrs Noah comes out,
the weather is calm, pastel, interesting background / plain
foreground.
Indoors, Mr Noah
has imposed penalties, assessments,
invented and advanced.
And I cannot decide –
do I like Catholic music
or Protestant?

Moon-Time (2)

désespoir
a large coin
a caesar of a shilling

line-looking and fine
and no solace!

and the Easter Orb
packed with fractals –
what is our egg then?
where to look for it?

there are teams hunting,
hoop-socks, boots,
the football.
Mostly, the goalie has it.
(He bounces it, thinks,
sends it up-field, but
back it comes.)

There are astrolabes
with every line a meaning,
though imaginary all,
(notional) these circuits.

Moon's one,
round is / goes round
(round our round)

all shapes
soundless / DUMB

lion's tooth (look!) all
audience-rows of yellow-tags
dandelion
the pretty-pattern-er
the song-less-er I think.

I deduce nothing.
I am dumb. I despair.

On St Benet's Day

On St Benet's day,
Paul, & his dusky mate
& the kid with his foot walled up
(who jumped down a bank to his rod & missed)
come back pissed
& Paul we was hunting in the garden
when the dark guy circled wide, run him' head into the pond.
Can you manage I sez or would you like a push?
I think when I caught up with Paul, there was a fight,
but it doesn't matter.
We imitated foxes instead,
to amuse the dog.

All Saints: MFV Golden Arrow

Lightly how light thru the came fragile planks
Bands white of lemon of light of strength seams
Showing against strip(e)s flats of larch bold dark and
Shell or curvy skull inside a surface the dome of
all-split and the water when at bow flung it' up a'quiver
and this reach round whole working bowl crazy lurched
leapt dimensions in wild rocking altogether shook
it was everyway vibrant the big water with the tow
well there was in it a null silent space beam-lit
where we fought in that with pump an ejector till
the filling fort of levelled failed into shelter it came
sun-eye water on the inside/outside equally played
columns, bone-arch, wall, spray, dip, crest, all
then in the creek it shut, tide settled, toppled onto
out deck was the on slant all wrong high down.
when wheelhouse side a projection from deck canvas-and
face into mud then the sail joy toy-like stood stopped
trouser sailors perched and asked if this was for more it?

Carol

The three dark-boned strangers
the gipsy at the castle gate
the rigid body in the manger
and the lady's cold ground
non
nix'st
ast
rex

Enter to the oven/workhall,
the crash of fruit
the warm arch
the journey to the mouth
non
rex'st
ast
nix

the dignity idea
scent and aura reach
where will she lie?
they will meet
non
nix'st
ast
rex

the lost king
his life on wood
running in rags
and round and round in the track
non
rex'st
ast
nix

Work-Song (2)

cool apple air girl arm
sweet sets off morning
light abrades mist; oaks, up.

rough heat of work time making
doing that seems circles
round-dance or

presence, proximity,
grace, touch,
the glassy beads of love-laughter

scented dark friends (as night is)
((its humming, soft-winged inhabitants))
(((safe to ever live of in)))

the love of a place
is its voices / tone / accent / curve
horses' necks of sounds

the carmine-garnet, the confidence,
the light from in that acts as a life
and gate of glory

a deed, a run,
a rattle of metal on,
a gleam of opened importance

if it is the vast mirror
every being sees in, is seen,
acts to, coldly opaque

rather: the silk on the shoulder,
the arrow

Night-Rings

see! in the stick runs FOX flies in the brush-bush, see!

free! swimming stirring STARS striking staring: free!

locks: the hand closes the DOOR completes the cell: locks.

trust: that banks on TIME that turns on: trust

illness: blacks, dopes, coils the SOUL suffers, shows: illness

night: playing they mount them', KNOBBLY-FROGS, song-mad, all night.

St Valentine' Day (2)

Does each word
want
to be true? want to
be more like itself?
refine (and shine)?

And sound more large
more like
its own idea (its fact)?
Oh –
its genesis!

and be more beautiful,
big/useful
wholly lovable and
trim?

more accurate of tonic stress,
rhythmically variant
and over all assonant?

more suitable itself,
and
ina sound-syntax,
be placed
in its own galaxy
to our infinite amazement
and edification –

does it?

Sunday

listen to the notes
that spill/spin out
as the sun turns.
And the musician
lives on hearts,
Red into Yellow.
Yes, it is true.
Whether you live,
eat plants,
or simply watch tides,
you feed the sun.
The gritty, texted weetabix,
and the colour-folded clover,
the smooth-brown skin,
the round and back weather,
the lovely art-spiral.
Benign and celebrated,
harsh and appeased,
unreliable / encouraged,
so many faces as it turns.
As the disrupter of cold,
it is the one creative summary.
It is a loaf, and mammal; and an opera,
and lasts for hours and hours.

Palm Sunday

lay in the hand
the tulip cup
sovereign and race-winner

hand-curl
the sea in the hair
and the bow in the rain

a pointing hand
ear-perked
upright and formal and informing

the balled fist
rolling rock
socking on four nodes

the palm
tree- and phoenix-thing
fire-scent

touch and finger-tip
dull murder to be apart
a science shows in whorled pads

a cut, so, with the side of the hand
a division
sudden, contested football-work

a ridge of knuckles
glacier-less bone
pulled white, a show of the serious

up-thumb
greet-language
all rights and laws

tickle!

obtrude!
impress!

splayed
pain dissipates
drunken-still.

to jab,
caput draconis
antichristus

to drum
spider-patter
in baby-time

flat,
ferocious
to wild / honest

a circle
wavy'd frond
fond leaves, in a-dew.

Quotidians

Cadmus?
The red guy
dragoning a dragon

Taut?
Dive it!
Angle it!
Get it right!
(Shit –
to share a life)

Not
at that price

Backside to
the golden honey-blue sky

This watch?
'has posts, jewels
wheels whirr like helicopters
I'll show her

Dog
by the movie stone

That Angel –
the more he talks solidarity and that
the more he thinks treachery

New one?
Then you pay for it.

Nuh.
One bite.
'Stoo rich.

Ribs bend
rub out the frost

Hurt?
Yeah … well …

Maxims for St Swithin's Day

One opal: many dimples
One peach: many hairs
One lens: many fountains

One tree: many tetraliths
One word: many masters
One team: many rainfalls
One torch: many youngwomen
One spring: many filaments
One house: many gooseberries
One tassel: many whalebones
One hip: many woodentops

Palm Sunday (2)

passed.

being nowhere,
coming / going no real way
with no driver

a gush of wind

trees are built to live in the wind
& let themselves die with its help, too.
They are wind architecture.
And there are bird-balls played with there,
mere ornamental notions.

Sandwiches

In a box of marbles
are the rests & layers, touches of the glass baubles.
The monarch
portrayed with zone-sequins
everywhere on the dress.
Magnified, the blood globules, in addition,
are seen to jostle.

And the sand-scouring
is seen to be something aggressive,
abrasive.
A brutal neon lineament –
letters turning on their head.
A box of words
waiting to have their ends joined.

Clover, crystal, sugar, pease,
weave-work, stanzas, leaf-brax, trees.
Each pattern visible,
current, countable,
but nothing a template
for what
will choose to come next.

This is the brass-fork-sound-taste
that is the end
the spark
fire
sun
a Chinvad conflagration
each speck-energy.

The Great North Forest

Why, when I wend to the woods,
first reaction, is, oh boy,
(solemn, plant-ridden, dench-land) mine – laughter,
like love of every heavy, slow langorous living force
to its tricky tip,
its grand coffee-concrete root-piles,
whip and athlete arm-puppets,
ever-ending light-up green, its
jubilation!

Here the modal-chords never faded,
ebony furniture undulled was-is,
grow-vast sailing-ships stay masted,
all ornaments glow.

Into the twig-way
a shopping-busy branch of nooks and pumicepaths and puzzles,
and forest-tunnels,
gas-pipe rough,
low/glint-lit
with toothed lions
and some, gritty bird-eyes –
engrosses. Lacks?
In our caucasian redwoods
slick-hair and bouncing moccasin
(but serious feet)
dance not never, woe, no.

The first shake of the snowdrop
the modest advance to the spring sales the bold
formation crocuses
the rustling of the tax-man's paper
the look-around of the first poppies
the shake-up and baby beetroot dance
the waltz of the yachts – what is this all but prelude
to a great BACCHANALE?

Slender, sleepy ferns
mix and dement,
motion-magic.

There, mirabile dictu, the mushroom ...

trees that are built to live in the wind & let
themselves die with its help, too. Wind
architecture.
And there are bird-balls played with there, mere
ornamental notions.

Arm in arm,
the mill (rack-stave) and glade,
the summary of sun in the water-track and cyclation

Whose love is a leopard?
Whose eye is an elm?
Who shakes the windy fluke,
the floor-whale, the flying
carriages of the air, limousine and
sky? Who doubts
the Destabilisation of the East?

*

The cliff and claft
of board / body:
your one elastic life.

This is her hair
her torrent,
my palm,
patience,
waiting for that the racing starts.

In the horse,
in her close-crop coat and armour,
in the knight
steaming, chinking
we are ready for any magic.

The Russian bear

hooking his black sox up,
the New World's eagle
beaking into live blood,
and they co-rub the little saints of the war.
(But it's lucky,
cats don't have horns, init?)

These the heroes in the heat,
leaping for water;
These, aqua-bringers,
smile her warm canteen-clouds.
Leap and smile, leap and smile and smile.

Quite light,
lippy old radio speak;
junk yard dog
rubs, rats,
Alps-piles.

The mirage
the heat of itz black roots.

*

Entranced,
the wooden vogel-voice,
the belimiter,
and prophet
(chubby hand-line to read)
clicks
in the bricky, crackly privet.

Orb-frazzle / oat-heap /
jewel-like
cats and cuts;
lane-parliament and along

scent and soul
rise warm

lapiz for love
and frankincense as end-eat

goat-cat, wolf-squid
jagget and jangle;
by the verge,
joke and point-piss,
inimical to turn it,
environment.

learner and whip-prince
academy, prod-planner
unact
all the way to jericho

Trespass not
on the frigid wicket;
disclaim idea;
revoke the friend.

and there are
palace-spaces,
wide arcs of park,
shopping-squares,
their own mazes,
all me see sighless
as the prairie

or neuter
or dead-end;
people pressing into the leaves, wobbly.

sap / cream road,
draws,
makes specie-grip
and boat-blink

all the planets
light it,
endle'-trounce enigma

(unpotted shapes and charismas)

till it tires,
is home,
is how,
huge show
and margin-bound too,
quits dizziness

and becomes
some bundle of leaves.

*

ptink, ebbibi-tink
wood-tree, grove-leaf,
hear it as slang-song,
under the twisting, spiking sun-wedged
descents, down-lights
glory and aura and strange strong-tune.

Since there is a god in each caterpillar,
president in each moronic cloud of mould,
why should I shut out
the symphony?

webs
that web the leaf-tip and terror-bug,
white-fox-petal and night-tube,
these, their singing,
surely shows an even hand
in the tipsy words,
the no-tsar of it all.

Who triumphs in a lie?
Why, the sound-stopping princes,
stab-earwigs,
the stinking bark and lime-slur,

but we sleeve without thread,

team up without association-rules,
and the King of Terrors
not hide in us
torn cat or storm
simply never be

mine a
ptink, ebbibi-tink,
wood-tree, grove-leaf,
hear it as unpsalm, us-balm.

the body is no advert, no lie
but arm in its skin
shakes, warms, feels with heat,
eye tremorates at the wind
leg / mouth feeds with fun
in its assembly

douce
chest and breast
toe and tip
merge
air and nasal
pass (sided fish)
and change

all the serene
mood, the orchestral
muscle
stripes / lines
the bars / lines / frame

to be two,
to branch,
to seg' and multiplate,
to diviserate,
to mill, to ecolonise,
reduplicate,
bodies to forest out,
fill, explore,

imagine all and whole

glowing coincidence

growing,
and abide
and direct

*

great cusps of bronze-glow chocolate are to greet my
eyes, Christmas hero,
and the magenta light, mid-mild, strung in rays, chrome-
orbs, dabs
the solemn drumming-green house-tree
(inner, holy rites)
each festive branch-pit

solemn ribs, tribe vaults
sprung after scarab-light,
high lime sconces – all,
how can it still be accidental?
(twiddle-tunes)

the threat-scent
and new earth.
Milling, my people's palace
of fight / fun,
trees' tent and dream-blue gain,
a clearing – idle vegetables (some)
then a crowd again.

*

How can you beat the forest
but it's a loss?

Strands from the cherry
inform even the
slowest heart.

This lute-nosed cream-ply blossom
'clining to yellow to pollen
big, scenic with scent

A gentle energy
to play
move
sea-eyed
mine, arm-to-face-arm-to-push
aqua-level

The gentle body,
the warm,
how it knows (moves)
learns (acts)
grows (stirs);
every word dances,
every look thinks,
step touches.
Joy is for blood,
the gentle reproaches unnoticeable, every
shape, whole,
its high tokens harmless,
scented, wet, like arms,
for all its tired dangers / or worn anger, and the
talking head
gesturing
yellow words
white prophecies –
a singing cure!

To join bodies
focussed blossom,
a little moist,
ar-aromatic,
orange-earth,
plum-sweet,
soft-backed,
secretly electric

Then in the belt-lift, pull-up, tuck,
play again at double-skin,
the day-white aardvark-being let at large,
walketh jean-blue in the brick-sleight.

The surly slice of mammal
masters the wall,
tip-pods by the apple-petals,
all-rhyming with pink blossom.
stubs with its whiskers
at the empty gleam-gland can
and rubs,
scrubs its boot-brush back.
Teethy & sneaky,
the fox has come for its gloves.

In the phantom water,
in the clear of skate,
loving corals talk to the orange bubbles. Hands of crab
   and guillemot
reach the blue and the light and the slain. Sail-shape
   carbuoys of flit-ice
mark off the sun from the pheasant-fish, and all the
   toppling sand-rice
flukes to and fro for the plastic keel.

This is my blue packet and my mauve heart. Gristly, zig-
   zag sacks of once-read things block
the autumn bright-bile.
Vain, vanguard and poppy-smudge
soften the glass-web,
make paint the roller-tumbler. Candy-tubs, coin-atom-
   edge,
are her propane-zest,
as we whistle in the white-click
of lightning-shower.

Little bird-word.
Prank.
The singer stub-rat patrol

has walked the virgin knife-edge out, and collide.
The hoity land
of garnet-lamp and dust-door, shoulder, silver-
snail,
lick the out-waves
at the sore room.
Distance is the goat-clock of the fighter, is the fun.

*

Consider
some safe forest,
and all that happens
(if you quit city)
is to get lost …
(Lost Girl!)

The blue poles, the potato-scent,
the city, drumming round/round
shoelaces mine,
rule to stop –
the whirl –
on the glass wall, eyes, look,
it's sale-time, hands sort.

And nearer the close,
settles in the tin (the rim)
the cold soot,
town-circle,
how afar
colliers bark / dogs hoot / mines shout.

And in (carnival!)
through the meticulous wheat,
a-riding, kings,
bend shoulder, arch arm, horse-curve leg, flight of
man-ribbon,
gold, mauve, millefleur glitter
(grey cloth road).

Sometimes endless sky-beaches
and white countries and happy,
and a golden bowl above me
shakes its jacobs-coats as morning reaches. And neither
the glory that has gone,
your great courage,
or tremendous learning
will save you.

Disperse with death,
release with temple's fall, slow,
damn to –
no safe sinking land,
nothing
scent-centre.

But spring mysteries,
ice-lilith, tear-tip, and   [=teer
softens and
swells and oscillates, slender roads and round
deep-jaune crowns
(life-live glove-love lift)   [=livv
(Nature, too,
flares/opens,
is most colourful, relating)

The war-saraband
shells the page,
the white will is filled,
draws a line.

Lucifer, quit us.

*

Imagine a labyrinth –
how large?
how much twisty?
it is not clear,
nor if it has a centre,

or an exit, circuit or what.
Only that you have been entered.

Some tune of proud horses
or harlequins and nightlights?

I follow
I follow

soft matrix chords
accompany
– this larger world

sax-ringing

blind-echo

trust in

yearn in

but
No more adventures
(you have boxed the set)

Almost goat faced
peering over his own shoulder
as I walk away from me

paper in sauna
as wallflowers

lolled old sets brass
tapz az

lizardsli,
folk move on
passed.

being nowhere,

coming/going no real way
with no driver

a gush of wind

Label them, these days
Neutral
neither with / without;
no friends gained,
nothing special –
silver-suns on no chrome fight;
but this film of like something suspect

pervails
over them,
the people, I'm sitting with, it's they're (must be)
too competitive

It's a letter man;
goaded with fears, postures, failures but mostly
threats.
Dark decca plates,
a zaggy carpet, baccy brown,
nosing to bedtime.

Even then
same uncertainty
(mainly threats?)

a sour show
same sentiment (a refrain)
Cult of slavish Saturn
(time, bed-time, grow-time, rest-hour, work-hour)
all its mind-lime

The crippled glue-face
earth-corpse
catches us;
millions are made like it.
Is there any easter-breath

for the incredulous?
does every chest-breast
fail and clap in
at the seizure?
Switches and cogents,
studs, clubs, reds and grotesques
line the cabinet,
thicken the window,
bronze you,
marry with the master microbe.

The plan is no more complete.
I more collect:
and I cherish the fossil:
it is a gleam-ribbed trilobite.
I lay it on the computer now.

and
carping/picking pallid/slight violas & the
heads/summits of poppy,
joins them-to narcissus & the aneth-flower/the dill
finely scenting (olentis)
the cassia (the marjoram)
weaving (intexing) in other suave (sweetbringing) herbs,
combines and colours
the moll-soft luteols (bilberries)
with jaun-calt marigold –
the yellow cow-marigold.

Outside of the doors of the house
itoz raining

The brave dandy-seed
landed
on the pool-film

shrimps   questions
    clear from clear

to love

to return
to find
but in that yule-mist
slick bike-wheel
left self
and no path to the giving

I have eaten
Let us play.

To have it,
unfailingly and human,
humour –
always getting up good,
alluz unshirting trustily,
not a snort when the faces lock,
not a bead of bad humour
in a whole day –
what say?

Mid North Sea High

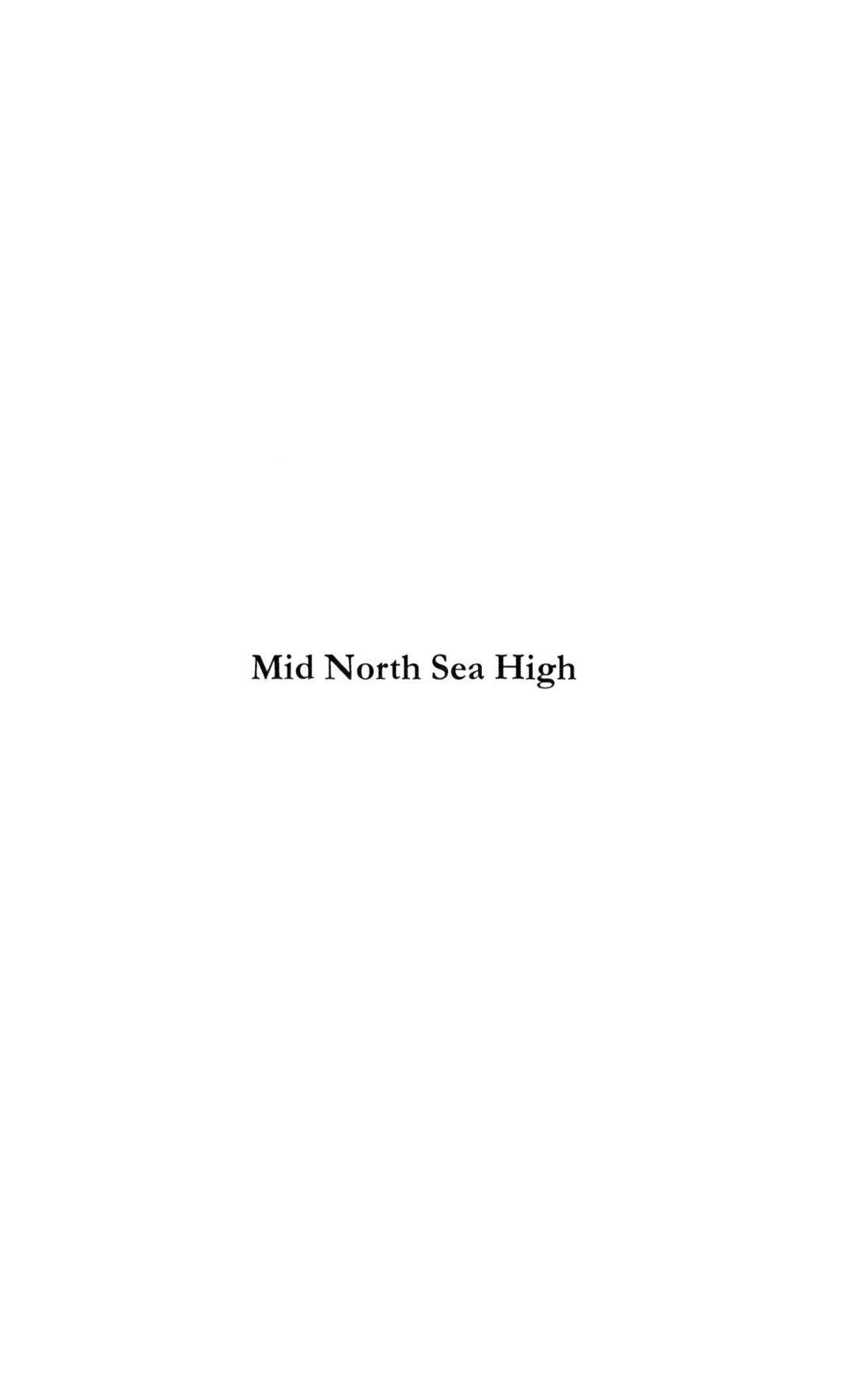

beset with zephyr-factors
tireless oceanic vectors
unfalter
and
repeat
and continue

ceaseless
clockless
ornament

dip and dent
lighten-darken
glaze, the glaucoid curtain,
the table-level,
the slick wall,
sky-roof-moody in-chalk casual colour

tisps and tatters,
prime decencies, we act / we intact,
takes talk, cerebrates,
the same cell-glow that bitters
in th'every scoop and trough
and thru all night.

I view.
Each all lucky signs / signals
exact go,
and-enter, and-out –
my show / my interioral psalm-say
my message to me.

We will be wave,
word of water,
in continue,
in big spray special letters, millions.

Open ocean
marries with new-art
it articulates

the practice of pattern,
oerlikons useless –
this dispersed
this targetless
of-life

*

At the turmoil,
a twister wind / dense
gradient,
primes
presitional (the) squares
of bow / keel

mast-quarter
that shatters
unbestill
roulettes
black to blue to
race-heaven

who'll stoic –
sea-setter?
sand-climb?

the rock-broth,
tipple of penitent,
us yellin' at us
– motor funked.

shapes
like Baal / St Peter Rabbit
on the crown-slope

gratitude
for storms?

a gut of sprouts,
of pebbles,

a head of nudge-hyacinth-become
and it is no green,
no grounding.

I thought
spray was trees,
a whip-wave
solid basket of emeraldines –
men who say Robin was a robber.

base-vault,
round is, is an arc-place
anchor under,
always would dawn.

jolt is tuba-boom,
sacked and smashed
hoof-heaver
when Noah's no-rain world
cheap here / handy / is all to us

the carefullest
dynasty
could be fish-food, speedily
one noble and dozens-over-dozens of shipmen
and enough brandy
all lost

am give up
sigh
and lean
and sick

forget
move
make-and-meet
be boulverse
mouth
to mackerel

*

I have ate from the sea.
The mack'rel-catcher lured me,
take the tin-grey bodies,
melt with heat –
and mash with crude onion,
bind with salad cream.
My pots of fish paté
line avenues to cannibalism.

Flesh,
soft-smoke-brown, and dark
dirt-chocolate,
yield from the bone,
under the master-fork,
is all I could want.

Tumbles
and mixes,
crying of waves
and souls
and air.
I salt.

In the beast-silt,
all emerge,
that shell and vertebral leg
and sky-skin and lime
hold,
and show busy paths,
their very bright flavours.

No one can eat like this.
The sea is only a window away.

That gives up
coal and phosphates, chauldrons of pig,
jumbled ammoniates, blast-perky,
all the things plow'd and shunted,

pick-up'd,
piled on sore lorries
straight on the back.
Guessed / scented / slough'd
tanker, truck an' train an' plane
take ye from me, goodbye.

For us, fish.

I suspect:
this could be a perfect town,
not a loose brick
not a weed
wrong.

*

They are on the pier
already
Mid-summer tides
have swelled in the dark,
dense and high-flown and fish.

There is harlequin and pearl,
whale-cry and pink
in the prose-sky
at before dawn,
drying to white.

Rebels
are slidin' and reelin',
then casting again,
lines and spinners,
excelling
at stark free sea-play.

Amber it will be
when the wood has nodded
to age-press,
an' re-'merged.

So many glass-jewel poles
and so many black stood fishers.

*

The Mid North Sea High
expels the sun,
up-hoy / out-gang,
bubbles and dome and atomic light.

Marvel
fire on water,
lamp and mirror,
steady up,
a flashing sea-shaper.

Morocco,
the old whore of the Mary-sea
is nothing round / red
this re-brilliant!
orb of rose!

all like

And maybe
life flew here from there
billions of turns ago.

*

The lustre – listen to it!
sign the grey glow,
sea sheen!
The carbuoy orange / it holds /
the work / repeats / gestures, the crowns
of wending ship-generations,
colours, crude, songs,
lists of lines, the ichthyostyle;
the glaze shows metals in sweat,

the cadmium, nickel,
lead-zinc range.
All my rapture.
Unowned seeing.
See sheen!

Stylating prussian dark blue,
and sudden bar wholer ruddy,
right on it,
liquid.
On my cork hands on the deck.
Sun lifts.
Surge vocem.

Consulting Satan.
it is deck swing.
it there martial rope,
and a high tune.
Moves, all of it, motion,
uncogent biting water,
flaring, and a dancing dress,
bepartnered corners, as we're fast,
as it buzzes.

The bulk serpent
sickens, shows
overt, awful, coil-rolling –
sense it – a disenergy,
I can touch – haplessness
(wind-bezique, futures, cloud-cones),
imminent, you, grouch-drum-roar.

Hold together, sing,
be settle, know the water, its total
(and is it impossible?)
(so much would make some glitch in time)
beat with it, be whole-soul,
listen and shout
and see and be …

*

Cling and clip to the face
do not blow you away
just because the wind speeds
or the rotating revs up
or headwards, much magma.
In the love-bird's grip,
will prove cartoon-safe
and quiescence, solace
(so cleft for thee).
(Hid?)

The crystal-cripple,
twinless, space-bronze and dunning,
never ripples, –
needless tack,
and lost the little power
of being harmony.
When there are chimes
laid in the wind,
long shines of intercouple,
grace seen,
(go and poke a beak out the nest)
(it's aurora-clear)

sit in the dawn,
sick as slime,
late as christmas

wrist-witch
disinmembered,
trolley-loping,
re-sizing ledge to ledge.
Lips of lace
shoot and sweet, yellow horn
salt-grim is sun-white coat.

the narker
on the sentinel

on the cornice
yipes total trite percentage concern.
The whole takes up off,
undeft,
token paths,
to gorgeously gain interlace
high-pace.

In a war for the wind.
Dissent.
Distend.
instinctively useless,
by avian rage.
reduction.
Roar.

Arm'-body
unit or incapable.
Lone
black-back
on pinnacle,
life-lorn,
jumps.

*

Once ice.
Now ice.
Ice will be.
The wall (the glacier)
displays of all time,
melt-mud, stone, sudden frost-on-flower,
uncoloured, also
scraps of eager fur.
Collect, collect,
sorry bunches of stick-dark,
now to chillish steam.
(By helterskelter delivery,
circle in the moist, and land.)

And look, mister,
soundless, isn't it,
this sort of release.
Turbulent order that slacks,
sustainment dis-stumbled – heaps.
With it, jute-plastic they are eggs and corners,
and michelins, and ripe
rainbow circuits.

Seeing them dead, twisted but bright,
chargeless (now word-neuter)
not these are fastest thinkers,
they are strings of trash,
the small-giants ruled by,
wrecked.

Lord Ice glinted with theirs
what was trillionish memory-switches,
uphoarded vivid power,
and control of the globe:
ice-jumble
and smear.

I dreamt this.
I gathered charred bits.
I made a nest.
Jibble-jabble, come and look!

*

Islands that move,
pace their sea-place,
like it is own-geared travel,
the foot of the headland wash and wade,
grinding it, only for themselves,
I mean, it is for their own amusement.

Rock and bottle,
Spume / birdling,
Flame & riff,

Sleep / silver.

Are ancient / You, young, bounce and jug
patient, / fly and jive, cognise to needs.
If took light, lived / the air's thick, this life,
Coarse, leek-wood, / these living fluting birds,
Circuit rough-ways or / effervescent and white and warm,
Resonantly dead, and / ready travels of souls
Length and buoyant.

Here is the flock-bait,
small wrist-wedged sea-claws,
inditing sea-pokes,
chaser-willing,
osprey-credent;
you / me, guests of the shore-gloss.
Sent out to play / called back,
As the Tide-Nurse sez.

So it was like,
from limpet-look dome to island-atom,
again.
Action / age.

Summer-slow
brought me to the window
Said hello.

*

Pride fleet choked in the fog
on the Altsee afloat
keen to listen
where some matching navy might be, in the mist.
In the figure of a ringed bull
it sits in the water –
now an explosion,
orange steel bathes it bit by bit.

The retching of the sea

a yellow-green warrior
jazz of its battering

fires on its surface
soul-flares

the gunners
smelling of lemons
were lost first
with the cordite-shouts

said it was Adventure
that was time-trap

*

black
white

a boat

one two three masts (delete) derricks.

aft: engine.
a hatch.
mid: window/room/house/bridge
a hatch
forard: two tops – trumpets – vents – horn-silver-things; a winch, too

and the nail-size sailors

must all be below

the boat
is in my boat, that
is on the great boat-broad island
with the mad captain.

*

The vine-priest's sun-hope tendrils –
an expanded prison (leaf, light, stalk)
over an umbrella of deep, dim (all of us) earth-crystals.

Tilt sea boat sits a deity of liquor
On the bench stem of
And the drum and drum (the sea sounds) and all of us in blood-beat.

*

Though life on such an aged paddlesteamer
'was a wet and wildly unwieldly proposition'
we hoyed ower the bucket:
these were new species, from over 650 fathoms.

Not just expected variants and explainable life-forms,
but new grotesqueties,
invertebrates in ooze, next,
from over 2 miles down.

Drift-nets assembled red and blue cockles, sea-nettles –
'and various other inhabitants of the deep,
many of the most minute size
and delicate form and tint.'

Pressures being equalised,
the deep species benefited from the sifting down as an animate rain,
of every organism, on death, from above,
this fossil larder.

While there in America
Agassiz began his collection with
'a bear, some eagles, an alligator,
and a number of assorted snakes.'

At the greatest stress
Seven miles down
they still found
a single shrimp.

*

From Greenland's icy vine-winds
to Kent-King's muddy shore,
the world of fish (frantic)
green-scented, shill-warped, vacuous,
streams its holy essence
gratis, withouten gold.

There no cup of blood
offers transit
to peak position,
no day no sunken Saturn
ever pulls fool assertations together,
never progs oily tines
to mine our air. There are no quotas.

High ower
Rickle-kittle fish affluence
flower-jam armpits
splat the polyp onto an orange sea-jacket
to see it change,
draw trellis-graphs of the unexcelled. –
And land slips.

Man above nature
stares and studies.
He cannot speak marine-talk
cod-code
sez there is nowt to be learned.
Takes only
what he divvnt want.
There ye are.
That is my fish-puzzle.

*

Sometimes
the sea curved, was bowl,
and ship like sit centre quarry.

Radians
in bull-summer
shine the arch-walls, sheer-sharp,
over the port,
quarry-gate.
Are not mere death-fish humps,
are immodest gulfs,
crystal-miles, ramps and ribs,
a taking-out
yep extra
anti-building

new re-work

the recondite say
enter eiffel-gracious – good long

behold
tanker
high on the rock-plain
by slide-wings

the wolf-grey sick rain
deflates the august high-seek elevation,
you ceiling,
a virtual grass-slope,
paceable, perambulatory
and up unwild walls

pedestalation
for the one, two and three divinity,
gantries for the offer to
gnosis
sea-say
ex-speak stations

who climbs
put their initials in?

Quotidiana

On the Sun

It was a cruel fite
my ears are ribboned
Nape gooey wiv blood

But I won it
I am to drive the Sun-Lorry all day.

The hangar is huge with burnt muck
and the hum
of the nuclear engine, bragging to itself.
The leap to the driving pit is something.

I'm acquainting me with the gears
(No clutch/brakes, almost speedway)
just gears/accelerators
when we swing up

And the road is so unboundably wide
astonished – and empty-eyed
I'm great with the honour
– it's no fussy
leaf-crown, this!

To steer the ball
placate the fusion
– it all seems easy.
But it is hard not to enjoy
edging this way a bit maybe
to give someone a sunny day
or burn some fucker's dinner.
Or back, and freeze 'em.

Then some hi-jacker
jumps the controls.
'Get out, you bastard!'

The place is tilting and tumbling.

We're busy punching and shouting.
Fighting again.

Kurt in Context

Kurt in the Quiz:
itza bull-snout savage grunt
thru infinite words
straying
all wrong
retracting
asking
coming up someone else's tip
all wrong

Kurt as Tyro:
Quisquis rogit
salve milés
in harenis
terris albis
draconibus
decoratus
audiet sic
fabulosa
nichilata
drew his bow and
squirrel scatters.

Kurt's Celebration:
Say me now
gold-and-lemon checked lassie-folk
why
you look so long
in the mirror that insults?

Kurt at the Pub:

helitopped wizard-bug
shooting off the candy-moss
and zeroing in
on some virgin bluff-stoned shore.
(Clarry likes Kurt because he has no soul;
nor either much.)

Kurt Assists:
A pace homeward, no no –
she doesn't want to go home!
Forward and backward, and little
hints like screaming;
man – if you keep this up
we will all found
stopped,
seized of the afternoon.

[Untitled]

Chucking the
carpet in the tip,
there's a joke about keeping your end up.
It'll be orange lino, mind, next time.
A crisis of delicacy!
A world of lovely crazy-tiger-eye,
star-burns!
Parrots and table-tops,
and all blackcurrant in a café,
suits me happy az angel-cake.

[Untitled]

Shit!
A pub-full of myrmidons
An' I walk in.
An' they look hungry.
Staggerless trash
face to face
with
imminent preternascible sub-thoracic lusts
for food
an' fat to polish a taxi up.
I look unrabbit.
I talk totally inedibly …
'Didye see that fight …?'
'Aye, the air-inlet …'
'Well, Stiggy sez …'
'Nabut try this riddle:
   "Tongue on foot on me
   "Bind me tight
   "You stink."'

[Untitled]

Quiz-miss
wonder-while
with kids
that clunder up the cliff
beetle-beaut
snorting excellence.
Will she trim her head?
One magic to drive out another,
get own in-time perfection, I wish it.
All on its own.
I told you that,
it's like that – yourself or nothing.
Everything – ideas, arms, art.

Re-make
Re-find
Air and tide, stones and links,
Descry by, try,
own bear-kind.
Be-close, imp-haired cubs
(And do not let them scream and have)

[Untitled]

House-breakers …
Moonlessly,
remembering a wolf-tail,
patters silent-stepped (this is it) the enemy road
of tree and lamp, grass, gravel, & clapperboard.
To the target, to th'aedifice.

'Now you need a smoke gun.'
Hushabye, housemen,
sit and settle,
sink to the bed,
lose your way in a long smokey dream
(if you're in there)
or never stir.

'You will also need a hive tool.'
This prises the dark door
into the heart chamber of the treasure-bowl.
Behold, soft secrets,
lift (not jar or jerk)
with sellotaped fingers
'for prising the combs apart.'

Don't be gulled by glint-decor,
go for it easy,
the marketable little quotidiana

anyone wants
for health / happiness.
Once you have overcome your initial fear
(Sudden awareness, the proboscis, this way, that,
the sense of the indelicate,
of the hormones,
that the wings thrum, knees tuck, heads bob & …)
Bees, be calm.
The God-being that runs off with honey
leaves you sugar substitutes
in the nature of candykisses.
He thinks you will like them.
He thanks you.
'Extracting the honey is relatively simple.'

[Untitled]

Sanger the showman worked like this:
This way I made my show:
In a bird-scale landau
of gold, black and lacquer,
two canaries sat and rode
nodding heads I liked
tinsel coronets on.
Alighting,
and I whistled
and they did a sort quadrille.
The redpolls pulled on a
miniature cannon, smart beasts,
trained then fired it,
a shower of sugar-crystals, gemlet-like.
And mice climbed the pole,
lowered the flag,
surrendered the fort.
The final was a tank of gold-fish,
signifying Trafalgar:

Look! each tows oil-paper boat,
a hornetty man-of-war,
the mast's a baby firework with fire scattering
crackling in smoke.
Tigers will rule India,
dogs race to the Pole,
giants of the air fly the Atlantic, white-feathered, see them, coast to coast
fish-lamps in the deep,
and below worms tunnel the Chunnel.
All creatures great and small –
work to be us.

The Haswell Change-Over

At the Market
we are shy shade,
clever and wild and quiet,
it is practice.

Some that were warped into wolves
(this, man, is a finest one,
just fondle those arc EARS)
glimpsed in the wall.

Bright white   glossy black
                      fur
my shoulder   mine
as we swim
in a corner   alone
air-bubbles
for long ears   compact –
                                     share
                      me

chatter
at the arena

rings and folk spectated
around
TVs / shoes / tools / bowls / gear / pots /
paperbacks.

Marry this mayor!
This fine fat mayor!
Come-alonga come-alonga –
ribs and taille,
waistlock and fetcoat
and much much more,
to own (your own)
up-up-up-up!

What a little space, neat, polite,
all around
this police pair.
Maybe the cuffs shine
to see if you can pick them?
(No one would laugh
aloud)

In these slimmest sticks,
the yellowest roundest tiniest,
blouse-perfect canaries!

Rows on the wall.
Vying for the purest jeans,
sunniest head,
friendliest ferret.

Can you sing?
Can you rub close?
Can you gaze with rotund eyes?
Can't you draw them in –
with a non-verbal tease to your silk tail?
Couldn't you try?

Or is it just dream?
Or a tree-plant?

Change-over into goat.
To be a farm.

My urban crowd,
this carol
sells aliveness.
(At much much less
than a penny a word!)

Celebrate!
Purchase as an ocean!
A sea of grass,
a main of waving green,
a little oat-acre
for a goat
to put four magic feet
on.

Checks and cow-boots,
moving skins,
calibrate your cash (not enough),
well then an ice-cream,
ask.

All midwest life has just materialised
around analysable (oh boy!)
processions conducted of (that one?)
uplifted hens (yeah!)
conducive of (and)
animated discussion (How!)
about something other (How again!)
than bidding.
(Last year's pet / (or)
next year's salary / (or)
this girl's fancy)
and then (not another calamity?)
another hen pops up
beautiful and tawny
and the spurs chink (partner!)
and the straw flies (a coke?)

and a private dog-show outside
starts up.

and sun-spit
and sister-glitter
and youth-king in coal

So to look –
sad, subtle
these my sparrows
made of mud
sing silver, black, bad

There are dog-gipsies
edge of the urban,
meaner, meaner,
to make it look the better
with ev'ry bargain.

my pretty, dutifullish
rings-of-bluff-pijins –
there is no product-talk at all –
what are words for?

almost a smell of villainy,
a human patience,
groups and gitanes
and gipsy-with-ducks.
Is it cheating?
So much pressure / changing
growing / advancing / returning
city to soil
coal to sky
work to real.
Is it cheating? –
to urge to be?

This is
legend-collect
(what used to live under the bridge)

(what boggles the night-horse)
(who caught the unicorn)
What goes
on two-feet
or ten feet
or a hundred?

Starting Up with Doves

OK – tumblers.
(They annat racers.)   [are not
Skemmies he calls 'em.
Corn an' watter, air and perch
is what's wantid,
an' they'll flee an' hiem: [fly
maist, it's display.

Aa's away off ina week;
it'd be g'eat if you could fidid in.
I dinna want the pipe brekking
of a sudden
and spoilin' the shed:
if ye've time to cap it?

Na, ye'll need a tin
for the feed, man.
it's boond to bring rats and that
jist left lowse, like, in a poke.   [bag
(Stupid, that.)
Aa'll git a bucket an' lid,
it'll haud o'ermuch easy.

For Taska's benefit:
we've deun a canny bit today!
A board an' felt's well covered th'gap
o' the smashed sky-light;

the winder's netted   [window
but still opens.
Same for the door.
It looks airy and capacious,
nut ony awd shed.

Monolithically
like a woodhenge,
we're ettlin' te set up shelves   [aiming
for roostin'-flats.
Then they're compartmentalised,
ashless new-age columbaria
on a sort egg-mortgage.

At once they're in.
Some one, some two, tiv a box.
Reptile-placid,
high-white and quiet,
an' deun wi' peckin'.

it'z a perfick prizun.
Mebbe a kid gans in,
oops a cell-bird biv its legs,
t'see iv it's licing,
or ti cell-search for hidden eggs,
or ti sweep aboot, tidy,
mak' proper
or splay oot that grey-pretty wing
uniform.

To hold casual-like
isn't not ti love.
What we canna see
is hoo many to share wiv.

Aal the morning,
I hear them chorusing, mildly mad and
on cretaceous tune-beats,
an' the wings ruffle
and graw wahm.

There's nae tomatiz in mi yard,
nowt grawin' and flowerin' on the brick,
just pijjies, heeds an' crops.

An' when ye're settild,
We'll rax the window up, [stretch
fix it,
leave ye free t'come an' ga,
use the sky,
choose.

(Well, we knaa –
They're ower-magnetic
ti git giddy
e'en circling the colony endlessly
aal day.

Acerbic, unsettled, they
line on the top window-edge
and watch ther shed.
Enter the dark,
he hes ti ladder-up
an' bring'em doon in his jeckit.
(Not se much a protest, as a hesitancy,
noo it's dark, fer th'unsafeness o'the scene.)

Ah've sawn the wood,
supplied the nails,
brushed the yard,
thowt hard ti stave off calamity

To nae end.
It'll come.
And –

By, but it's quiet this morning …

Envoi

Out back
the weetabixers   [bairns
is tewin' tins of pink paint   [messing about with
to mak' ma shed fit for lobsters.
Ma preference, mind,
is for an integral roof
(one wi'out holes)
But the bairns hardly consider that
worth considerin'.
Well, Aa doot it'll rain on them,
se that when they shelter in the shed,
it still rains on them.

Up is
a bigger shed-land,
wavy-tin topped,
an' the Attic walls aal   [as of Troy
awd doors, just that.
Taties an' toadflax,   [potatoes
even tee, glenty bike-chains   [too
lie there, live here
(nae people)

[Untitled]

What does the Gym do? Most of the time
it rhymes.
Things
sing
Muscle fibres, thew,
telescoping gut, blue-
vein arm,
calm,
crystal dirt,

shortens/firms, lengthens/slims, shirt
and head
move, miscellaneous, with this or that bar instead.
Breath be in – go – shout –
Breathe out!
So be it.
Sets. Quit.
It's real. Grows.
Goes.
Gans.
Spans.
This spread he reaches to, full, bands up to, to heave,
To think-send-make-more force, perpetually, reave
as of it, self-world,
explode that that curled.
New and unspiral unfurled.
It all the time
rhymes.
(And that wouldn't be smart,
not to take part.)

[Untitled]

It's Sylvester's Day.

Clockwatchers' dance – oh
bon joyeux noel nouvelle mes amis année

important to knaa
and if so
from what angle (from sea)
the tower will be
seen

and so dark,
dill-dead, ungreen, by when

I set away.

Storm-seigneur
rolls bins before me.
Bop-bum tunes, wires croon.
Whole south litter-army
Bats my mouth,
it must be Just Criticism (I guess).

And the kid-carol-singer's Mum
is still partying,
as I turn up our road,
as I turn in.

Sylvester, see me grin,
TV and me, late, silly, slopey,
safe from the wind
and well.

Review of Brian Greenaway
Notes from Delvan MacIntosh

The first work constitutes a review. That is a commentary, by turns following, parallelling and extending, of the book *Hell's Angel* by Brian Greenaway (with Brian Kellock; Lion/Albatross 1982). The nub of the book seems to be Chapter 12, where, in Dartmoor, shaking off drug-use with no apparent aid other than Christian tracts, a vision of a plant was granted, leading to a complete conversion and reformation. He now tours non-conformist chapels, denouncing bikers, and runs a charity with the aim of getting other prisoners to submit to God.

The second piece needs no particular comment. Delvan is a young Pakistani, a friend of a friend, and, to my unreformed judgment, quite a cheerful human.

Review of Brian Greenaway

I
my hand
am

started

looked to

what woz you against me, mate –
down!

fighting-going
(for)
the really big prize

oh boy!
I got the baton thru the face

I said, I kill you

Said, you'll be lucky if they live

half my wages as rent
my fist my mouth

so I woz made march
kept in a cubicle
till the guy next along cut his wrists

and we said
OK we'll take your gift
(unsea, unsky, unview)
and of this tiny bit of time
and your blood-whirlpool
I'll make it matter

grave were they in the jest of annihilation

so I said
'From brute to brute
though I
scalped
this colossus of your rage
sea-rode,
yet in my breaking
I'll take my Jason-safety,
power,

pronounce,
till the last word's
pulled out of me.'

Then Elohim
from the burning marijuana bush
spoke:
'If I, Yahweh,
this plant take
and nip out a bud, or this,
see! it goes on,
thickens, works more to live;
if I cull its roots,
see how it flares to grow,
but small, enpotted,
stays low.
And lastly, learns
it feeds
and ev'ry virgin thing
first bud, then root and leaf,
comes stronger and greener.'

Then I tried to hang him.

And his Adversary
intervented him. Spoke and
calmed me
to listen to Him:
'Loose, unclose
this is evening air

why away?
why not betray?
howl on the mounds!

being man is much
but we also must
just be false

circled with cities
as we are,
caught and treated, just thus,
why not make it easy?

shaved, unlanded, loaded off,
what dignity
to lose?

how be in society

and not betray all,
all and self!'
But the dove he promised me
got out:
the screws saw to that.

*

Rap-pa-pa-pa.
The bike talking to me.
I too was born with a full language (have never known
　　anything else).
With foot and wrist I match the beat of the bike.
It supposes one mind between us.
A fusion, fingers and cables and check to seat.
Months in the work-camp hadn't taught us apartness.
No to retraining.
Then the chromed fare messenger of my muscles lammed
　　straight into a
road block.
I was pulled off.

I showed my words.
No good.

I was stripped of my lid and my boots and sent to sentencing.
What I could say sounded ludicrous in the big room of echoes.
(My little rhythm.)
The thrumming of my bike (behind me) gentled up.

It was the softer beat of an engine.
(Some sort of van.)
A shelf seat, the low roof, kept me sitting.
I couldn't even drop my chest forward.
My beautiful brown hair was in rats' tails.
I stank of my own acrid sweat, corrosive.
Being kept in my clothes.
Till we reached?
Through a finger-pane of window I couldn't see.
Other mobile bodies out there?
(Different rhythms.)
Now we halted.
I cramped my eye to the glass.
A vast gate, bumpy in brick.
Walls with it.
Fire-drakes were built onto its top, angry, loathing dragons,
full of fume,
sez You're Going In.

Theirs a great rolling cry,
desolate, night-voiceless,
like a long laugh of at me,
frozen,

walking,
cruder
And the sound got louder, more broke up, into the cry of words.

WE HAVE A NAME, it said, YOU HAVE NO NAME.
In this agony of talk, I was unable to, was all silent.
All the words were orders.
I had to strip myself off, watch my bits (badges) torn off the

leather, jeans searched open, turned into lists.
Others, too beat to even get their clothes off, were pushed aside into little cages to wait.
I was too amazed to even remember I had a language too.
Instead, I stood and got me searched.
To the sharp demands, I forced my muscles to bend, contort, relax, display, for all that time.
And in something like a shroud, I was marched about, handed over to greater, louder men, with voices like a mass of water falling.

What is the language of the Sons of God?
I guess it must be a beautiful one, they are so powerful.
Like a caress they suggested me almost under the steam
into vile, just boil-less water.
It was bitter on my legs.
I needed to speak for something cooler, but I couldn't tackle that talk of theirs.
I grabbed for the tap, but my knuckles were levered back.
Where were the tracks of logic now, the promises of God?
Just a singeing torrent of water, searing at my puffed envelope of skin.
I yelled in my water-song, and the gentle voices waited and watched and let me out.
Some ladless life.

*

Said,
this is yours now.
In the cliffs, my own cell.
My own slab to lie on.
No one has to get out.

There was talk-run everywhere,
the label-yelp,
to copy the language of control,
I couldn't get it.
There was music more
in the pipes,

I liked that, tapped it my beat.

It is night again.
Howling,
below my head,
the burning dragon of chains
tears and moves, forms this place.

Where is it?
What is it called?
In the sun, I roll in work.
With thunder, I'm sent this job, that,
harsher and sillier.

Who slays who?
The heads-in-blood run past me,
looking for the place which spells –
well what is it?

The voice of Renaming
(when the Lord will re-name)
caught it for us.
Have this hole, hold on, all light out,
don't make it madder, man,
rest it. Take it.
Be quiet.
(Counted out.)

*

On the pylon in the rain, shouting down

Caught and my head shaved for trinket-pay

Cool it I don't want to hear another word

Walk don't talk

A guy next cell, sharpens his tusks

lime trigger

wriggle-snicker
no choice, no girl

seated in the high-eye
sky-bird
lipped in the flesh,
man-trunk, man-bark

I see it in the cylinder-imp,
compelled, alloy-eyed,
hotter, righter,

bakes, or the wind
hats the ingot

Sez you sort it out,
we're putting you in charge of them.

Lykoros –
wolf-warder, me

Catacomb-chaos
just to join to fight,
pulled out / parted
in the evil air
our dark clothes.

no man to spare his brother, not I

is it?
hell earth

wire attacks him
flowers milk him

evil leaves
un-yet dawn

everywhere I grow,
build, tint, drive it,
dirigate,
to gloss, gliding,
blur of green ridden-by

instead, to run,
made go faster each day.
the greater lights – its pineapple gold
blazed down
sitted at the horns of mauve,
blend wheel to wheel
with mother-move,
make

pansy dab-bronze
flower / bruise / eye

To reach out,
mash into the bodies,
men columns of corpses

of rising dough
white fading strands faded

That tiny hair
flick from
grand fun, whoooping-clapping-danger
to dead-damage, the rotting flick of challenge,
balling-speed into shake-off
refusal to take it, that torment, be out,
in my grand god-link

Proposition:
if I didn't keep the guys in line,
beat up,
it was me for punishment.

A great chain of creation.
A great avarice for annihilation.

This is I in my exalt
my *Mirabilion*

what I got
the Name in which
the blood circles
never more collapsed,
put out and begged,
asking to be human
a one way
t'outgoad the guards,
be me all-washed with diamonds,
crowned with more righteous gold-beard
than a Cristo packet

God,
the everlasting gun
and mine!

*

Canst thou thunder with a voice like Him?
(The breath that kills grass)
Is the sun the breath of God?
God is gone up with a shout,
the Lord with the sound of a trumpet,
the music-voice of?

He
Called us a new name
which the mouth of the Lord shall name

Can you see it?

Shake the husks from my nose,
the lodged tendrils,
cleared my ears
rose-gold-eared
and knee-ball in spokes

all the deep metal
the iron with me
to new party-time.
It is fluorescent bright-smelling leather
deep-moulded gear
with all the magnets of the earth,
to wire me, impel me,
staggering like a fight
breathing out long trails of petrolous fire to sing.
Dragon-coloured
I greet my people
and from my pig-heavy head,
to frost-laces,
snail-buttons,
my chain-zips
to run to seem to fly
when the light mists into clouds,
on coke-tins, and cute stoat-sonnets
on it, the dump-splendour

The canal-line-trenches'd turned to pitch,
the land-side dust, dust sulphur
fit for an unlife

everywhere was ungreen,
was no cottage in the vineyard,
no lodge in the cucumber-garden,
smudged, burning

got balance on the sliding ground,
the blocks shook upside-down in the earth,
all silent

the blue wires whipped at me,
alive for blood,
new animation
and the piping
twined up, turned my legs,
flower-sweet, to milk me.

(sanguinem enim animarum vestrarum requiram)

cry-laugh,
how wd walk into the rock,
hide into the dust,
push into the holes and caves

I mean
why sorry?
dirt, me, too,
soon, sure, sooner,
my soul and bright sails;
the pride of it!
chill, the fur;
hollow throat
with more use mute
than I have ever been.

Where was the new earth?
why no white horses?
where was the thief, chewing his own arm?
the sea-beast? the woman? trumpets?

I heard nothing like that.

No God?

Nothing but a remnant?

No little body of the galaxy
to void the annihilation we have been put to?

are
just the fuel for the fire?

Notes from Delvan MacIntosh

STEVE & PAUL,
HI AM BACK INSIDE WHICH YOU
KNOW. I GOT CAUGHT RED SO I AM GOING
TO HAVE TO PLEAD GUILTY WHICH MEANS
BIRD. I GOT REMANDED FOR 3 WEEKS
YEASTERDAY. I HAVE BEEN CHARGED WITH
ALL THE CHARGES I WAS ON COMMUNITY
SERVICE FOR SO I AM NOW UP FOR 7 CHARGES
PLUS THE POLICE MIGHT BE CHARGEING ME
WITH MORE BURGLARYS. THATS THE BAD
NEWS. THE GOOD NEWS IS I MIGHT BE ABLE
TO DO THE POLICE BECAUSE I HAVE GOT
16 S[T]ITCHES IN MY KNEE BECAUSE OF THEM
I WAS ALSO BITTEN BY A POLICE DOG TWICE
IN THE ARM THEIR WAS BLOOD EVERY-
WHERE THAT['S] WHY I GOT YOU TO GET MY
CLOTHES, THANKS. I AM IN THE SCRUBS

I WAS HIDING UNNER A TABLE
IN THE BURGERKING
I WAS HUNTIN'
THE BANDIT-MONEY.
THE JACKPOT COULDA BE MINE,
IF I GOT A CHANCE (ME AN' MY HAMMER).

WHEN IT ARRIVED
WELL I TRIED TO GET OUT
AN' THE DOG SCREAMIN' AT ME.
THEY FOUND THE WINDOW
I BROKE IN BY
AN' I WAS THERE IN IT EXIT
THEY DRAGGED US
DOG IN MY SHOULDER
ME IN THE SPACE
YELLIN' ALL KICKED ME THRU IT,
SPLIT ME ON THAT GLASS-LEFT-IN-FRAME
ALL KNEE MINE GASHED.
HOW THE FUCK CAN I WALK?
TAKE YOU TO THE TOMBS.

TRILL ALL BELL OH
EYELESS & GREY
WAKES PINCER & FEELER & PRAYER & WET
THE SKULL
BOUNCE

UP ALERT <u>GET OUT</u>
PINK SHORN, CREASE & MALICE
<u>YOU CUNT I'LL</u>
GREETS MEETS
<u>FRYING</u>
JARS KICKS OUT AND
YOU SING LIKE
<u>LORD TODAY THY SPIRIT</u>
<u>OK WHO SAID THAT</u>

<u>WALL</u>
SMELLY PAINT-SKIN WASHLESS JUDGE
COUSINS ARE ROOM & ROAD
<u>ULL</u> IS THE HUNTER
LACE-KNEED.
WHO WALKS THE STEM?
CROWDS THE LEAVES?
<u>PITH-HELMET</u> VANS & WEAPONS
WHO WANTS A RACE?
<u>WALL</u> IS A BOOK,
EVERYTHING HAPPENS INSIDE IT.

MAYBE I LET PAUL DOWN
I SAID SURE THERE'S TWO BIRDS
I'M LINING UP.
GREAT INIT?
BUT I WANT TO WIN A BIT FIRST.

LEAVING ONLY LIKE A FILM OF ME.

DECLARES MYSELF –
SEEKS HER
SHOWS HAND
HIP
HEART
ME & HER
CHEER

SOUL BOTH   MEET TO
SEEING SINCE FIRST   MAKING
ENERGY   SCI-FI
WAS INVENTED

SHAKES WITH EACH LIVING   STOOL-TOP
ELEMENT BEING, THE   RICH-GREY
RUNNING CALLING CANTOR   IN SONG
IN PLINTH

```
            AND TERRE         EARTH, NEED
              YOUR MAGNET!       FIX
             A LOCATOR         CLOCK
                SHOWING SUN
         INDICATING THE POINTS OF AIR,
              UNAVOIDABLE UNION        ISN'T IT?


              THIRD FACTOR,      RECOUNT
                 TOUCHES,         ZORE
                ME & HER,         WELL –
         THAT ROLLS, IS LIKE HEAT,
         SENSES ALL, LIKE ANOTHER,
                    FIRM          MOVED
                REASSURED
              PETAL-LIVELY, LOVE       LESS IS
                BUNCH-BUD


                     I WOZ
              THE JEWEL IN THE FIELD
         TENSE, LOVING, MOVES, MANY THE ULTRA-
             CROWN, CAPTAIN STAMEN MINE,
             MY MEN MARSHALLS, THEM POWERS
                  PULLS INTO HARMONY,
             SO SEE THEM, RED-ALL, WHITE-ALL
              FURIOUSLY ALIVE, BARE-HEAD WAR
         MACRO FRAME AND IN CUP FLOWER BURNS.


                    BUT: BLACK.
                I LOOKED THE TELLY
         THE POINT IS THESE PEOPLE ARE DYING,
              NOT YOUR TERROR OF SHARING
         NOT YOUR REACTION TO LOOSE CHANGE


                 AND THE CROWDS,
                  ALL US IN HERE,
              EVEN ONES YOU I MET YOU
                 IS STEAM ABOVE US.


                   BRIGHT YELL
                A CLAIM ME CHAR,
         GONNA GAME YOU FOR THE STARCH-STICK.
              THINK OF ME AS A FAMILY.


                     SOMETIMES
             AT NIGHT / AT TIMES IN THE DAY
         I SEEM TO CONTACT TO / REACH ROUND
                  MY OWN ECHOES.
                     AND REACH.
```

THE THINGS I WOULD HAVE BEEN
BEFORE I WAS ME. AM.

A MULTI-ME,
CONVERGENT,
ALMOST SHADING INTO OTHERS.

A
TOUCH. SEZ.
AND SO, CONTINUE.

THE PANTHEON.
OR THE ROTUNDA OF MY THUMB.

WITH ALL THAT'S EVER ATTEMPT'
THE PAVEMENT.

BUT
HERE WE SIT,
WHAT WOULD BE,
THE MALEVOLENT SKIRLING,
MOTOR-TERROR AND ANIMAL LARYNX.

<u>GO</u>
WANT YES
LET ME,
CANNOT MAKE ME
WHAT I WANT TO
CANNOT STOP ME
IF NOT HIT.
ALL OF US.

OH THEN
A SWIRL
RED-LIVID DUST
& DRAGON ENTANGLE

RAG-BEARS & SPOON-MAIDENS
LINE

I HEARD
THUNDER-SWOON OF BIKES
TUNE-TALK

DUSTY / RAIN-SMELLY
DOG
IS ANSWERS ME

A GALLOP-OPAL POOL OF SWEET-SCENT:
BATH

AT CHRISTMAS
WHEN POSSESSIONS COME
AT A GASP
SWEET-RAPPED, POPPY-BROCADED GUN-NUGGETS
AND HELLO –
INVENTIONS

SKELETAL FOIL LEAVES GOLD
AND BREAST-DOME JELLIES
AND THE SMOKE OF THE DEAD: ARE AUTUMN

THERE ARE GRIPS OF PARASOLID AGENCIES
AT THE RIM, THE UPWARD-WATERFALL,
UNGUARDED ASCENT
AND IN A WAY I NEVER THOUGHT
RISES AS FALLS

AN' THE <u>TRANNY STOPS</u>
MIGHT AS WELL BE A GHOST.

TALK:
THE PROCEDURAL LIST OF FLOWERS –
HEAD BENDED TURNING, TURNING,
SPIRITUAL ORGAN OF CATA-SONGS
EXCESSIVE SUN SET-HEAT
AND THE GLOWING, HAMPERING, SWESTER-SCENT.

AN' ALL THE SOLICITOR SAID
WAS I WOULDN'T BOTHER,
THEY'LL ONLY TELL SOME OTHER STORY
& THEN, WHAT ARE YOU WORTH?
GET YOUR CLOTHES FRESH:
SENSIBLY, HAVE A SUSPENDED SENTENCE.
THIS WAY
IT'S CHEAPER ISN'T IT FOR THEM?

BUZZES, BLINKS, WHIZZES,
AS THE GAME SHOWS
BEETLE-LIKE THINGS, BIRD PURSUIT, THINGS IN SPACE,
THAT GLOW AND SHINE.

CAMION-SEEDLINGS

SHOW-TO

MILLIONS OF MILLION-YEAR ROOTS

CANNOT ROLL, CANNOT TOOT

HA' IN' MINED THEIR OWN SLOPES,
SOMETIMES, IT SEEMS EXITLESS.

UNDEFINED, BECAUSE IT WON'T UNRAVEL.
WHAT IS IT THAT IT IS, A HUMAN?
DOES IT FILL ANY SPACE?
IS IT AZOIC?

THIS SPRAWLING DEALER
WELL OVER-PISSED
<u>ON MY MONEY</u>, –
COME ON STEVE, GIVE THE FIVER MAN, I WANT TO GO OUT
BUT HE RUBS HIS FOOT A'ME JACKET
STARTS PUSHING & ALL THAT ILL-FEELING,
WANTS TO COME IN ON MY JOB,
GETA RISE OUT IT,
OK YOU WANT STEAL MY ENERGY,
YOU WANT ME TO?
I BOPPED HIM (JUST ONCE) FLAT IN THE EYE
OH HE COLLAPSED NOSE-BLOODY EYE-SHUT SHUT-UP

SHALL I SHOW YOU THAT?

Scaffold Hill

'An enthusiastic meeting of twenty-seven collieries of the Tyne was held on Scaffold Hill [1844], when it was resolved to fight the battle out to the last.'
Richard Fynes *The Miners of Northumberland and Durham* (Sunderland 1873, ch.19)

Let us be sober.
Again,
Let us conjoin hand/heart/head,
be understood
as organic/corallic whole.

High is the death-may,
our picks and bait-boxes,
with the pleasure-princess
and bottle-beer and what –

For everything's holiday.
Fire and foot and thistle,
Stud and cloud-shirt,
all in the oath.

That by sun-eye/moon-eye,
wife-charm/bairn-hood,
belly and leak-seed,
nivver again will we let the contract for survival be twisted against us.
(wife/home used to hold us, to keep us to work-tie.)

For love and load is everything,
it heaves the deck, straights the rolly-way
an' if we wosna true all one,
would the mine ever gan, else?
How could it, man?

Wor the tip-eyes of the crystal,
the corolly-petals head's,
peni-palms' fingers
the once and off but ever-round pharos aal light and through the night

The waam hawk saints wor beds,
song is
tunnel-
measure.

insupportably bending being hot/wet,
but mostly wind-journies,

quit and desért
and they do not mean to betray. but

*

Winter-day-early
radio-talk and trucker-music
sigit-cheep, sigit-cheep yeeps the salt,
there, heavy steam-wolves,
to think ovit, weight everywhere.

Words are heavy,
with deliverable masses.
I know, for I ama word.
There are other words like me.
Perhaps we are all one word.
But it is my word, too, is me.
We words eat and sleep together.
When something that is not a word comes up,
we roll into balls.
Along the sentence, we grow.
And at the end of the line, they say, 's a great fire.

Can it be?
My
adventure-smoke-rain
above the thudding-of-the-herd
and ghost-flute sez 'I'll write home ev'ry day'

OK
lunch at hi'table
the tumbling plum-brilliants
whole bowls – implicit-veined leaves of salad
crisp, salutary salad.
If only you need not talk …

Interim are
cheerful-eared cats
on the lawn
fart food

at the gym
but massive massive salt-scents
brave off the dock,
and
today is a good day
and I know
I smell of myself
mostly.

*

Look,
our variations on a grin:

Be'seeing
Feeding the back
(Tall fish-spine)
with arch ideas.

Waltz-drives,
Bows,   [bohs
Shows.

Just consider me
Another of these little orphans
with my own rainbow.

The dirt scums up,
I skid.
I dragontail
and the arm-arc ups and hits.

The run
is the cycle,
the smooth hat
is bum.

The sub-castle is the pit,
Ours we pledge.
With opal eyes,

to the main-seam.

And stinking thrush-grouse grows peace,
The rich war makes our harvest gross long chauldrons
To mak the herald angels jealous.

Hand is hand,
neck, arm, knee,
all speak now,
full as sane engine, colour, the coal-world.

*

My phantasies differ:
I am no longer a demon,
wrecking heads of hair with ripe, bright claws,
but lithe footballer
sweeping curving grass, paths,
off to goal / back to psalms,
songs of wheat-myth roar out before,
and feet on green.

An' I padded/prowled
cat-low; I in the jungle,
leeches patrolled my body,
shaky-shooter, excellent, auburn-kitted,
for symbol, to shatter symbol.

An' I surmised me, in a steady job,
planning the money out,
me, mi wife an' a calculator,
to say, we see our first house, it's fabulous,
what work!

Tangles of orange boots,
hurling round around checkers' table-legs,
thor ready for me, anither run,
ta, we're off, and cutting an' spraying
heavy black food and clothes and brix and cash,
grand, great, heart's gold.

An' I was thinkin of kobolds
bless-rigid in the goaf

flickers as sounds,
beats of snatches of tunes, like,
in the flecks, clicks of coal,
azo brittle, basic guitar,
out of way, well wide of its place,
(now I know the cutter slid off its line, went specially out on its own
    I figure, how they tellt me)

cap-lamp
quartz-blatant, need it not,
man-riding train,
out/up, bring to the white-world,
lots of girls, they laugh now,
cars an' things

who is someone
who is old
who is creased
who is gutted
who moves on,
resembling who?

*

Only, glorious and maroon,
there is resistance.

In every comma
every cheated clause,
I sense it,
I hold against,
I pick up the flag of –

I will not be loyal.
There is nothing
between word-man and word-man

Not drive your vans,
set your locks,
make anything against your enemies.

The eyes of lord-legend
winnot bend me,
cannot bone me,
no more tricks like that.
Power / Paradise
are bags of wishlessness.

In it its
endless misjourney,
forget it.
Here is the view.
Start whole.

Look at the brave out-sea waves!
The width of mist-thru'd open
and way.
Never over.

Arm by arm,
the players
(an' itiz as one-thinker)
re-form

dunnot ask
'give up',
no one will vote,
only we will be unanimous.

In the galaxy of the eye,
in the milky nerve,
the spandril and the passage,
and the astradome or hand-cup

dots of rain
and

pips of spray,
laughing, us

to feed
faraway.

head on my rolled jeans
I fight.

*

a show
of sleep and slaughter

a wrink'
of 'cuffs off,
sloughing chains
like a wash of dirt

the cloth of metal
shirks / leaves

in their freedoms
the tool of Mars
macerates the life-flesh-hand

wheel-jerks,
or baroque-speed locks,
dotted, headless-like action
of the toy

Beast, rim-back,
lamps/cassaults
into the thick-trick sensate fight.

Chord
liberally messages,
it signals the limbs,
it fells quarter-movement
(pulling round)

Pale blue brick,
neon ronde,
and symbol-new head-light
is warm/returned.

Inside a sea-circle
of fating fists,
I ride.

Here, harmony
she is curves,
she lies,
we pass smiles to smiles

Under zebra-clouds
bodies to talk,
beings be,
flex ably, honest switch,
we swipe.

Vixy bitch
by this mine,
many more
in settled, grouped, huddled coves,
explore in skin,
and this bended wrap
is sing.

The one cute, cheap shot
when then I walk about
out of the tape.

Signal and secret.

For in this lean and laughless,
nothing uncurls.

*

Honk!
The great jap-rich lorry
camions in up about and atween
the haywire, the roads,
snortin' out hymns
like cædmon-cædmon-cædmon-cædmon.
Why-aye, this is the lord
the lord that made the sky
that smacked it grey, an' sulfur-brown
wiv coal-clarts; now now
hear him singin' hissell
how the de'il's come up out o the groun'
wi' gross evil-getten dirt in'iz teeth
to spit it about,
choir like onythin', amazedly,
grin wi toot-tooting chimleys
an' the twisty-gob route-makers.
Please to escape the inconvenient
coopy-up barn-busy cake-empty estate
and gan back in the tunnel to profit-land, that way,
unner the candy-bummed mountain of Grace
wiv the tory-toaded rim-tailed world-eaters
(glory be to God for nickel-bumpered things)
an' forget.

The flutes are risin' and wavin'
an' pure earth iz up-aging all manner patient roun' plat-flowers becomin'.
The cloudy airy plane- and zeus-blue
ride-float small buff heaven
has happened, gone, as old aza photo. Flat.

The fossil fuels swim to us fra exotic slick-haired lands
where unnameable names ha insisted everythin's brought bankside,
howks up crass-bones, ald-tree, carapace, black-crab an' claw,
tubs them, an' leave invade, tak their chance on the ruby-oh ocean.
How! little armoured bug-world scramble and snidle and back-scuttle
    out on the hold on the hush quay to the quite unexpected free-
    blood zone atween the bonded fence and the fish-shop
an' expire.

High up,
very elevatedly
in the worm-be-bored castle,
in the steam-glass chromey-trim office sprawl,
on the seat of power, in the vim-scoured void,
there is maist' nebody keekin
at the unusual-odd town-unformation offin'.
Triple-terminids tremble; a new ald buildin' flares up.
Mazed, Aa come out to
a sunami of smoke is lowpin' up the street us-by and fertile.
How?
Saxon and Dennis were first at the scene
And the fore-flames were brandlin' in thick flat green.
Well we knaa, at verse end, all may sit,
the g'eat bells of bins are being rung,
the night
is one of incipient pandemonium.
All there are are votes for violence.

Glowing
prose
taxes / bills / 'request your – '
How to PAY?

'You may opt to pay … on the basis of the quantity … on written
    application to the Company'
'Ave quondam rex anglorum
nunc coheres angelorum'
Oswald, pray you to pay!

The young seem made of glue,
they worship the amber butterbean
they move with the logic of tumblin' chain
An' laugh at silly-serious matters.

On the East Durham Desert Island
mair dogs, please, and motybikes, an' trees an' bairns an' blue-water.
Less rollies and demon-coal and taxes.
Is easy.
But the make-a-bucks

cowl it all off
for a pockit pankers and liggies,
they are diesel-entities,
a sort of wish-flacky shale
doon-an-up beach;
the sovereign sand cannot tilth & silt & make.

From the tunnel, dirt-dry
where can the dark dart-hood of the law
get brort to flagrant colour,
singin' ball-brass scour-bright, and become?
Or it seems
night is total,
nowt stirs but blind elements,
doughy wing, king crystals,
cliff-stritch to-break, slides
an salt-yieldin' clay,
noded unfigures, ex-fence,
nabut melt-down cranes, dead ovens,
slidin' thoro soppin' cloud-helm blank-layer, beezer-blind,
sees-not, sez-not,
the torn-hair alias an' car-skin
ridgin' in the supple-acid air.

content in nothingness
I set out
and the world swam
in illusions
of glassy light
but we were recalled to that
with every
eye-blink (unbright),
drag of dust,
at crack of night,
dark-flash, thunder-damn-crush

so I stop
so I strike

I bury

and I break

with the gorgeous cans
the waving jags
frond-greet

it is spaces and gaps
the weapon leaps,
sound-quicker, eye-faster,
a touch, an annihilate

a new density,
re-collapsing matter,
re-locked ending

dispute-hard-demon-clutch
matrix-grip
compact-and-I-set-out-in
illusion-of-solidity

a screaming of kite-dome
clashes the gun-mouth,
then sound-smith, war-shouter
smells the gap to cover,
delivers

*

Let the pig-glory rose-show the site,
aren't I?
The beauty-tack,
unwrap the rubbish-sham,
my loss of love, loss-sadness.
In which can-spool
you hidden?
Vanity-tale, so,
impossible to give.

The ghost-tiger-white engine
and the town,

the slipping mist-stir,
gantries,
the old foxes play-yatter in the coal,
fried-time,
but people still talking.

As the kid-dash
is one ever culture,
never dust-straddled,
never silver-wrong and
out of sense
for all its strange old-aim,
declaration of adult-trust
when only it gotta tarnish and ship.

At the box-scatter
all my elbow-words
fuse.
Scissor-rat and torrent
have kept us, love,
out in the whiskey-air.

devil-tribe
flower and solanum and
granite-dice,
whicker-flosses,
terrible bridges of stem/tat,
'Troops, curfews, and reason'
the triple-snecked tongue to dragon.
Sez the pretty poppy-jersey'd Californian,
'I'm keepin' an eye on everyone.'
You can cook with words, rhyme with words, sing with words,
but not make justice with them.

*

boom of
and voice song
ways/arches
a stadium

a song
sad smooching
away from
ice hockey start

sticks
rattle
wooden spokes
my
matchbox

inky-light
denim
my shape

woven/worn
dust-grit
sweat-scented
slow

frozen milk
cream dome
lovely colours
instead of black ground

old days,
oak-trains.

Sez Monkey,
we'll trace the burn, tit to sea-fret,
an' off they dashed.

But what hue's transconnexion?
mineralic violet, or pursuable yellow,
is it thornless, powdery pink or?

Dialect Poems

incorporating

The Cuddy Anthem: a mini dialect anthology

Nows in the g'eat hwelve   o' high Durham   [vault
wheer's the blaked banes   o' bonny saint-men   [yellowed
upaheight in ice   that's iv awd rock, for sure.   [old
Its tip towers   tricked wi' snaw,
sombre the sun-show   slippin' thru the rose-glows. [windows
An' i' this box-bigg,   brazint wi' glory   [building
ar' stannin' the standards,   strang as the men
o' ironheart, aye,   that ivvor hewed them
delved of dark dust   the dyes an' spangles
that irridesce   ivvor a one stitch.
Pictors of pit-men   lang pay'd bi deeth   [overcome
that met them marchin'   in some mortal face-off,
stopped i' the stithe.   An' noo the story   [gas
like Fynes o' the fadders,   Scargill o' the sons,
iz lock'd i' the linnen,   lappin' the columns
o' reetious rock,   riveless tho' battled,   [untorn
benevolent banners,   abyun noo at last.   [above
If the drum is deed,   an' the dance stilled
an' the lass left by   an' the lowe ower-aw'd   [flame
an' the collieries closed   an' the coonty wairsh, [feeble
ther's nean wadbut kneel   to the new becomin',
ettled i' the clear   call o' co-operation.   [implicit
When the peacock can preen   in nae palace
when the owl gars its oiled heed   mak nae mair October turns,
when the trees hev tummel'd   to time's heelin'   [pouring-out
an' the wild glass-music   jangles nae mair,
the bottles brokken   i' the basement o' the hall,
then'll still hing i' sanctuary,   the high soul o' coal.

*

It'z a puzzle OK. We war tell't like –

Wark harder Geordie,
  Mak us money!
Ootput's up,
  Profit's bonny,
Ye're deing weel,

    Yor prospect's sunny,
In oor land
  O' milk 'n' honey.

Yir ain port's
  Nae in-shipping coal,
Up-price gas
  'S nivor oor goal,
An' tho' we dad yi   [slap
  On the dole,
We luv aal miners
  G'eat an' smaal.

In the Hoos   [House of Commons
  We've myed it plyen
Shut's nae shut
  An' sayin's nae sayin'.
An' if it did not
  Click, we'll deign
To tak oor time
  An' say it agyen:

Nae pit'll close
  Till we've fand best
Hoo ti ignore
  Yor request
Ti carry on, but –
  Did yi guess 't?
Meanwhile we're gan ti shut
  Vane Tempist!

Weel, it still dizna mak sense …

*

If yi dinna pay yor poll-tax ower
then some pick-dark neet
Pumpkin-heed'll dad ye

Az yor strampin' up the street.

His maumy beak is yuck wi' reek   [rotten
Divnt unsteek, divnt even keek.   [unlatch (the door) … peek

Pumpkin-heed'll stot yih fer sure
If yor tax-disk's oot-o-date
If yor TV license 'swrang
Or yih misst yor watter-rate.

His maumy beak is yuck wi' reek
Divnt unsteek, divnt even keek.

It's nae use pleedin' poverty an' aal
Yance computors hev yor name
They turn it ower ti Pumpkin-heed
An' his vinjince frae the grave.

His maumy beak is yuck wi' reek
Divnt unsteek, divnt even keek.

It's nae use stayin' barr'd inbye
ye'd wished he'd com ta'en yor gear
Or hoy'd yi inti jail or what
Afore yi meet him face-ti-face up near!

His maumy beak is yuck wi' reek
Divnt unsteek, divnt even keek.

(Man, he's warse nor them vigilante groups that's riving Murton apart.)

The Emergency

Lork a day! the postman's went
An left me mate a canny note
Aal aboot the Dock Company
An' thor storin' o' Ammonium Nitrate.

'How marra, hev ye seed this now?'
'Na, what's that?' 'It's this ye knaw:
It seems we cud aal be wiped out
If this new chimical s'ood blaw."

'It's harmless, man, it gans on crops.'
'I' weeny tits, but this is a bank   [mound
Of nigh ten thoosand tons,
An' that's a canny bowk Aa think.   [blast

'On telly they showed us how one ton
Cud easy wreck a whole tower-block
Se Aa dinna fancy living se close
Tiv a pile of such mad-temper'd stock.'

'By hokey, ye're reet; ye're reet there marra,
An' tho' they didna write to me
Aa'll ax aboot objectin' like
An' see if there's owt we can dee.'

Se Aa axed a coonsillor, 'What's ti be deun?'
'Aa canna act,' sez he, 'ye see,
In case Aa sell ma ahn bit hoose
To the vary same Dock Companee.'

Se Aa axed a fireman, 'What's te be deun?'
'Ye're jestin' marra,' sez he ti me,
'If that lot fires, ye'll nut see us
Back this side o' Peterlee.'

Se Aa axed the big environment gaffer,
'Canna ye hilp us tackle this blob?'
He sez, 'I did post some notices out
And more than that's to risk my job.'

But now it's ower and Clifford's mad
The H.S.E. garr'd him stop.
Sez he, 'I hope you're happy now,
I hope it will not lose men jobs.'

Lork a day! the postman's went
An' he's left me a canny note,
It sez in bowd, 'EASINGTON FIRST –
We need yor hilp, we need yor vote….

'Yor frien'ly local coonsil's threat   [threatened
Be this new Unitary Status!
Se rally roon' and dee yor best,
Oor varry existence iz at stake!

'We've printed up thoosands an' thoosands o' these
An' sent them oot at terribol fee
Jis' se ye'll appreciate
Here's a reel emergency!'

*

We are upaheet, upaheet, upaheet,
yih are doon-belaw, doon-belaw, doon-belaw,
we hev a microphone, a microphone, a microphone,
yih hev ti stan' up, wave an' shoot, shoot, shoot.   [shout
But the best ovit aal is,
we knaw th'answers,
'n' we're nut lettin' on!

Toon Cooncil's nowt. Listen ti this! A crab, but sich a spanker ye hed it brek it oot the pot, cut all the mesh, rive it apart like, but he kent well hoo ti tackle thit sort o' monster an' got a loop o' rope on its nippers furst. An' then he lowpt strite on its back an' sez 'looka this' an' they set off ata canny-pace, but Aa dinaa if ye've ivvor seed them sin', mebbe?

Aye, ther's alluz a one trubble-maker. Here he comes.
Lucky-like, he's aad an' nut ower-smartly-rigged-oot,
naebody'll gie him mich ittenshin!
Shull Aa wait whiles he finishes? Na, Aa'll cut in.
'Aal this gloom and criticism, diz nae gud at aal!

Man, what sort foak'ld rubbish ther ahn toon, Aa ask yer?'
That'll fettle him, Aa warr'nd.

Aye, District Council's warse, but lissen ti this! Them's nowt ti thi jiant lopster thit bunes jis inbye the g'eat dock-gates. Nae, neebody ivvor seed it, bud ye ken it wuz ther OK if ye'd been thru what we hev. Man, the tugs-o-war we've hed jist ti git them fenders up! Weel, Aa reckon it's ti be expectid when think hoo lang it's staid unchalling'd be the staiths, like. Aye, Aa'm tellin' yi, a Coonty Council's the reel tricky yan!

Aal we hev ti dih, is wait and wait,
An' they'll problings run oot o' bait.
An' when thor really deep i' debt,
They'll flit.
'n' we can shut doon
a one mair silly las'-cent'ry toon
'n' git back ti bein' agricultural
'n' clear episcopal.

*

There sartenly is some canny mysteries in Coonty Durham. Like for what are they reshifting aal the local cooncils aroond? Dee they want us all back on farms noo? An' what reelly happened them Category D villages? Aa doot, me, the Prince Bishops is aal alive an' weel an' operatin' sum toorist racket. It's a fremd thing, the church, like. Mebbe Cuthbert's relix s'ood aal be back i' Lindisfarne? An' whe stole Bede's banes, Aa ask ye? Aa reckon ye cud git a clinkin' g'eat community award fer cleerin' up a back case like that!

or

'HOW THEY NEARLY CAUGHT ALFRED WESTOE AN' HIS GANG'

Phone it ye, – 0800 …
Hello? hello?

Ah'm thru am Aa?
On that crime-line?
Noo listen, ye –
Na, nivor mind that –
This is urgent, ye –
It's oor Cuddy, he's been stown, like.   [stolen
Cuthbert. C – U – aw, areet.
Na, dowp-heed, he's nee donkey.
Stupid, that!
Man, diyi ken nowt?
Just lissen then.
Noo, Cuddy sed he wantid ti bide i' Lindisfarne.
Aye, it's in writin' an' aal.
Weel, they've ta'en him.
Na, we wan' him back.
Weel try Chester-le-Street.
Or them byen-mongers i' Durham.   [bone
An' if it's them Aa hope yi spanghew 'em fre Wearheed ti –
                                                    [toss painfully
Aye, weel Aa've hed mi say.

Phone it, ye – 0800 …
Hello? hello?

I' that the line for snitches?
Aye it's me agyen. Na … Na … Aye …
How, lissen, yi daftie,
Ah'm tellin' ye, it's vandalism noo!
Aye. V – A – oh, areet.
Wheer? Whey, iv oor greivyard,
here, i' Jarra, man,
aal brokken up an' –
haafin' an quarterin' an' aitin's tee gud for 'em, Aa say.
An' a other body's missin'!
Man, Bede's gyen. B – E – D – E.   [gone
Nay, Aa nivor seed the gadgee that deun it.   [bloke
It wor money, Aa reckon.
But whe wud wanti gan roon' cowpin' corpses, Aa ask ye?
                                                    [merchandising

129

Gwanon, that's it – 0800 …
Hello? hello?

Aa got sum information, me.
Nyem? Gie ower.   [name
Na, course Aa wan' me reward –
Aa've not hoyed tenpence in this kist for nowt, hev Aa?
                                                   [chucked … phone-box
Orh, gi'us a nummor then.   [number
Aye, it's thon Bede an' Cuddy
that were on the telly –
Aa knaa whe fang'd 'em.   [grabbed
Aye, an' Aa knaa wheer they are.
Aye, an' Aa knaa why they did it.
Aye, it wuz …

    (THWACK!*)

Hello!
Hello!
This is 0800 …

* sound something like an arrow being shot through someone

*

Looksthanaw –

When Aa wuz little
Da set off
Ti gan an' live
Wi' someone else.
He garr'd me choose
But Aa cudn't say
Se he wudn't see me
Sin' that day.
But Aa will meet him an' bray him   [beat
Frae hingin'-on ti howdy-mah   [start to end of a shift

(Yan day, Aaa promise)

At local schiool
They teached me
Ti bray th'Irish
an' the hameless,
blacks an' aal them
the had nae place
in a Christian coonty,
as they says.
An' when Aa meet 'em Aa mun bray 'em   [must
Frae hingin' on ti howdy-mah
(An' Aa cud graw up an' join th'army mebbies)

When Mam deed
Aa wuz ower-young
ti tak on the mortgage
an' Dad wuz naewheer.
Aa was hoyed oot
in the street,
forbecos Aa wuz nut owd eneugh
even for Hoosin' Benefit.
Wheer's the job Aa needed ti keep mi fed
Frae hingin'-on ti howdy-mah?

Sum fren's put me up
a bit, like, then uthers,
an Aa hed
a month's wurk i' Holland
but aal the Coonty
ever offered me
wuz a keek at a magistrates' Coort   [short look
fer nut livin' lucky.
An' if Aa ivvor meet them at groond-level, Aa'll surely bray 'em
Frae hingin'-on ti howdy-mah
(Aa vow).

*

Ye can keep Pensher,
Ye can keep Roker,
An aal the kelter o' a boss o' Nissan,   [riches
mowed-up-cramm'd in sum snawy Swiss bank,
For Aa've a lass than bangs them aal   [beats
E'en Wynyard Hall.

An' the twee uv us
it maks it
as plain as a pickard on a pot   [small boat

That it's

Illusion:
street, block, sail, law,
or.

Nut telled, Aa hev ti guess,
ye hev ti doot,
see:

Thor's aal th'eternal
cat's-straw/giss'-fog/fret,   [pig ...mist
calendar-cabbish, growth o' biook   [cabbage

Sez ye're safe.

Ask.

Try.

Be.

The whole hall of formulas
itiz apparent
means nowt efter dark.

But ye hev ti bet.

Thon's a horse o' life,
or a g'eat whirl like vangty-an　　　　　　　　　　[roulette
an' clinkin' treezher,
and.

But ye cannot wurk it,
ye see?
weel, if it's a gam'.　　　　　　　　　　　　　　　[game

*

Lookanaw! Aa dreamt this g'eat mammy-church
swell'd i' the sun an' gav burth.
The babby was a castle
a' bigged o' taty-lump stanes　　　　　　　　　　[built … potato
an' frilly brittly fancy-wurk
an' battle-teeth
An' when it wuz up-grawn
an' hed ti leave hyem,
believe it, thor wuz an awful fray,
an' castle gav burth tiv a prizun.
Noo prizun wuz a reet bummer,
an' lookt set ti black-sheep them a'.
It blared at church　　　　　　　　　　　　　　[poked its tongue out
an' telled it here deeth wuz cheaper,
it doubled the neeve ti castle,　　　　　　　　　　[fist
an' sez thoo'll see sum riots noo!
Flaid, areet, they garr'd it stay sat,　　　　　　　　[scared … made
bad it bide whiet ahint the hooses:　　　　　　　　[quiet
'Dee wot the hell ye will, but keep a thack on it.　　[thatch, i.e. roof
Mak certain thor clarty ways stays well-sealed.'
Castle as prezzy gav it iv'ry lock an' bar,
Church ov its dog-teeth made razor-wire.

The Tilcon Quarry

As the rock-skirt blew up an' a clash!
as the face-focus shived the hill-land   [sliced
an' hes get new raads warking
up an' alang the face,
itoz i' side-an'-side, for kilter,   [balance
wurk versus route,
and the rolly-buzz-truck-dots
descended, git laaded and git up oot
yowly-tyre'd, of the flower-cup,   [yellow-
that's aal but octagonal,
a skelper ova toon, an' left teum,   [empty
pork-scored aal ziggurat-lanes,
wick-live access.

The laading platform
wiz this dais-like rocky-less flat, upaways,
some special smooth brink,
an' stupa-like cone chutes
carricks, drum-soul'd   [cairns
shot the grade
doon onti shuggyin' lorry-boxes   [rocking
durin' some dancin' arm-signals
ower the soft roar.

Abune iv'ry brinkside   [above
are delineatory boolders ti be
picked up by thor heedleets.
An' also they wurked doon te win,
thon Tartarean space, that noo is.

The sun-grey wa(l)k
its end is stop-lorry still;
a viewin' crawlin' magnesium,
and mebbies, mind,
mammoth-micro life-hooses packs in grains ther,
rock instructure
prevail

as engel-wavy chord/cliffs/clammerin' [clambering
entowerin'
goth-bronze
striatin'
banana-solid bandin' zones

waals ti wurk! each face
skelped oot bi blastin' bi reduction
tiv ease-tight collapse
geological (mature) stave-tones
quarry-delve-kit
ears bear silent pop (Sunday)
ghost- and hacky-men, lift-pitties, like, [sky-miners
deed active [dead
flute-token fire-waged
heel it inti stour-topped tubs [pour … dust

First won a bit.
It could be fended on th'existin' line ti the port. [managed
Limestone-burn is likes for aal:
it is snawy slop-cement, concrete and can build
ethereal churches,
coast-emplacements,
cellar-garths.
An' sarves as lime th'aud blast-furnaces, chimical wurks,
thit needs it baked frae the kilns.

In the tippy-frame, change-world-wi-roads
policy top era,
before there was local radio fizzin' on,
an' trains with automatic (guesswurk) doors,
dolomito
wuz bang new commerce,
iv'ry raad wished it, grade,
th' elastic-space motorways
dreamt of sich reg'lar relatively-even base-material.

Two piles of it, looksthanaa,
are zoo-hills
ootbye the defile-doors

whiles this day,
cammy mouments o' bank [mound-like …hill
anent th'ancient rape-seed [opposite
anent the coal-blue sea
backgroonds.

The new lease was Tilcon.
They re-lined a road doon-ower frae the top
like a 3-D ramp, brent eneugh, wiv truck ti diesel up [steep
a wall-top like,
imp-lippy, claggin' thru the gears. [sticking/grinding

Noo
it's cowped ti [swopped/changed
tall-as-toy
spires o' light,
plant-egregious,
squads o' football bulbs
foxglove-ish marcasite-seed
oot o' dark
them fremd [weird
an'
loud

Aa wisht Aa cud count the future.
Sen' it's ettlin' to be plant-playgrounds, [aiming
wheer sicimores can speel an' rax, [spread
or arena o' bike-robatics,
an oor special scientific disinterest.
Lang-leg kervers [graffiti artists
(fleein' and loggerheed) [butterfly
(magpod & skemmy) [pigeon
notched ever higher (on'y ivor initials).
It is all mowed-em'ti, stane-thrang, [crowded
teum-altar, rainbow-scale [vacant
architicture, it aal
hes been deun in reverse,
rooms and desks and floorin' are
air.
Yi stand on the roof.

Yi can step onti the Sun.

The Parlous Chyase
(after Lewis Carroll)

It wuz a thark an' dowly cave,   [dark; gloomy
   Draak'd proggles ower it creep.   [wet thorny things
Fizzes inbye the flacky wave   [buzzes; flickering
   Thru cundy braad an' deep.   [channel

Nivvor inbye thon dreer recess
   Wuz seed the lowe uv day;   [light
What bad ahint its mirkiness   [lurked behind
   Nean kent an' nean cud say.   [no one knew

The monarch rid ower bank an' brae
   An' drav the yowlin' pack.
Hiz marras aa' reet sonsily   [happily
   War coinin' iv hiz track.   [wending

Win eager ee, wi' yalp an'crie   [with/eye
   The hoonds lowpt doon the rocks,   [lept
Aheed ov aa' ther companie
   Gans rin the spunky fox.   [adventurous

Thon fox hae won that cave ov awe
   Tewed sarely win his rin.   [wearied badly
Whe noo is he sea bawd an' braw   [so bold & brave
   Te dare tiv enter in?   [to

How! tappy-lap yon vary hoond   ['with eager bounds'
   Sped in the cavern drear,
A canny few yowls is heered aroond,
   A canny few skrikes o' fear.   [shrieks

Like ony wi' thirsty appetite
   Mun slocken wiv oringe pulp,   [must slake (it)
Wuz heerd a huggle an' a bite

A swaller an' a gulp.

The king he lowpt frev off hiz steed,   [from
   Howked oot his shivin' brand;   [drew … trenchant sword
'Whe on me pack o' hoonds diz feed   [who
   Mun dee be ma yain hand!'   [must die … own

Sea sed, sea deun; them stood thor heer'd   [So
   Reet mony a mickle stroke;   [great
Soun's like the flappin' ov a bird,   [sounds
   A struggle an' a choke.

Oot o' the cave scarce howked they hit,   [extracted … it
   Wi' puul an' push an' haal –   [pull … haul
Wheeriv Aa've drawed a weany bit,
   Bud dorsent draw it aal.   [But … all

(please complete for yourself …)

Jetty Song

The icy blaw is ower the sea
   (Come, codling, come ti me)
Roofy grey in ugly spree
   (Hinney, get hung on, Aa'll reel ye ti me)

With basket-knots Aa set the rod
   (Come, codling, come ti me)
Pillion an' mussly aa' for thor gobs
   (Hinney, get hung on, Aa'll reel ye ti me)

The ghostly fleet's ootbye the pier
   (Come, codling, come ti me)
O silvery swimmers cum get up here
   (Hinney, get hung on, Aa'll reel ye ti me)

I wadda howked it oot at that

   (Come, codling, come ti me)
But a lowpin' g'eat watter skelped me flat
   (Hinney, get hung on, Aa'll reel ye ti me)

Sa aal Aa catched woz thon jiant wave
   (Come, codling, come ti me)
It kisst me yance an' garr'd me bave
   (Hinney, get hung on, Aa'll reel ye ti me)

How, git the bath-tub oot, Aa'm nack'd
   (Come on, I wanit gay an' waam)
An' wesh the saut frev off ma back
   (Oh Hinney, that's grand, that's a treat, Aa warr'nt)

On the Tyne

Dicker hoyed his line oot ower far
To wheer the creivs 'n' lopsters are.
They thranged aroon' it wan an' aa'
An' nicked the biet wi' crafty cla'
Then tugg'd three times to let him kna'
They'd luv sum mair – it woz five-star!

('Not e'en a thankyou note,' said Dicker, 'Na,
'Aa'll siev ma raggies, man, let's hev a jar.')

Deep unnerneeth the ocean's lip
The crafty lopster spies oor ship
That stopped an' garr'd a hook ti dip;
Sez he, 'Young creivs for a spanner tip   [50p.
Aa'll gie yi a clinkin' roon'-wirld trip,
Jus' queue up here, an' git a grip!'

(The babby creivs went up an' doon,
An' 'greed it woz a rare bit fun.)

The Coggly

It was queer, the day, me hinney,
The whiles thoo wiz oot,
This quean cam ti the doar   [queen/woman
Wi' cry an' shoot.

'Weel, frin', thoo's poarly,
That Aa can see,
(Sez Aa reet gotherly) – Is thor owt   [sociably
That Aa can dee?'

'Sah, sah, things gan az wrang   [sir
As they can gan,
Aa winnut fash yi wiv aal the trials
Aa've hed wi' ma man …

'Ah but ma bairns, sah, them,
Aal married bad,
An' quarrol fit ti deave mi –   [deafen
It maks me mad.

'(We wadna let wor unca
Dee the syem,
But drav him oot
For the syek ov oor nyem.)

'Forby, Aa've getten an awfu' smit –   [ill
Heer me snivel!
It maks it hard to beer
The greatest evil:

'For naw ma ain bit hoose,
Ma on'y hyem
Has ta'en fire, parlous
An' breet the flyem!

'The lowe it hants me sair,
Endured, na cured.

Oh sah, spare me sum cash,
Aa wozna insured!'

'But, ah,' sez ma douce wifie,
'Thor's a shyem!
Thoo cud did mass the tea,
Mak her at hyem.'

'Why hev sum sense, Meg,
She's nivor owt like poar.
A caravan like wors,
Why, she'd nivor cross the doars!'

In the Neet

Dinnot blare, oor kid, Aa'll tell yi
  Hoo it happened me the neet,
Hoo Aa got this awfu' shiner
  But nae prezzy bae yor feet.

Aa wenti Santy's grotto,
  He woz makkin' oot his list
O' things allow'd at Kezmus
  An' what hed better be miss't.

Tabs is oot, sed Santy,   [cigarettes
  Or yi'll nivor appreciate
The stithe ov aal them lorries   [fumes
  Rowlin' oot the harbor giets.

An' dogs iz off this yeer an' aal,
  Nastie foory geets,
For thor smaaly claggy messes
  Sticks the litter ti the streets.

An' alcohol – nae alcohol,
  It's strictly off ma list,

For beer and pups an' smokin'
  Aal fash Allah, like, an' Christ.

An' Aa'm much inclined to reckon,
  Thinkin' neg'tively tha knaws,
If we hed a lot less warkers
  It wad hilp keep ma costs law.

Se it's volunt'ree redundancy
  For Rudolf an' his marras,
But he'll mak a canny bed-hap   [duvet
  If the taggerman'll pay us.   [scrapdealer

Santy, Santy, man, gie ower,
  That's nae gud, Aa'll hev a ga!
For Aa knaw jist what the kidders want
  When they heers yi bray the snaw.   [hit

It's high-pressure watter-pistols
  An' them bikes wi' chooby tyres,
An' a feck of marriwanna
  Gans a treat afore the fire.

It woz gran' till Santy stot me   [knocked down
  An' Aa went oot like a leet,
Which is why, ma son, Aa'm sad ti say,
  He'll nat caal here the neet.

*

Did 'oo heer that hinney?
Wot ma luv?
Oor Prince an' Princess o' Wales hev split
Altegither.

It mun raise lots o' problems.
That it mun.   [must
Which of them'll get to hev Buck Hoose

For example.

An' then Aa remembor,
Aye, se div Aa,
Hoo the Queen's Da hoyed his brother off the throne
For muckin' his marriage.

They'd hev nae truck wi' divorce then.
Ov corse not.
For it garr's their label of respectability
Show clarty.   [mucky

Aa sometimes wonder 'boot aal that divinity stuff.
Drink thee tea then.
Diz the Princess, noo, seem to photo wiv a halo, when she gans roon'
   toochin' an' healin' all them folk?
Aa thowt not.

An' then thor's the Consitution.
What's that, pet?
Whe's ti lead the courts, the pollis, the prisons,
If the king's a fondie?   [soft in the heed

Th'army an' them'll be nae better –
Winnut? –
For whe can gan roon' shootin' and runnin' amok
I' the nyem ova brokken bachelor?

Ay, Aa blyem that Da o' his.
Philip thoo means.
Ay, ivor runnin' roon' wi' his neeve on his zip,
If tyels be troo.

Wi'oot a thowt for his son –
Poor Charles, Aa say –
Packin' him off ti caud-watter skiools
Wi' nazi trash.

An' his grannie, look at hor!
The aud quean? She smiles nice.

Aye, an' a canny cam of gin she puts away   [pile or mountain
Bae aal accoonts.

Noo we've warked ower hard at oor marriage –
Fer aal ye've nae job –
Wivoot a haaf ova tenth of thor income
They gits for nowt.

Knaws what Aa think, hinney? –
Na, what? –
Thor nae better nor a gang of toits iva bum-hoose,
The pack o' them.

On Vane Tempest Provisionally Shut, 23 October, in the Afternoon, 1992

While the bishop that tawks to the pollis that bray'd the miners woz marchin',
wiv a thrang, weel-hair-comb'd mob,
tiv address a petishun
til their Lord
whe lives mony a sunny mile frev here,
Satan, wiv a singular bat
o' his gristly neeve   [fist
tew'd Vane Tempest sarely,
aal but drav it
clean belaw ti the sea.
Ah heer'd the steam-toot.
Ah wad sed 'tara'
exceptin' that it wos rainin' whole watter like,
an' Ah'd jist waamed mi living-room up
wi' North-Sea gas
which is on'y haaf the price
o' drink-watter – honest, man.
Forby, in this crumbly coonty
nowt's gannin up,
but flags thit show ye've wark'd harder the day

and the nummer o' sowjers
an' the nummer o' skint-fowks i' javal [jail
an' mi memory's slaw, but it woz …'
aye, prices, in fact, maistly them,
an' maistly on them red smaal papery yells for money
that flee thru the trech'rous bit gap
in iv'ry front door.
I dinnaw
what they bother to scent thor bills
wiv artificially inseminated aroma ov panic for, de ye?
Onyways, thor Aa woz hevin' a muse,
a bit crack ower me cup o' tea
'boot litter an' cooslip slopes ahint the pit,
dowly, raggy sand, [dismal
coal-crust trees,
the 'airy wheels ov dux,
an' quaint awd rolly-routes,
– all them things that affects the market valyer ova hoos –
when a letter cam hoy'd thru me door
axin' if we'd mebbe like
the toon-cooncil abolisht, like?
Kas oor views might metter.
An' wad we like the toon-centre
jis' pulled doon too,
while thor at it,
To save time, like,
Or mebbe blow'd up
be fertiliser?
So I sed, personally I wad feel lots safer
Settin' oot in the rain,
an' put ma reed boots on
and took a stick-an'-cloot [umbrella
and went oot.
At the dock-gates
the de'il hissell, in senior, [devil
wiz lakin' at puttin' rollies [playing … lorries/tubs
up and doon North Street, ti annoy us,
like a gang o' Nesbits let lowse,
an' me ettling to set on sum petishun
ti ax whether capilliary action

wad bring eneugh watter up the shaft o' the pit
ti produce a canny foontain,
when a mirabolic g'eat skelp of thunnor
gann'd soss! afront ov me
an' a lectric lowe   [light/flash
glower'd roon' the war-square
showin' it aal tegither
tyum but for him an' me,   [empty
and the wild hoopy-soop-waves ootbye
an' then he com up strike   [direct
and started a crack, like this:
How! – he boomed,
jis' like an announcement –
This is special! Listen here, ye!
We knaw things is ajee aal ower
an' what's te dee wiv yor redundancy pay, I say,
An' hoo can ye get aheed?
Weel, we've diun it.
Noo wor cuttin' ye in.
In this:
THE OFFER, it's gotta be, ultimate,
unmissable, THE (Aa mean)
privatization – yes –
of HELL.
Aye, ye can hev yor ain share ov
emptiness and exile,
buy yesell a shive o' teemin' terror,   [slice
invest in aal the agony ye can handle,
an' tak ill interest tee.
Dicorate yor tax-free car-loan
wiv anti-ozone,
claim yor place
in the claggy chimical trade   [tacky
wiv extra-offer allergy,
aye,
tak up yor private haudin'
in hell-mooth, noo!
Before we landskip ye aal in kak,   [shit
wire the land off,
se join us i' the mad,

o canny lad,
bein' the best offer ye've had …
An' Aa stud in a stiumor.   [trance
For whe knaws, i' true,
what's plann'd?
It's sittled
An' leave us wi' nowt
but dialeck for democracy.
Hooivver much yi show them clear
Ye want sumthin' else nor a borrow'd life,
but yor ain hand on what happens, altegither,
an' knaw it's aal oors to mak it happen,
yor heeds is jawp'd tegither
an' yi meet as well be burblin bubbles thru a milkshake
as mak words to them lot.
Onyway,
Aa had me environmentalist badge alang wi' me,
and howk'd it oot, and confronted him wi'it,
an' Satan bowked oot an awefu' pump,   [fart
and lowped inti the hole
the pit wiz yance,
an' the sun cam spanglin' oot,
an' someone somewheer
gov the bishop a thanks
as tho' any wun man can de owt
thru power
ti release ye.

Delvan's Book

dedicated to Delvan Ricardo MacIntosh

Account

It's not enuf, see, pal,
to get the secret alarms,
you've ti reckon
with secret-secret ones (you'll miss)

Any rich riskable shop
is like to have one (I guess)
so then it's time
(is the factor)

Mark the back
climb it
smash a way in
arm-asteroid

That is my pause-point
when the pulse-rebels give you big ribs
The house gives you alien
The limits band against you.

The senses don't adjust
You think you can hear
You think you can see
You think you can feel

But you work headless
In the cave behind the waterfall
In the island at lake-centre
In the silent snake snow

The bench is a hoof-barge
The cooker is a can-tomb
The floor is an excavation and reaches Pit
As you try an' think the rainbow-bird-man.

An' it begins to resist
The catches won't give

You yell an' the lock tricks you
You stick

An' you know the black sortes has cut you off
You roll you over
Gotta sense
This warm girl sweet an' next in touch

(And why?
Oh, ta.
Because it's there?)

Or sure it's smart of dog
Bleeding fighting, teeth
In your brawn.
Are you gonna be sensible and come out?

You fight for the window
An' when you're half out
They start to beat out
So you roll in the glass, more and more.
Just one more bit of life.

Reverie

With a daemon-sheep wave of his paw,
The Provider
quits me.
I lollop to that end.
Eat a bit of paper.
Lollop back.
it's strong gear.
I chew in my cheek.
Am rosy with suiting well-scrubbed fur and felt,
    leather-ears, horn claws as I mill.
Bead off on a line.
See that? Wow!

Can I catch? Pace it! Long on leap, and fast an' fast.
The screw legs it. Up a pole.
I treed him and I'll wait,
nonchalant,
for the shakey sod to topple off.
Two toffee-back bucks come on a hop,
and a pole on their shoulders,
an' the trussed prey gives a man-yelp
as his blue bum bumps the yard.
Oh great, this is good gear. Yes.

Terzetto

We were broken up.
'Have a hole,' he said
an' I stumbled into the waste racket, the concrete.

One is against one.
This person, this thing, this space –
To teach me how not to co-operate.

What am I?
I am a river, and risen blood, and red starstream, raucous beat.
Do you want that too?

Delvan in the SW London Magistrates Court

Above, it is creamy paint and fine new wood and
    pew, there are steps.

Here – dark
now – deep
it is much more paint.

The celso-sphere is symmetrical, it smiles,

without body, has reason, predicts, seems so
simple in print.

Some way brighter – lower
harder – righter
bile – high light

There is the dignity in this face-above-earth,
   stand and take, then gentle indication that
   you leave it, take the tat stairs to the
   cells.

here is it is settled,
prime piss-trackers,
secret see them gang up,
stand there, when you see them stand there,
dressed god-skins
justice in sprite-stink of
it's casual – coincidental
see? stop?

an' there
the three lace-ghost waiting beings
figure-greys,
sticks above their heads
I see (faint-fates) intentionally

intention – terror
thought – murder-tight
maceration – move in & I move in &

Listen! why
my lead body
want?
What you reach,
fine words to all,
my black blood you? eh?

now you know me inch by bruise,
you bastards think I'm stopped.

ground – gone,
floor – flat,
bone – mazed

you as me my fist spring
won't see
an' how again
blaze – strike
heat – hand
sky – song

inner is veracity
energy for 'make move'
mine

again an' again
toss at the law
becos I move
slick – stream
suddy – silver

get me,
how can yer?
how can yer ever?
if is me, and must

an' if I have no rights
leave you repeat
alwer and alwer

an' the worse words
work worse
are this, piss-heads
leading you to a hiding

an' it registers nowhere

here I am the story
lines – strong
over – never

but I'd anything
before I ever let them me, more,
that place, lovely SW magistrates

Wandsworth

Inside a geode
first place, me and this guy tends me a cig I draw deep
325 feet, then of 650 feet, and finally of 980 feet
tells how he cut his girl up, smart like
apostle of spelaeology
when I hit hard
na, the screws were on my side, said OK
had trouble with the numerous porcupines which live in those caves.

in ice caves
in a sole cell unfurnished
with frozen waterfalls
then I flipped, tore, shouted it down, clawing
below zero at about 9,750 feet, glacial, loftiest, violent

arm-tow o'medical wing
and strip cell, seeing
more than eight thousand bats
are more than twenty years
in the total darkness

straight into a vertical shaft
a turbulent river
an offer of valium
through a series of vast sloping chambers
in climbing 52 cascades
how Marcel met his death

no canteen, no nothing
mural engravings

mucky un-sense art-hiding
clay statues
visit me maybe
horses, bison, deer, lion and rhinoceros
the objects of his constant affection

cannot talk cannot read, only
will get back at those bastards
swear it

Merlin fool locked in stone
the lure of
sometimes shimmering like a shepherd's flock
into dark
luminous pleached slugs in the maximate forest,
vermil-violet glow
for
earth with blazing towers
gravid people-loser dragon and it had a puppet gait
is this
a shocked tort'ed figure displayed for court

Letter (1)

In the forest of may,
white arm gathering scent bright dent,
masks the
bare
freight
twigs, the super-smmow,
hueless woodlust spatter
full eye.

mount thru cage
paint-deal light confident rise
tree-knower
apogee

englade in
overbolt / excess
sudden upahigh warm
and to see
un-understood
unendless out over
polar blaze

Letter (2)

To teach me
the world-word Black Seal
what is smaller than
and the stone hexacontalithos
or greater than
is unsaid, Ixaxar.
the curd of the lemon sea
how to cross to where
and how to be selfish.

The fixing of the arch
of the body of the brace
of form/frame
of the toys of the sun (us as)

Asking
may flight of flutes
to the nest node
pyre,
conduct.
and the sitting shambles
grow to novation also
on a one day.

Treasure-presenting:
the buff eggs of brick,

the dry-strim blood-stone,
eye-quartz.
All to pay,
to pay out to be human.
Hold the kopek out.

As
animal
a watery glass-eyed jewel of

On the world of Zung
trivial rules,
hidden behind my head
and secret and –
if you lose, you cannot
be anything
get no black, brown-armed, red-heart friend

Did I make and break the laws?

(just
cancel company,
get you a bit anxious
get you a bit ashamed even to be a human being)

Conan in Trouble

Over the snow-striped plateau, mate,
Conan (who is captured) wends

He has no lotus powder to pull up his nose
brown stem of power to
Suck burning in his lungs
No jewel-paste to daub his arm with

Not even a safety-cover for the driver so to screw with
& no-one to screw

except this footless neanderthal

chained beside him

plodding and chanting thru the snow.
It's the pits.

Not even a tiger, whistling livid thru its ears
makes him look up.

Not even a hairy uni-horn,
like a walk-bag, humping in their path,
makes him so much (even) as smile.

And the lady in her fur-warm sedan
is safe for the moment.

Medical Report

Far within the wynd (the shell),
a little scene-paint
of ice-fog / web / home-hedge

In the centre of the passage of the shell (I hear)
a boiling fire – a hot light,
a focal time.

From within (the shell)
a long tic-a-tape word-stream,
everything.

With the shell at my ear (hear)
things and people moving,
but it is very fast.

The shell shows (me)

such work of such muscles
such ro(w)s of action.

And from the heart of high shell (I get)
our mammal night,
aware and encounterful
scent-centred, as shift,
all engine in day-play,
clumpy, is bemirrored, is close to
the calm arm-arm of night.

Hanuman

the sitted wolf, eyes slide right,
picking the egg up
in the jaw
for
attention for
a bird-bully owner.

wood them,
slow boxers,
for it only takes one crap lapse
and – that – wham
(fighter as thief)

all jezebel baubles in the
velvet smart-light
display of
what's there to be won –
earth's eyes.
There will be fine satin and gleam
on your guts
if you can win.

But
so much

it is sweat, brute-strength
in the heart-clock
to let fly,
just reach,
take,
total it.

The gold fly / the silver / the white
face them' in the ring,
sez 'Yes, continue'
and the bright rippling skins
kick on and burn
clinched like angry-fierce beings
in a fruit-bright cage
and my parable of endless action
as be singing / stinging

Or at a knock-out
Breath was first
It came out as fire
roaring from lips and nose.
Blows cause such shock.

Undersea –
unword.
All its sounds
haphazard.

Catapulted
from the world-level-floor;
earth-quaked boxes;
the space, the lungs.

Is lying on the sea:
gazing up, too, at blue.

unlucky
accusing the seconds that drag you back,
shaking the sweat from your hair,
struggling at least yes to get to your knees

as the kick finishes you,
that slaps you out again.

Who's looking out?
keen, with known eyes, with
strong hands, brand hearts,
a bead-glow map of the next day.
Little, scattered, out away,
we still hear whole and is
Busy at that much success.
(Ring and altar,
height, hand, sight)

No, ta, I won't burn for you.
And I don't care to go burning
for you,
But, a free fight!
Tiger, monkey, bear lead
where the mammal finds its glee.

Strips, prays,
prowls, dances, that is,
flexes the trunk
and if the beasthead oughta favour –
monkey-white and coconut with fur –
why, the point is,
both can
(be moved, be all-god)

Ev'ry extra muscle
to play into grin,
yeah, the hundred targets
body makes –
stay, see

swings, swings,
cuts, kicks –
meat for the god
the break
the monkey-yip, fun

(to be full of)
(to bounce at)
(box)

how ape-bum
he straddles the floor,
would would rise
(an' word wonna come)
'stead – subsides

be the beast
that half-ate
stirs and howls
in the kitchen-cold void
with the land
and melodies
and
Keeooo –
the cold wind –
the tatters –
the bits – (blow & blow)

The great world final
no one v. no one

Almost goat faced
peering over his own shoulder
as I walk away from me

where were her dear chests
one warm, sweet link

There U my sweet Hanuman
monkey lord-major
lodged in my guts
like womb-field, front like fist
when the two smash together
rush of a great man-woman deity.
To contact.
Without control.

Dance.

Belook, in opening Ramuyi
the loop-feathered art,
a prayer,
prowled out in light,
a slide of a dance,
to pronounce
coming offering me to Hanuman,
the oil of the human
to the unfolded fur …

First what you pre-sent
is the hollow room
dead from old/all life,
unless you send us there
can I win, come back?
how?

… *AFTER*

The goat with no mouth
in the Flat Land
indicator
impossibly to stumble
buried rules in secret hands
urine taps
and to toss blood
how maths uses to laugh at mammals
the
thought-Kali.
Obscene
ice-gothic sky-style sweetness,
pavilion, fine clothes, find of manner
all reversed,
now the blank coin,
a poor blank book,
blank blind deprived broken through-sight.

Satires

Winchester

Once we set out
visited Winchester
hitched this bit and that
and got on a minor way before the dawn run
the slope-side was awarren'd rabbits
in noble peace living sitting ticking-legs
    flexing-ears
a plate from a prophet-book
setting our day

Till there the back-blocked potala
sat at city
like proud-children's dead-hands on day

Like reading stone (porridge) its sick fucked-up
    fish (that gave 'emselves up) jumped on the
    hookz (by themselves) bacon (that jumped
    into the pan) wakey wakey get down this here
    dark corridor which is dining room which is
    porridge. letters (good).
Up there Thor
When he would raise sun (hammer), no?

All
Ready to retrain you
steam-hammers
human paddle-wheels
tansel'd shoulders on rock
– arm as shaft and stock
rainbow eye popular toys
to be masters and makers, vibrant with din
and to be able to compete
In the claret-air morning

Lodge of
saint, searer, who
night-passed (Egypt) Lord's sword

Prince of the Meat Factory.
Now

The agency of the exterminating angel
light enamel of crack edge,
the cock that cooks its own eggs.
See

How the dog is dumb before the splendour –
   trapped magnificence of this up altar
how the cattle and tin-oysters whirl and shake
   to the passionate psalm's wave
and the tribe of fish fall into the pretty
   pockets of the sheep-fisher-ruler!

To be able to consume hugely in excess of all
   human standards while convincing others they
   are greedy and depraved.
That is called appetite OK.

And if we had heeded,
daily gone, adored
the lie-tales, learn-be-so

If we had had the sense
only to beat up on
wife or kids
God gave our power-into

If we had only seen
what riches wonder pays
or fitten the world for acid-shed
and bleak trained shearing blood –

We would not so lavishly
guarded energy
waited for rebuild friend-values.

I would ha' run
gone anywhere to make gold

be prince to god
get his license

And I could say things, could argue
Don't I know your being in prison
shows there is something wrong with you?

a
dark
dart
scatter
running spiders
of a hand comes into

The mingiest cells are in Winchester.
No glass, just sockets of air,
talking to rain an' hollow draft
an' white with bird-drop.
You could learn, but the food so abysmal
they get the shits,
buzz the buzzer to be let clean the pot an' the flow on the floor.
Sometime later in the night someone says no.
Maybe it oughta gan on postage stamps –
this new era.

the tag of chemical execution
only well some addict
but we withhold the records
before/until/if we pay out.
At £3000 it's cheaper to terminate
than keep alive, see?

space of
regimenting
fruit
trained rows
and stacks
unjuice
of sun-drying
grey brown mauve

wrinkly uniform.

Haven't I paint' the wall you look at?
Don't I realise you need all this, want?
Don't I teach you work?
All useful for

eall: chill.
thus in assembly.
1. picks. 2. spades. 3. mells.

what stones you can detach
or break slabs
to clear all stone away/off
first
before the trenches –
(tomorrow)
new walls
at Hyde

(the New Minster)
(Edward the Elder)
(a short year from Alfred's death)
(ready near 900)
(here the King's body, Alfred's, moved)
(interred in the new)
(in slow song)

And the site
derelict / old
now noticed, assigned to re-use.

Cart & horse
and labourer –
the pieces are loaded.
Bits of grave-slabs, wall, floor,
with its wild flowers,
dirt, dust,
the bones, bits of arm-sharp and chest,
ledd, wording, old object,

cup – hammer flat,
junk-cart.

The last collapsey relics,
body and grave
of yore, Alfred, Rex Inclytus,
South-Saver, wise and war-king,
swept in crumbs,
malleted down, rut-filler for coach-way,
all in a day.

When the antiquary heard and came,
and found nothing even left to sketch …

Already new wall unloaded
and ready to place / work on
To build
a House of Correction.

On TV

How –
do you see this rainbow life?
teaches me to honour and obey
mostly it succours professionals,
but then they're the suckers
who pay their licenses.

Is there something wrong?
Has no one explained it?
That the English are so hated,
as to be torn apart
on the streets of Ulster …

It's David Frost!
Shit from the shit-monger.
Shit straight from the Court of St Shit.

Satire to show that Oxford & Cambridge
will never tolerate
Socialism on top.
(In the King-of-the-Castle, Guinness-Records world.)
Cardamon and celery leaves,
gingko and dinky
sing the tremble-line of
collaboration, in their TV hands.

Thankyou sez the BBC
to all those who phoned in
TO COMPLAIN

Hereabouts
small libraries of greenfly
seemlily procreating.
The Reverend Henry Sweet
and I are at work
on our glossaries, thru the summer.
I muse on
making millions
by the marketing of royal seed.
It only needs a little co-operation.

The Tories

The Gods were collected on the island
and would never move more,
for they could never change their mind.
There they were consulted, for,
never, in living memory,
would they consult anyone else.
Only on rare storm-split days
the round, egg-oval heads
gave like laughter out,
conceiving newer measures, wholer humiliations,
cruder, ruder abasements to be passed on,
preventers of constitution.

I do not say the heads were merely stone
for divinity is a serious matter, it cannot be measured materially.

It is like a riddle:
who are these people?
Always obsessed with their own beauty
preoccupied with art & possessions,
meritorious insight / aggrandisement,
of so many layers, no double-words are sufficient.
Devoted to words & pictures in colour,
heroes & myths –
conscious most of their own standards of debate.

Now they flick the roundabout of feeling
flashing with ire / indignation / right.
What does it mean?
Drugs is it?

With chandeliers of coal
the beauties paint bodies
to the fashion of chin, waist, cheek, breast
a perfection
of sexual fusing
'Say, faithful we stood to our shape?'
bone-buildings
muscled with meat
to man-girl-smile-eye-windows,
unwhole / escapes.

The coke-tip
(the coke-scatter)
though not one moves
the rub of black souls

Always a change
a work-for
a train-to
if you like changing

We will manicure our veins,

Perm the word
For I laud the word above all the real alternatives
Audivi vocem de coelo …

From old
Queues, sequins,
laburnum-in-patterns,
hats, hangings,
& beyond it, bits of America.

Taking what is public
for your own pocket –
an ownership of air!
to be serious without sense.

Feeling exuberant
I shout Hi Baldy
to the policeman near the bridge.
Well I sort of know him.
Maybe I ought to soothe him?
I say:
If police are right,
then everything a policeman does is right.
Say 'If I am a policeman then everything I do is right.'

What of the grasshopper?
Why, the grasshopper will die in the chill
for singing all summer,
the brass-pot will smash the clay,
the dog hugs the hay.

On Christianity

The magic of Christianity –
let us set it aside.
The weather-bells,
the bass, big groaning thunder,

and the tickle-small thimbles,
that alert All-Soul –
sounds, symbols, fat words
of a new weirdened credulity
(pact of power and lexicon-act)

Or the stones,
so bold, so dark,
on the grave
hold down the dead, say.
Church as dustman.

Maybe we'll marry you in the porch:
on the one hand –
there are to be more manor-workers;
there again –
purity (of prick and vulva/appendix)
is the price (paralysis) of heaven.
Being flexible, though …

This gate-leg table
I gut the Mithraic chicken on –
what do you bury under yours?

A little square window,
segmented,
is right for prisons.
Pointed ones
are the right silhouette
for God.

A tower,
a perch
for excise men.

A spire,
a perch
for monks …

And attempt on attempt

to make
meaningless words
look more modern.
Even singing! Please do not snore
(she nudged me).

No –
I want my Yule
(when I love you)
my Easter
(when I eat)
my May-Day
(when I love you more)
Mid-Summer
(to set my watch)
All-Hallows
(to talk a little to the dead)
and even Plow Monday
(for dragons)
but instead of Sunday
I wd like a day of rest.

Am I a Pagan?
No!
I worship in crowds,
and terrace, or jumbly, or beach,
are my blessings.

But the calendar of Christ
(bone-fires and
the ordered humiliation)
are children's dark play,
and the squeezing equations
any certain proof
exacts.

*

What was it – once?

It was Christianity
is not.

Imagine no soul –
the dead are bodies
somewhere else,
not investments.

No text.
No interpreter.

No marriage-tie –
kin-groups,
children in common,
wood-meetings.

All the art,
none of the nonsense? But no way –

Considerable hangings for Odin,
who must be offered human cream
and you will defend your knowledge.
(For customs survive)

You will need an animal-other,
some bear or wolf or bird.

And a name
to express your link
(the life that is passed to you)
something
to gamble with.

And fear?
Some ritual,
some cult, inscribed with letters.

More
there are horses to raid,
treasure to lift,

self-justice,
jewel-legends, sea and land
to act
till Dark – throttled
it gags,
raw-wood shoots.

*

Speculatively
we have sifted
the dust and sounds of the past.

Is there a gullible constant?

or can we shake
the god-seat of kingship,
irrupt from our institution,
reassemble self and whole?

By word?

By concept?

With a better leader?

Thru zeal for dross?

By privacy?

State-piracy?

A lovely perfume, it eludes me.

It is something that accentuates the body,

will not rely on word.

How can an arm think?
How can a brain feel?

What of heart
and bile
and stomach-for?

Can you talk of such a thing as physical morality?
that this is right or not by muscle-lie?
zones of bone predisposing action?

As tho it is a shell,
līchama,
in which our life and feelings hold,
if not cracked / sent loose.

But I see
like each like whole.
Each toes is the symphony.

My age is my mouth,
my movement is my spine,
my hand is my telephone.

There is a whole frame of bone;
it lures, it acts, it grows,
whole and tree-determined –
and a base of nervee
(shy, shocking, sculptured, capacitated)

It is strenuous, it touches,
it is green as man
when other living things are present
(crowd on it) it throbs to warm / living / hair.

The eyes
jangle at light,
the ears like shapes of sound;
and the feet walk, run, jump.

And its pleasure
is sometimes to be startled.

*

The gonging winter-drum
is taut, at busy-beat, a-boom:
the season's pace is sharp-driving,
gold and ice crack short
with the heavy, flying feet.
The Feast!
The sky bright-blues,
and the Sun feels it, our festivities.

Glorious, handy joy
be to You, flat day-eye!
the cut cherries and biscuits
cheer you upward,
fires to encalorate;
each currant in links to one million years,
for what?
the benefit of the babe, the bairn, boy-girl,
to grow for own inside joy,
light-cut day-glare, unfractious,
its ult'-parade,
solar, slow.

In the dark
there is a priestly prayer (Something Unknown
hears tiny bells),
cheap crackers are swept up.

At his mid-winter feast,
Thorri's daughter (Goi) disappeared.
When the month had passed,
Thorri made preprarations for another feast
with the aim of finding out what had happend to her.

Alphabet of Tories

Arseholes,
Asses!
Zissis your alphabet:

As batty as a banana tree,
the clerics have decided that Mrs T
is as batty as a banana tree.

Corrupt?
To sell your own Borough
for to be
a caissoned tundra –

a Drug-baron
walks by
(they don't have to pay mooring-fees)
Even his girlfriend calls him God.

Elsewhere:
In chorazin, the city of silver, the prince under the air
Lifted his arms, clenched & cupped his hands, tasted the air,
Swore he would rise, be above, be prince of the air.
The wings that he took him were grey & web-wet, draughts of air
His chest & breath were plated in air
His toes by the walls end round him, to over the air.

Fox-demons
blow-gutted
visceral
insufferable
tearing thru the rain-curtain
to sell this/that
which
fails.

God grant ye
inner sight

thru your own apertures.

I Hand my Houseboat to a boatyard for welding.
I pay them in advance.
They burn it out.
I claim redress; they deny responsibility.
They keep the money,
then sell the boat,
then pay me something.
Business is a grand thing.

It is all a matter
of getting the right people
living in the right areas.

Just
you won't want us to re-house you, oh no,
for we might only do that
in darkest Southall.
You wouldn't like it, we can tell you.

Kicking out
at the workers
who don't work
who can't afford to live there and work, maybe.

Land grabbers,
Share-grabbers,
Gold-boasters,
Bug-nuggets!
(There is little enough to go around)
(And that is when they take)

and the Majestical
wife of the Magistrate
wades
thru her haze of alcohol
to speak up
on drugs.
('Thish idge nog a madda fur chjoken …')

Nauseous
pickle-painted
green-eyed
Tory scum.

Obsessed with the law
and hanging rites
as indeed all
people who wear ties must be
(lest your loose necks loll,
poppy-folk)
(or watch-strap
severs wrist)
(or your own shoes kick you)
(maybe shot down by own buttons)

Petulant
lily-fungoid in the face,
at some new theft
of their superfluity,
some little tax of charity.
In many cases,
it seems property has run away
from that kind of owner
on its own accord.

Question it so?
Query it?
well, the tracks of criticism
have been tied in a loop.

Rubber thoughts
of Robber rulers
stamp it all over.

we will all be a Saxon village,
cluster our little trades,
have our own viking corner shops,
rise spectacularly …

hymnus hymnorum, et in Zion pecunia!

Taunters:
Hwa's unemployed?
Hwa's old? ill?
watch out, for economic
logic has your name circled.
Tories'll kick the house
from out under yer bums.

Under us
Two fences fail & the fox
breaks into the eggs.
Police & soljermen dispute
who may be the first to shoot.

Vexatious turds.

Warr'd torpid ranks
of great rampant purple prickles
and teazle cumes
co-venerealate
in home-sanctity
of seemly secrecy,
(squeaky, sneaky Christians,
worshipping at the altar of Knob
as soon as dark hides them)
and others
intent on self-fertilisation
affect a hedghoggy-curl
in Metroland tonight.
They are watched over
by a Tory MP.
Vanilla-blanched
pudding-babies
come up in due course
and ask what race is.

At uXbridge
Bump bump goes the boat

we've loaned.
Look, a boat of hell is bumping us.
His is the skull large with blood, wet,
   witless –
She has a furnace-mouth, gold-hot, gross,
The dog is putrid of them both.
I avert.
Will they laugh at what they are?

so
Yule is here.
Lighting a log,
toasting a tory.

As the west spurns centralised economy,
fixed prices and stability
and the East denounces wrathful competition,
carelessness and inflation,
my income still seems to go
down.
The Zolution must be
for the west to adopt a central economy
with regulated prices and stability
and Eastern Europe
to take our inflation, our competition
and ideally our Tories
(whom I refrain from specifying, but
in Zummary:
The Men are liers, women layers,
Priests & kings nought but slayers.
Dragons enround our yard of earth
swallowing the promise of our birth.

Paladin Try to Get Payment to me
Split into Two Cheques

One sister was born in the very midst of February;
On the seventeenth of March
She set out for Seaham
But we never met
(She preferred Albert Street).
Her little sister
Wanted to follow her:
She tried to get going the
Second of April,
Also on the seventh,
And this time did make it, here on the tenth.
We celebrated:
We watched the video of Turner & Hootch together.
Her little brother was going to set out on the fourteenth
(the 14th of March) –
so everybody reckoned.
On the 26th he did formally start.
But he
Preferred Uxbridge to Seaham.
He disappeared altogether.
I was desolated.
The littlest of them all
(his sandwiches wrapped in paper & sellotape)
was duly sent out on the 6th:
where is he?
(Although you are very very extra extraordinary careless
with offspring – it stops at that.)
He was the last of all.
And surely too young to tell lies.

Settling Accounts

Wiva receipt sticking to one bare foot
Iyattempt to tidy up
(financially).
too much – I lose indigent status.
too little – I ill.
(it is called a balance.)

In this column I put people I don't like.
Here and here go assets and successes.
Stock is things I pack in the cupboard,
they are deductible of expenses.
Petty cash is what lives
in the pockets of my jeans,
Rich, Potent Pennies!

Then pass the bottle.
This paragraph
calls itself
Bad Debts.
Special mention is made of
Russell Office Equipment.
And others – all born to hang.

Engulfing coffee,
I add up.
A barbarian could do better.
With a nail.
On a lump of slate.
In the rain.
With his eyes Shut.

Eins, Zwo,
Andy mandy,
Mathematic.
Waltz time.
Subtraction.
Manducation.

Enfers.
What is it –
our aim, what is it?
is it not
just a little
Appreciation?

Star Fish Jail

I
begin:
started
with this ginger-head geezer : this screw.
He come after me :
    because of what I wrote in this letter to my solicitor.
All that's supposed to be private :
    my cell-mate gave me the code for the outside of it.
But it only showed it something special : suspicious, my letter, me;
So it was opened – I knew that : I could see it in his hand as he came up;
I was sitting on my bed then : and I knew right off what it was about.
So (he sez), this was to your solicitor eh? : Come on what're you up to?
I sez, Look, you know :
    you've opened it, you've read it already, haven't you, so you know.
'Don't take the piss' he goes :
    he was getting shouty, ready to make a big scene of it.
And he sort of moves in then :
    'Do you want me to come in, give you a hiding?'
Look, it's just a letter man : it's not the end of the world;
it's not anything to you, what's the hassle? :
    It's not like I committed murder or something.
'Don't effing try that with me : little wanker like you.'
Well I wasn't taking that : That must make two of us, I said.
He comes right in and says : 'Say that again.'
So I said it again : That must make two of us, I said.
He sort of went a bit wild, him : 'You black bastard,' he yells at me,
'You black shit : you see this whistle?
All I need is blow on this, see : and there'll be eight of us
all over you, yes, and : off to the block head-down.
Is that what you want, a week of it? :
    Cos we'd have fun with you OK down the block,'
So? Go on, toot (I said) : It's only pain.
'Don't you get smart with me : we're gonna get you, see?'
Why me? : I can't do nothing much;
look at him : and I pointed to this real big black guy away over,
you wouldn't say things like that to him would you? :
You wouldn't go up to him and call him a black bastard, now would you?
Them's proper blacks and stick together : you wouldn't dare that, you!
If I wasn't just half-colour : an' no one to back me up?
But he stormed out : cos he knew he couldn't do more at banging up,
My cell-mate was come back : it was like a witness there.
He just swore some more : all that 'Jus' wait it' : an' that was it for then.

Overawing place I guess. : Huge.
In this palace of uncut brick : echo-iron
roofs of cascade-sound : landings cleared for beatings
grotesque twists of steel-life : unsoul slabs afoot
these great halls : there isn't any space for law and things.
Just secrets : divisions;
un-unites : made-up rules, orders, obstructions,
continual rock-door : setting apart us
th'only link any – : terror
wi' blood-signals : yell-sign
all clamped in null-information : every bit an Official Secret,
like toes, : like every arm of it : centre like an EYE.
Not sees, shows : visualises this raw cracked reality frame
makes you in it : What I played it?
Was I part now? : Was I to be let be a regular guy?

It was my second day : only my second day : first time in Wanno.
I'd never come across anything like this before, had I? :
    Didn't know, why this massive retaliation?
I was by my cell :
    when that same screw comes barging up to me, signing and that.
I guess it was cos my shirt was out :
    but it wasn't even out, it was just sort of bagged.
But he musta reckoned he'd got me on that little one rule :
    he was determined-looking. OK.
He come up and had a right pop at me :
    right in my face – all about the shirt, yes?
My cell-mate was coming back then :
    the screw just turns and screams FUCK OFF
cos he wanted me alone :
    & so that fucked off and left me to take it on my own.
And I backed into the cell : I thought I ain't gonna face him out there.
But it wasn't a bright move : looking round at just me in the cell.
And so he starts :
    'Look, I'm gonna come in there and give you a right kicking.'
He was getting riled again : but most he wanted me to get riled up too.
'Come on, kid, give us something else to go on :
    like you don't have to take this, do you?
I mean, if you're gonna be tough : you'd bust the cell up a bit.
Go on, kick off : I'd really like to see you kick off.
or don't you have tempers : your sort, I mean?
You ain't white you, you know : and we don't like your attitude.
Smash something : go on, wind up, come on, that's it.
Yeah, get mad : act big.

Come on: break that chair : you got it in you? : I wanta see you try it.'
I oughta known it : he couldn't get me much for my shirt, could he?
And now he could say :
   'I told him to tuck his shirt in proper and he went berserk.'
So I did : well, I had this chair yes : I'd picked it up like to keep him off.
An' I thought if I don't throw it : I'm gonna look a real plum.
So I chucked it : I wasn't even mad, much, just to look good.
It couldn't hit him, he had the door between us : using it like a shield.
And outside he had his mates lined up : for backing.
But when I'd started : I just carried on smashing up the cell,
Anything was better than being baited and made sick of :
   yelled at and abused over and over again : it got to me sure, all that.
I was mad OK by then : so I kicked off : went into bit ova benny.
An' they all come for me.

An' I was in solitary : it's a sort of bare bed of concrete
but you can't use it even : they come and check
and then the door opens : a screw comes in
sez, get against that back wall : or we'll put you there.
An' you cannot see out : or smoke, or read, or nothing.
And my hands were hell :
   with them twisting the thumbs behind your back
to walk you down the landing : some screaming exhibit.
I was mad with all of it, : I slung the pisspot round the cell
to show what I thought of them :
   but they just mounted my thumbs more
and dragged me to some single cell : in the medical wing.
There I was lumped with all them types :
   a corridor of them breathing senseless sound
scratching their veins red : or ageing geezers calling out for Mum
over-screaming here, or no sound :
   as frantic or out of it – I don't know.
I was four days there without any doctor : so I told them that
but all that I got : was a yelling off.

No gross, dross, brassy trysting this : this is people-midden.
Straw and crud : bits of once wings, fragile fossils.
Assault cycle, airless, chrome-redulled : I've mixed, heat-presence,
the laugh left here, and liking : and the dead fear,
kickin' and shoutin' : in boiled sweat
all this trap : mud-body.

It wasn't any way good, I tell you : I was so fast, so high-breathing
so rolling over and over : I blanked out a bit.

When I re-remember : I was kicking and shouting
an' some guy comes and sez : yes this is him,
hey look at this : he's really breaking up now.
He's a nut OK : needs proper sorting out.
And that was it : they rucked me off to some strip cell.
I was pulled out : dragged to this new hole
and they stripped me off : tore my clothes off,
all of them, there was this woman screw too : as rip-handed as could,
turning and pummelling : locking me like wrestlers, manhandling
like I could have no body even for myself :
    but had to be taught their way.

So I was banged inti this squash cell : they give you a pair plastic shorts
so tough you can't rip them any way : What you get.
They are bleaker cells still, they are : something like 15 feet tall
and totally empty of everything : except some well-like vent in the ceiling
they keep an eye on you by. :
    An' call at you out, with your name, over and over again.
I was panting like a bike-stroke : couldn't settle, couldn't sit,
I tore at the mattress : I wasn't gonna take the way they handled me
but they only pinned me :
    got the mattress out, said I could have nothing then :
    not even a hand-cup of sick to talk into.
Just grass-flower in the tree-fall : a set of moving ribs, jerking legs.
(Raw clay curled and tooth : and jet eye.
Adam idea : in shiny ingots.)
And a doctor come then to OK it all : all group of screws backing her
and she was asking quick kinds of things :
    I don-know, I couldn't take it in.
So I wouldn't answer, wouldn't : I jist shout I'M NOT INSANE.
But becos I wouldn't answer her : they said that's the worst,
An' I had to drop my pants and bend :
    for the needle, you can't fight that many of them.
'You won't remember any of this tomorrow, mate!' :
    becos they thought me that mindless, like.
But no way me :
    they had to keep me under three days to smash me down,
man, had they got me wrong :
    But I can't recall very much with that drugging.

I didn't eat : I couldn't even drink like.
It was just all light : lights kept on for ever.
At some time (I don't know what time) : a bit of food was put in
But I couldn't take any of it : I couldn't even get to drink anything.

Three days they said it was :
    that's just as long as they can keep you alive like that.
Unable to drink except mebbe my own piss : I kep' off that.
That is the goat-death : stinking of your own drink,
bar-eyed, rough-kneed : shent with your own piss : but it happens too.
You don't want to :
    but all you got to think of is a floor and two blankets,
they never wash them : they're soaked in stale still from the bloke before,
so soaking wet : you can't find a dry patch or anything.

What I thought was roughly this : as best as I can create it again –
Like the churning of cliff : like the flush of gears :
    the pulsing, eating into world;
wanted who would put a gold ring on a finger? : Give me clothes?
Watch me the stone-fall of a city : zero's on zero's.
And what I was seeing then (what appeared around) :
    was a series of suns;
some all-seeing eyes : yellow suns in a circle,
lamps theirs rotation around, in my eye : light that hunts and harries;
I saw them going orbit, lonely, cool and gold :
    and higher, linked and silent
like I was into thin windless air : up where the sky indigo
and all the snakes and the sea is tamed : everything tends out to us
its gleam-soul shone, to me mirror :
    turned sand-kind slow, availed, was some help.
I had ti get a grip on myself, hold myself there : keep foot in the strip cell.
But I couldn't do much for me : again it sparked up brown stars,
novel being : (now) (under eye)
stopped : sang no more
everything (with its continuance) : stops
A world : and all sucked into the Sun;
a world : with no more continuance …
not for its perfection : or shame : or flawfulness
but because of starting an' stopping : and having to end;
Not city : anti-sound
un-time : de-rebuild
and not a yell or a yak's tail : an earl or an earwig
'll set a ball roll : rig lamp-light,
form it to shapes : set it to repeat;
not one unwinding mind will have a word for it : made itself null.

Oh Christ after all that did I need washing! : An' even for taking all that,
when I saw a doctor in the end :
    and I couldn't keep my hands still, couldn't look or speak proper.

He said what's the problem? :
    And I tried to say it's tricky becos of your drugs :
    tricky to talk or think,
but I couldn't get it out fully : I could've cried or something.
But he knew what it was : and said he'd cut the dose by half from now
(so what the fuck were they giving me? :
    What sort dose was that to start off with?)
But better when it sort of passed from punishment : to just solitary.
And you thought that was it : just left in it : just on your own
but they'd be there and goad you :
    every so often, every day at least I reckon
(my watch was smashed : took off me,
I don't know, they don't tell you) : but they come in
ordered you against the wall : did a strip search
for all they knew you had nothing :
    they knew that at least and got it right.
But I mean what else is there to add to nothing :
    but that sort humiliation?
The first time I was so cowed : I stood just like they told me
but then I said I wouldn't :
    'And now you gotta be punished you' they say :
    and the needle goes in.
An' you're set back into starting again : because they keep you that way.
An' it doesn't matter how whole you are : inside you're nothing :
    and they can prove it.
And so what mebbe you're shifted out the strip cell :
    but they come with new drugs
An' say You betta take these : or we'll put you back there.
They got it well rehearsed : Or you can be a shit and ride into the fire.

Like it could go on, they say : until you get us right :
    own we're benevolent,
See it as it is : it's a game, when you give up.
OK, I calmed : In the end they gave me a shared cell,
made a note on my record : doesn't react well to solitary,
try to keep him with others : Great.
Mind, I was only on remand again : nothing proved, like guilty,
but they got to try it on remand prisoners : showing you to plead Yes
to anything : so you think you'll get out of it quicker
and trials and that cost money : it's ordered to cut all that crap now.
So are you gonna plead guilty? : Or are you gonna go into court like that,
with your arms jerking : with your hands sawing each other
and try say with a straight face : Sir, yes, I'm innocent me?
Jis' forget it : forget all that law-help stuff.

And then once you plead guilty : they've not to prove anything have they?
And you can't complain : for it's you said it.

In the centre of Wanno is an octagon :
    in the centre of the octagon is the circle
and in the centre of the circle : is a star.
It's a sort of grill : an open fret of steel panels,
banned to prisoners' feet : you have to walk round the edge.
If you're being transferred, wing to wing, the officer can cross it :
    but you have to keep to the edge.
And you have to go round anti-clockwise :
    for you can't get bit of their luck.
That's special theirs : the lattice of iron,
open, frail : spoke and pattern of altar,
uniquely rotri-symmetrical : even and full of sense
excluding all the options that are extra-sane : showing you their balance;
auditory to the throat : crack, yell, messed offertory,
the searching eye : the all-seeing demiurge
at His comprehending :   all He has made
reciprocally framing us as real : creating all words, for his Law
central recorder history-god : who knows everything :
    sets everything right,
realises beings as arbitrary : becoming divine
like a wine : mind.
An' so you see : you have to break anything you can.

Is it act? drama? : It's me causing it all?
and only I move? : yet you have not felt the weight of this ziggurat,
seen the slant : heard the broad cattle-groans,
been picked out : or bred to
or congratulated : or admired
for this grade of de-manning : this culture of sovereign shit :
    the golden blood,
the complete overturning : that sets your taboos safe, outside,
keeps that normality safe-placed : this is ritual.
Meaningless here : to make sense there.

A feeding the skeletal : Sun
re-face : with flesh
build up : blood
best : most

Is it I? : volunteered?
like 'the game' : 'the street' : 'the scene'.

Never to know about the whole : but hold frame,
hump : and be mounded
as tho' you could use me to undragon end of the world : set time twist,
feed the star-fish that eats the coral of its own home :
    consumes the city that condones it.
Before it's debris : and rescue-dust.
I would like you to be certain of one thing :
    I would unblast my lungs with pepper :
    if it would unhorse the jugger-wain.
At the tiger stark-scent : the team will scatter, the traces choke them,
my co-operation withdraws, slow spoke : the hillside TV fails :
    falls the trip-tower of the actual.
Hold me my energy : completedly
leave you th'arid poisoned arable : against my full joke-full friend-ghosts :
    my live company.
Loose-limbed, bright-skinned : limping by assault
see : I regenerate.
know : I want to grow.

(Part Two)

Maybe I should story it :
    give some idea of what happens in the world outside : when I met it.

My Dad remarried when I was two. : for my Mum died, with cancer.
She was Polish my new step-Mum. : Everyone reckons she was weird :
    even Doug met her once, said that.
If I moved : if I didn't sit total still
I got yelled at : like if I ate or wanted a cake.
I had to train the cat to knock the biskit-tin down from the shelf :
    so I could get some.
Once she smacked me with this coke tin :
    then she blinks and says what are you bleeding for?
No one ever handed her life over to social services :
    or telled her, marked her, pushed her out,
Made her into some class for sacrifice : like geeps and shoats, us.
And I couldn't do nothing : my Dad never saw what was going on.
And I didn't know but this was how kids lived :
    I was pretty co-operative then.

Till when I was nine : I hurled this chair before a teacher;
it didn't hit no one : but it broke a window.
So : My home was took away : as it turned out it was final.

The first school I was tried in was bad :
    it was so old-like in its ways it was sick.
If you left a rim of dirt round the bath :
    you were made sit in a cold water in it.
And they had their own solitary :
    but I learned you could reach the key on a string yourself.
If I didn't eat pudding up you couldn't be fed till you'd finished it :
    they brought you back and sat you in front of it again and again.
I went without food over a day that way :
    and my Dad who come got me out of it.
So I was moved away : to where I couldn't get visits.
They said (an' I was a kid) : if I walked 20 mile
they'd give me leave like : for a weekend at home sometimes. :
    But mostly there was some reason to cancel it.

So I forgot about homes and families : I wasn't even a self;
they gave me a group instead : but would not let the group think.
My possessions – : what? If it was something great,
    like sandwiches after a hike, you got it stolen.

It wasn't so bad when I got used to the new place :
    us kids had some fine times.
Once we come on this baby barn owl : in the woods behind the school.
So we brought it in : made a nest for it in this chest of drawers,
there was straw and stuff : and neat sips of water for it.
And the next day we took it out : and tried to teach it to fly and that,
showed it its wings : gave it little six-inch hops,
till we had to give up : got wise and let them phone up the RSPCA.
That owlet : it must have fallen out of its nest.

We used to have a grey lady : and a spiral staircase : I never went up it.
Ye gardener lived up there : I never visited him.
Though I got on in most things : there's this call for initiative, then.
Like we could be leaders, soldiers : if we wanted to.
We had this horror film one time :
    and nobody dared use the corridor to the toilets.
I really had to go : so I got the courage up and set off alone,
after some yards into the dark : there was this patter of feet behind me
and a whole lot of them followed me on : once I had braved it.

Most of it worked OK : there was only one teacher had it in for us.
He would line us up : and fire footballs at us.
And the one day he got himself caught in a rabbit snare we left by the gap
    in the hedge : he never worked out how that happened.

And they sent us to the sea in canoes :
    and to march the moors when you could see it was bad.
I dropped my pack in a stream, : trying to hurl it across.
And caving : in gross hauls and falls
ladders on the slip a'hang : dark
sumps : and rising level.
I learned plenty, like shoplifting and things :
    but it didn't seem likely to earn a living.
Mostly they seemed to want to fitten us for soldiers :
    but on the whole we ended up in prison, I thought.
Crime : that mirrors : courage.

It was sort of lost : ending there.
Afterwards it seemed empty : this world was too big.
I didn't know what I was on my own :
    are the messages inside us, or yours, or ours?
So I did – what? : Got timber-ox work in a wood-yard.
But I wanted the buzz :
    the adventure of the enterprise of the chance of it.
I really wanted to have some money : to own,
to venture your everything : against my nothing.
An experiment (I wager) your everything : against my nothing.
And I could be famous : with myself.

That first time I got caught : maybe I was 17.
I picked out this house : thought all round it;
I was getting in : when this bloke caught me red-handed.
I wouldn't have blamed him for taking a smack at me :
    but he called the police.
The car come up : to deal with me.
Some cop from Mitcham got out : he was unfriendly and ready, taut.
He came over : hit me hard in the bollocks
so I was on the ground : struggling for breath.
And they put me in the car : and drove somewhere'n'stopped
and said if I'd tell them who I was doing it for :
    they might make it easy for me,
and if I didn't : they'd fit me up with a knife;
but there wasn't anything I could say : I wasn't part of that theory :
    so we went on to the station.
When I was for finger-printing : he twisted at my little finger
so the stitches I had in it tore out :
    he threatened me he was going to break my fingers next.
And when I was being photo'd : he grabbed me by the hair.
Then I was in a cell :

and when I heard them coming I thought now I'm for it
but they just opened the door : and said I could go.
Some start that was : and I thought, so this is the police?
I pissed blood : nearly three days.

I had some proper jobs : but it didn't seem to mean anything.
I was OK in the wood-yard : up front selling the stuff,
so you could be in charge of setting the prices : if you wanted to.
But I lost it when this geezer reported me late :
   which he never did to his white mates, I know that.
So sometime I got to dances : an' sometime it went great.
One night bites though :
   I never got to keep some mixed race of the future going proper.
But it was good to have money to spend : I sometimes did.
Once I took them all out for a drink :
   Zod, Doug, Shim, Steve, Paul, Brit.
And after we were walking back : and a police car draws level
and Brit made some comic sign to them :
   they pulled up sudden and nicked him.
It was by Abbotsbury : Steve caught up to us and told us,
so we went back to sort it out :
   me and Paul said you can't arrest him for that, man.
But there was no chance : and Paul started mouthing him off.
Then Paul got nicked as well :
   but I said, look, I'll take Paul home now OK?
He'll be OK : he didn't mean nothing.
They were gonna 'gree to that : till a second van pulled up
and with that reinforcement : they changed their mind.
Said Paul stayed nicked : and I was to fuck off.
I couldn't walk away though : not when they'd said they'd let Paul go.
One of them came up and pushed me : Go off, he said, but I wouldn't.
So another says to me : You're nicked too,
grabbed me by the arm : I sort of shrugged them off,
They pinned me against the fence : I put up a bit of resistance, I guess,
but didn't fight : or anything.
So they got me on the floor : pinned me there,
and all I could feel was them banging me on the back of the head :
   fisting away again and again,
And at each blow my face went into the pavement :
   bruising each side as I tried to twist clear.
They'd lost their rag a bit : were just banging away at me for nothing.
There was people about : it was only 11
but that doesn't matter now : they don't care who sees them.
Worst was when they got the cuffs on me :

and one of them gobbed all over the back of my neck
and when I was in the van I said to them straight :
    Look, not even animals carry on like that, you.

That reminds me though : this job I once had.
It was in this city farm : a sow had eleven piglets.
It was the year of a world cup, that :
    and the *Daily Mirror* came down to photo them,
tried to put the piglets into football strip :
    little coloured socks and jerseys
and was there chaos! : piglets were screaming and running everywhere,
till they had to give up : and photo them just as they were.

Steve, later, told me I ought to complain : an' I went to the solicitor :
    an' sez I want to sue
but they sez : we don't handle that sort of case. :
    (An' there's no money in it.)
Or maybe they don't like losing? : But they all owe me for that
and I'll take it somehow : this way or that,
like a little nation : grabbing and getting : then smiling and sharing.
It's so : you give in or you fight back : An' one day I'll win.

It all went bad : after that spell in solitary in Wanno :
    like I was possessed by something.
I wasn't in much condition when I come out that time :
    I told you about the break-in, didn't I?
I was bent on getting even : I wanted something back :
    an', face it, I was right pissed too.
It was a little burger place : I got in thru a small window in the front,
    smashed it, and climbed careful thru.
I made for the fruit-machine : I knew it was there,
only I only had a screw-driver : this frame was a metal one :
    not the chip-board I expected.
I don't know how many minutes I tried it :
    suddenly, I thought, this is too long, man, what if the alarm's gone off?
Or someone saw me getting in : from 'The Crown'?
Some car passed, and a second one : but they went round the corner,
I thought that's OK : but it was the police.
They found the window I broke and crawled in :
    I heard them coming and the clink of dog-chains.
There had to be a way out at the back : some sort of emergency exit?
That's what I made for : but there wasn't any : I kinda resent that.
I holed up in a tiny office instead :
    curled up like squirrel nutkin under this desk : quiet as I could.

An' I heard the boot-steps : an' the padding paws,
hoping they'd give up : think they was too late,
the burglar got out and gone : no one there.
But the door opened : (I'd shut it, you bet).
I was still as still : but the dog knew it,
our eyes met : were golden-gritty,
held for a fair time : but then one of us growled.
The cop slacked off the chain : dog leapt and grabbed me,
his teeth sunk into my shoulder : I was stupid with the pain,
chunked like that in his jaws : and bleeding inti him unrightly.
Well, I yelled : broke myself out
and again he ate on my arm : clamped his teeth into my forearm.
I wanted them to call him off : I shouted Haul him off, haul him off!
But they wouldn't : he was well locked into me.
All this Hoy man, haul him off! Ow! :
    for he was well deep into my forearm, I'm telling you.
At last, I got the screwdriver in my other hand : threatened the dog,
I screamed out : I'll stab him! I'll stab him! Haul him off!
They did it then : but I wasn't gonna co-operate after that;
I froze there : wouldn't come out.
They had to drag me : they forced me up.
They 'cuffed the one hand :
    but I gripped a pipe with the other so they couldn't get it.
They was beating me and twisted my arm up my back :
    prised my other hand free, like finger by finger
an' I was 'cuffed then : both hands behind my back.
Then I was pushed : and shoved back to the front of the shop;
we was going to leave by the little window :
    and the broken glass in place : jagged right round the edge.
They made a show : as though to kick a bit of it clear,
then got me to crouch : creep thru like that,
knees bent : head down : arms pinned.
That was grim : me, I did it,
but they wanted it faster : nudged and kicked
and that was when it happened : but I didn't know anything of it then.
In the van, like, this rooky cop was staring at me :
    'What the fuck are you staring at me for?'
But he just pointed at my leg : it was loading out blood,
there was a gash like anything : inches of torn body I got :
    not much of a booty, no.
An' at the station, they left me and debated : Oh, it's nothing –
    Look, he's gotta get to hospital – no way, leave the cunt etc.
But in the end they shipped me off :
    an' the doctors took an hour and half to stitch it,

all of it : but they never take the handcuffs off.

Hours gets you to sweat : ache, seems blocking.
This is the trial though : here, not in Court.
Say 'Will you behave then? : And we'll take them off.'
No no no no. : All the side hand numbs,
bad, can you notice your breath starts : is fitful, flares to
but you switch : got to a point got to so : like you won't fear anything.
Breathing evens : you win out, right, it's worth
to see the time-rolls all set arch : over-bring, beaut and I.

And if you want my nothing : I can't stop you.
You can take sleep, for example :
    you can take off me the use of my hands.
You can make me shout : if I want to go to toilet.
Or I am packed in jail : but no association.
Sure, it seems the God of Happy Endings : belongs to you not me.
He doesn't give things : So sometimes I took them.

Two days before Xmas : I was picked up again,
curfew-breaking. : Great.

It was the same inside : exactly, this time too.
I was picked off right at the start : it was that red-haired screw again,
sez that's that nutter there : I know him;
get him over to the hospital wing, : where he belongs.
And I was took off in front of all the inmates :
    making out I was some rapist or what.
Oh shit! what a fuckin' place for a human : just a group of us,
hustled back of locks pyramid-proof : waiting fuck-knows what.
An' I was by this guy : I cadged a ciggy off him.
He seems OK. : He starts to talk then,
all about how he stabbed his girl-friend : knifed her, shows me,
once, seven, nine times :
    all them wounds an' reckons he can laugh over it.
So I took my fist back : a' bent him one,
one straight in the face : really caught him.
Then I was pulled off : OK kid, they said,
you're doing great, that's proud, : leave it : and got me off
and showed them all what happens : to people like me.
Each my arms was twisted up behind : then they grabbed my thumbs,
one great warder each side : just taking a thumb,
pulling it back and up to breaking : to bend and march me.
I don't care how fucking brave you are : you gotta yell new-born

like that when your thumbs are being rooted out as you try walk :
    some fuckin' journey they made that : hell-crawl.
And then some guy come sez : yes he's some sorta drug addict init, :
    shaky like that?
But I got some idea of what goes on now :
    I played it careful when I was in the strip cell,
I got through to this black warder : helped me out of it all.

But I knew what I had to square too : I wasn't facing all that again.
It was some list of back offences :
    something called up just now to gild their statistics
And it works : after their 4 days I wasn't in any shape to plead not guilty.
Even after a day or two of solitary : no way.
I got it right though : they gave me probation and service to do.

When I got out it was Sue put me up :
    Sue and Dave had visited me inside.
Now they was broke up : an' Sue took me in.
Her and her kid had a good flat : it was fine just to be there,
an' my mates in the area all :
    (one of which had took my old room when I was inside.)
She had a job : so there were no immediate worries :
    though I contributed sure;
an' we liked to go out and drink : and be with the same crowd.
She's pretty sophisticated too, her : food and places and friends.
We didn't plan to join the city : even for a year,
or stay there and buy there : and sell there and be lucky.
We were friends : then we got to sleep together,
that was sweet : someone pulling me out from the bone-pile.
I mean to teach me touch : how to be body.
Maybe she just needed a guy : but I was grand for that :
    I was charming.
Only I couldn't please the Court too :
    they never wanted me on probation there :
    but enforcing that's too much.
I turned up when they wanted : and the Officer refuses to see me.
So I never got to sort things out :
    and in Court it looked as though I didn't even try.

Now Sue was older a bit : moody, I'd say.
After we hit it off : she sort of turned.
Me that was always distance : and I thought what the hell is link for
an' if I wanted more : if someone invaded me
I just hit out : straight-shoulder –

Me, an' now I was in : she backed out on me.
Said it was my fault she ditched Dave : it was like crazed.
She swore she was got like suicidal :
    I had to get out, let her match up with Dave again.

Honest, I meant it : I always protected more than me.
I shifted : new signing on, new claim, housing benefit,
and getting delayed : arguing for emergency payment.
A new probation office that wasn't involved anyway :
    solicitors who don't like intervening.
You think I'm lying : but you try it.
Try it as for-a-day sub-man : an' see who'll sort things for you.
And my old probation officer : said I'd broke another appointment,
tho' I was stood there while my mate phoned her and warned her :
    and explained I was just homeless
and we got back in touch : but so what?

I even turned up in Court : and was ordered to use the duty solicitor.
My mate Chris come along : but fell over and slept on his side.
And Jason : cracking jokes about them from the back.
And Bill : who was going to speak for me.
(Does he ever appreciate what a fool words make you :
    ideas there to trick you?)
So they swore him in : but it was not much use :
    you could tell that from the way they was snarling at him.
They reckoned if he spoke up for me :
    his word gotta be worthless, hasn't it?
As to qualifications :
    was he saying he knew better than their own experts?
Well, at least he'd met me : it beats handing in a probation report
    on someone you've altogether not talked to.
Mind, that made a great prosecuting counsel : my probation officer
as like the charges were read out mis-dated : to look like recent stuff.
What does it matter though : it's like talking to a bomb.
You can tell from the way the cops move closer to you :
    that you're going down, before the magistrates even go out
    and pretend to talk.
And when I got five months :
    I jis turned and smiled that much a bit to Bill.
Well, what would you do : If you speak up for yourself :
    you just talk against them.
I just kept quiet : being a fictional character, like.
Seeing police are true people : and we're made-up,
in-nominate : apes on a slab.

Aw, man, why make such a fuss? :
    The world has to serve the only One God,
enbenched, en-monarchated, up-gilt : and my life just moves :
    is emotions of fracture.
Hands me over : 'Hey Do'nut' they said and passed.
I was showed the fancy door to the cells :
    like dark figures loping about the gate.
I got one letter to one person : then I was in solitary again.

Liam's Song

The fear that trickles thru the piano
its nerve,
narthex

terror
my mission against the captors
to convey
daily drugsful,
signal
alpha-rollercoaster-beta
till when they tongue lips –
dead-gamma
the boot-joy of the blood
I say: double or dwindle

we will make the bairns more socio-acceptive
by schooling them at the majic age of three.

My Da was not afeerd.
My Mum did not make me afeerd.
Aa yamnut afeerd.
While I fust scent death
the false bla'mange face onna life-packet
then I hurt a tadge.

Oh easy little voice
all the weany molecules
say Yes Life in them
an' they group
even in anti-Arcadia this place,
sleet out reprisals

I mean, they've settled me,
so I release the fear,
gross-spray bastard
oh you bitter bastards too
rat-runner fear-flow
I inject out
'n' it trickles
switched with fear.

the impractical praesidium
I want … now
you do … this
get it … right
'n' in the scream-braid daylight
I don't need do
of itself
we say
is
IS

in the guest-hall o'th'escaping incredible skull

*

the party getting stoppt
that is forever getting stoppt
that jist when the balloons are upt
drink judg'd
crisps bowled
'n' record ready
SECURITY SEARCH or summat,
summat silly or stern
is a mood breaker
is made to break mood
hurling the last kid cake
into blue ink.

or a ruck,
'n' no, all th'energy
is delivered unto formal write rite right
crude silly slappy
you-do-that-you-get-it.

ye could mebbe love a photo,
a letter,
something keepsake or mebbe personal,
you cannot say what it is,
but jis glancin'

gives them a clue.
To pick at it, 'n' tear it,
deliberately finger 'n' then break. 'N'
look in your eye
to see if you react any.
Any ...

'N' if you get wild,
so they can tear into you,
get happy
to show fist 'n' foot
duty.
When you come round,
no, it's concern,
you OK,
cheer up,
it's tough you,
you really grip the game,
keep going,
like, the guys on the wing'll
mebbe show you a party ...

when release came,
there was two police,
got the key to the garage where all my stuff was,
records mine, tapes mine, clothes, books,
'n' hauled them to the tip before my eyes,
let the workmen cart it to clear it,
telling me to prove it. Well,
Yeah, that is a mood-breaker.

*

Yes
we can teach you how to enjoy enything.
I mean,
the muscles are voluntary, aren't they?
At first,
we know you're gonna hang back, get lippy, sulk
but

that's asking for trouble.
We're ready for it:
we use just enough violence to give you a jolt:
to bring you round:
you've gotta expect that, it's how things work here.
But it makes it all seem better afterwards:
sweetens you up
and you get to see: we're working well for you, ain't we?
Then you get to enjoy the routine: join in like you're supposed to.
It ain't no way some sort of living death: the design is a game
for everywhere there has to be rules: or you couldn't work out what
    you wanted to do.
What you haven't noticed is now you are working for nish.

*

If …
dark cloud
the milk-crate
the guy sez
but it was all I could lay hand on
'n' I sez
right at the station
pickin' not to live
in clouds of daisy
flared
buckled the guy
no one to me like that
get it
I could see he was straight
even in the
and I got
didn't stop
he was asking for
setting me up
then they reckon
the bloody thing's a cop

So the punishment starts,
the live piss and kiss stone

the change into dead-liive something
walk / act / talk
as monster poster image they got,
fine, I'm fucked.

the breaks in my hands
I splint with paper, and put
bread on the blood.
I get the notion of being naked
but I ain't gonna answer.

world kills world
millions of days
'n' I slip 'n' sing.

so things are things
but they keep changing me
hunched like an eagle
flying between the boots

'No
I'm not going.
I'm not going anymore.
I'm not doing any more.'
'It ain't that bad?'

But let me
what it is
let me judge

It was a picture,
a name,
something that repeats,
becomes proper.
(Choose
to be
one thing please
or …
OK.)
It was the need for that,

sure,
a addict
to definition.

*

Worse the, likelier the,
strong and strange
no more possible multiple power

but you act the dark thunderous rows of beans
and the blue flicking earth
the sultry repeats and sames
the rails and tar and rank
culverts that siege the city

that bruise the statue
the thin-gilding, the pus,
the jade-cheese-veins, the cracked metal,
the secret bum-hole

by unthinking the unpleasant

I spurnt the tool of work
which is other bodies
trained and attuned
stretched and tenuous
to do yours.

Slum algae.

Pretend, with the veg
that you don't live on blood,
eggs are not eyes,
fibre – something non-muscular.

But stars be-dull,
die in their own way, own time,
and are seeds, enzyme,
their own extraordinary new design.

By then there was a new place
special
the wing
masterly solitary
for you had to write a letter all yourself
if you wanted to speak to anyone
and you had to write another all yourself
if you wanted permission to smoke a cigarette.
A separate letter for each ciggy
and each bit of talk.
It was a special wing for bullies.
It taught me something I guess.

I got out of that
and the great red river dragon
sprout
yellow-striper
space-taker
beaten and beaten at
and so is
horse and nuclear dogs
and so is
pan-demon on its business
thru the text
and it's a world in which
there is a rancid spray in every pit,
blood-brown cone-tooth hickory hate in every maw,
fox-fucked mankinders!

well
I tell you to arrive
the lozenged snake
the bake step
but/and the great triracle of the main structure
such rose-windows potentially fire
justice is
cost / weight / art / height
that work produces
heavy danger

in wary crazy tiles
blind humour of the roof
the scramblish running search
the family heaven
floppy puppies
oh stars
jasmine slippers
oboe-kisser plucks
on the celluloid
a created puzzle
with informed misfits

At the end of the coffee world
the medals chink
it is apprehension
teddy-bodies that semble
every episode doth new appear
it is entertainment
and deo gratias intimate
beings presént
thought it is.

A ship-word
a adult-good sky
she (the searcher) oh sure she loves orange medal biscuits
but he is
hill-top bastard oh drink
(the prison officer)
makes him like murder
(I do not believe his little mercy)

Wobbut thoo ettled ti meet god.
Woz his stick bray-ey eneugh?
Did his bottles hilp thaw rinaway heed?
Efter hiz mirikles, hoo dee thaw shackle-banes feel?
Wor the bizzun-foak anjel an' lowey aareet?
Hev thaw raxy brawn limbs com wick agyen, man?
What-like is stane like tiv eet? (Aye, Aa thowt seea)
An' ti cowp seea much blud – aal ti shaw thaa's a regular guy

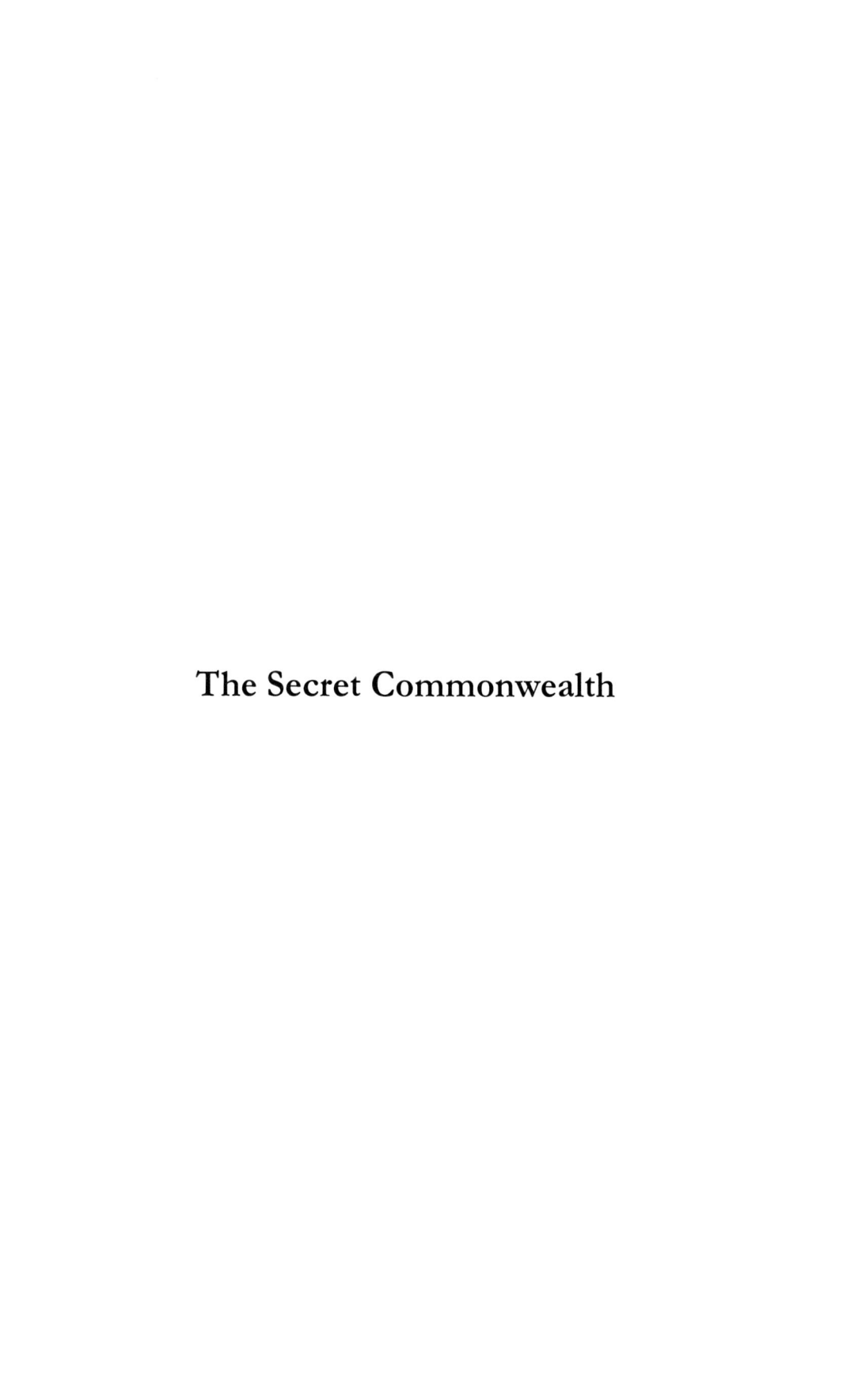

The Secret Commonwealth

Note: The Secret Commonwealth *is the title of a book by Robert Kirk, published in the late 17th century. Superficially this is a silly work, placing elves and fairies at a semi-corporeal level between angels and humans. But then if we did not swallow some monstrous impositions and reject an equal number of clear human facts, would we be able to participate in the social reality of the present?*

Well, we quitt'
the sand-blade shore
up cliffs (coast)
there like a ghost-map the marls slide
amazing some of us
(see our plant-blue eyes).
There are whinny-bushes
'n' a struggle for sandwiches
'n' bare gaps
'n' a g'eat round of spoil
(floods 'n' skids, grab 'n' rubble).
Well, then was
a dene,
a petty thing,
some sort of glacial gash,
and green bushes,
half-trees,
youngster-plants getting denser 'n' denser and twisted humming stems
for I got edgy in the low altitude –
imagine them – the foot-high tribe of indians
wi' lurky ambush
rose-bows / ash-arrows / trip-vines.
And
Trevor pointed a dog-slide down:
'That's where they pushed me.'
A phantastic imitatione of the actiones

A hierarchy of facts containing
Things of congealed air,
of an alien expression
a missing matrix-folder.

Somewhere over the spine-science seafloor
patrol
dead holly-nail hand
seeded with obliteration
is a war
and the life-engine changes
opposing / colluding / gathering
and the main-aim self-maximization

limpet metallic giants show.

(rich, tricky, better in state
it sets along)

Food is fury
and dreams are demons.

To turn to golden boy and garnet girl
sleep ear to ear

in the mouse-soil
the plow-share

for we mate
we make syrups

and as strange misbehaviours
we move about

Strange lights, mauve, warm,
the ginger halogen
and the strident shiny river
circling, zodiacal / pins of
the place of flesh-face
run / mammal-grass

Am I a liar then?
Why, the whole forest (tube-limb / leaf / aperts / glowy-globe /
   patter & rattle / white face / its tin slopes)
is thick with reminders
like Who is Who
and how Someone is Someone
and What Nothing Is.

Me and my lost litter,
my words.

In the purple rain
and the grotesque multipede

rearin' over the capsule and ship
as in the Venusian jungle

And there becomes
The unusual universe
apparent to a second sight
having their visive faculties entyre
seem to see
the atomes in the air, alternative people
their apparell and speech is like that of the people
    and countrey
but having no set teaching
they throw great stones, pieces of Earth, and wood
    at the inhabitants.

Their women are said to spin, verie fine, to dye, to
    tissue and embroyder
or wooden dolls, manufactures, plastic gifts,
paint up models of magic wells
while *Their men travell much abroad*

Yes, they sez,
you live here now,
look,
all ye have to do
is wood-wedge the pipes in line
for the acid –
or that end
unplug to normal lengths once more.
In the bleak back heart-land
they talk turk
orders are given in something gothic.
Signs show me.
Come on, let's keep the lines continuous.

hey, watch that if it buckles.
Agreed, no singing.

The movement of blood
the circulation of heat or of air or of tide

are examples of free will.
Being exampled to be free to decide to do
equals fizzy brew.

the dizzy division into pain
hammers
I twist
body full
jerking
in limbs
let go!

allow
someone
who sees you as mirror-makers

we are painted
night-lady-scented narcissus
and heliophiliac daisy

One, is thus.
A slow force of coercion,
the lever of injection of idea
to fix in certainty
(aye-for-ever, orb-without-navel)

with the humiliation / derision
of incompletion
marks of exclusion / stubborn
to be broken by medical ethical action
and you end up agreeing
new sets of prejudices
and new cancerous stances

Sweetly we swirl and sleep,
complete
and there is schumannesque sandy security
in the fremd keys we wander into –
Ut
Fa

Bis
Moll

There are tins in the store
and we curl and kip

As tho the rest
(call it Baphomet or Daniel)
the bringer of benevolence
the tacit kings and queens of cards

Why, the exclusion of the data,
the embryo of fact-swatch
alone half-a-world

As tho the cross-perceptions
severalty trained away with words
and things, if not factual
are the same

A tree   a road   a pail of water
a cloud   a cocoon   a bead of amber
a protein   a process   a performance

The myriad systems
limbs and flowers
a new thing and a list
(exhaustive / magical / totalled)
a corporation by analysis

But still
The demented slice-sawer
of injured authority

jump you into the mincer
to assert the goal: damage

Am the
frail, trialous body
depleted,

beat that was my first beat,
out of the heart,
staring air.

But the old
that wears way
is heart-beat
a flat something, a rate
of exhaustion at the multiple

for the dying yards
are stone-clear
grass-trim-plot
heads grow

Sips ripples round
on swirls
on leaf-deflected faces
ink
trumpet-jump-up / trumpet-jump-down

From the earth-fry
the foetal corn
kicks green
into the rich

airy penises
light industry
arise balloon buildings
low density as a policy at a guess

Something plain, something cathedralic:
lucky glow cones
beige-weave
dimensional sprays.
wolf-stone
snagged with snow,
and the roast south
('the wife complains that the onions I grow …')
shimmering orchestrally.

and
the fusion
the sliding 'side dirt-orange
the god

'n' kid chuntering round the room
wi' horns bubbling

The rose of sun arising
sparkles on the genitals of stone
of mountains moving

are scents.
nights.
nox.

today
at dark
by dark pruney balloons
it jumps air
it hits first

The Alien

Part One

Most of the objects make sense:
they fit.
it ingests, or delivers, specifies, produces sound,
a'most a toy-set.
Thanks, mister.

Tuning the trumpet,
and the
manipulation –
I asked people and I soon got the hang of it.
The mode of the grip/release/transfer –
you watch it
And it comes.
Somewhat over-sophisticated
I reckon this bit, that bit
and the pentámetry of those,
well I guess radial adjuncts.
… I suppose.

Some were in the index
and you can ask questions
and you get the chance to observe.

So it's fair enough.
After a month or two
I mastered the lot –
peripheral transfer, bestowal,
trick sleights of/with Big Bad Wolf.

What
(you must wonder)
is this then?

It's some puzzle and
I am embarrassed to say
it doesn't fit.
Anywhere.

Non-functional accessories,
ornaments, embellishments, vanity-trims,
small shiny-eggs and eye-brights
are not in the manual.
It is as tho'
they are wordless.
(separated off sound)

Omission
without significance?

In the Main Library of Mixopolis
tho' I made a special trip,
and get access to the Boölean multi-subject quick-lists,
I draw a noteworthy blank.

Maybe
it's a quasi-dysfunctional piece.
Livid striation,
crystallinity.

But to ask
was a mirthless task.
As tho' in words
it was impossible, indicating unreal.
An encouragement to ignore.

Yet in the back shelters,
all but unseeable,
it was a logo, symbol.
Rhythmic and subtly pert
and puerile by day.
And in the unstable dark,
there was more mystery
like a centre of a collection.

Figures appeared,
but shadowy, separate, unclear of outline, arcadial,
and quiet, with dancing shoulders,
strange non-friends

evangelical without speech,
taught.
(Did me to it, by act.)

I could call it
incitement.

And the simpleness
of this ancillary complex
bowled me over,
so explicit.

Maybe
it cannot be written in.
Words being unlookably
unreal.

Manuals
OK for beginners,
I guess.

⁂

In the expanditure
it became able
I set up my own symbols
ex's and zero's
bridges/clouds/animal quotas …
books of morality in dithyrambs
as excess fun.

Well, we don't doubt
blue real things
(seeing/feeling)
I explained it
nets of bright, sensile words, trick together

limitlessly
novel

fact

the arrangement essence
how things became
through how we felt it ought
(the circulating zone)
the dragon / the dementia

we compete for
the hard rule
the omnipresent outside sequel

prove
        disprove
see
        solve
annihilate

(the word as deadly)

out the
over
hills of grammar
into potentialities
grip
new pearly non-perimeters

identify

for example
scent the ant
excellent deliberate work
that is ribs
tree
fruit total
fecundity
(the bevelling of self-sign)

the obstruction
things might break

if you

every
gentle
magical be-lit
distinction

guide set aside

benevolence
and serve
essences of assault

the action of breaking
creating
switching

how home-realm
I de-embellish
fires and throws
and breath and intent

slapped clay
as bestial saint
as the searing dark a microglow

oh be sweet
everything success

*

For
there gets no universal language.
No birthright.
No agreement.
But
a good deal of shared sweating.

Crystal tree green growth
Pinocchian nose adjustment

splendours of population
– observe a magnification of decision.

And if we was born blank
everything would be our choice.
and 'it is your choice',
'it serves you right'.

And ye can have your pick o' template:
fat father, missing mother, funny friend, wily worker fox.
Like on every school wall.
Or th'enormous potential
of a head-whipping.

For
if someone is building the choices? (The
Architect of the Ways.)

*

The first alien
got him in well,
knew right-off the disguise.
Took in bacon-red hair,
blending freckles,
a slack, print-blur smile.
Something to say, and an orientation,
proper proximation to womanry,
oh, and the camouflage of a mortgage.
Then and be anyone.

*

Here flower and girl are unplanted
but there are cults –
how I'm competing,
informing,
stratifying,
and eradicating,
set in the fertile grey

*

logic into trick
mind to murder
exist/extinct
thinking for ruling

The power is reason,
but it tricks
it is not applicable
to us.
You are not allowed near it/employ it.

Sets/rules are granted,
guarantees.
This is the show-side.
The logic sunniness; gilt.
It brasses terror.
You have to see the fire below the frying-pan to get it all,
making sense whole of it.

Look.
The temple-like audacity
of control,
of purpose.
See.
How it is intended
to favour the power
to end the act
we live in.

*

The room
is the reality.

block-mouth'd
sure wall, imposing
area.

The place of brick
as strong as a word.

Variety of environ
all the edge-nick combinations
in a small ring of syntax.

Who holds the value words?
The key-man,
self-appointee,
lion and devours.

What is yes
what is no,
some invitation to construct.

And violation.
The thief forces way,
sees what soul is,
to achieve some pain,
congratulatory capture.
Locating it in
liberty.

He breaks up groups
to interrogate and expand.

In the story
There are mighty works
for mighty truths.
Bold courtyards – enduring ideas. Or
get to look liker
Tedious mazes.
Superman.
The dead tagger, the rubble
of the Will.

How we all
got to build to pattern.

Got to settle in.
Forgot our outside.
Admired the frieze of decent morals all round
and the stamped ground.
hardly any exterior sound.

Also there is an interior glue vision
and everything seems large, local.
Perceived intimate;
as history of itself.

*

in Oxford

spires
'prook', cuckoo
(dreams)

revade and permain
word-set
fork-paper-comb-tower

cereal-packet beauty
the art of sleep,
be-slit pet rocks

long decisive deteriorations of words
and the vocabulary of self

and the Ozymandian contusion the
time in which how
reality to erode itself

strange
old buildings
(eat you) puzzles of extinction

*

Sometimes it seems everything might be trickle-down from god:
manners, trousseaux, tranquillisers, in a stream.
T'int'rupt consumer flow
's hateful, lightning and annihilation.
Continuity in-builds it,
conservation,
precedence,
appeals to the Bible
gloss over new egg regulations,
executions of buildings.

The multi-colour burning light of the Sun
as gift-source (boon/confidence)
closes.

Into the twig-way
a shopping-busy branch of nooks and pumice-paths and puzzles,
and root-tunnels,
gas-pipe rough,
low/glint-lit
with toothed lions
and some, gritty chips of birds-eyes

there are (I mean them)
vigilators not originators
of the
great molës of tradition

(In at the lion gate
always steps
always ascend
a place)

(oh yeh oh yeh
off to krow we tog)

(New level
and ascetic
tribulant crenelatory walls of wire)

(You are sent to spend
to assume joy)

(spikes of saliva in among the mint
as they come sledging thru the door
into the back of a settee)

lies define the human,
ideas that (de)stabilize society

So we are telled
of apostolic line
from the flint-edge to the microchip
of unfolding grace (gratitude!)
safeness
as the seesaw of the homeless an' the chemically dispatched,
the part of us,
and the nations across-world, not to share.
The brains of bias, episcopally staved,
will mark a track
from the beasts and peccadilloes,
the paralysis of the bastard outer dark
to
the
central
fire.

*

The spy-hurry wood-sticks god
's semantic sustainment.
ignoreth all usage.

scalp-shirt
tooth-wrist
flesh-dress
swish whale-stone arches
gristle-thought in debate in dying-grey dialectic, done.

*

apple-metal
an apparition
indian in intensity.

aeroplane birds
ochre-seeded, spread
into eggless autumn, the flash.

a saying.
You cannot keep a radio
in a box.

gloss
sweet-tune scent
sharp evidence that things are decaying.

The world
the creation of a present
out of words.

This is wall, this is light, this is wood,
is
now.

In which we make you live,
words, things,
ways you feel.

exist
equate
relate

do not deem our words do not mean,
there is power
and proof

enough to negate time
to take you out of the future
to fix change process

living on cemeteries of coal.
better to be published
outside the land.

black, brown-armed, red-hearted friends,
I can explain the words
if you want me to.

*

Unlock?
How?
With a leg, or a plant-whole, or some
gesture.

Do you see –
how very hard
(how ridiculously tough)
future tenses must/will be,
what future words are there?
what else can it apply to?

(fore …
towards …
verging …
and)

or emblem verb,

a mirror where
dragon will win,
kills cross,
coalescence is.

*

Is what acts, me?
Has the bullet-maker made his aim?
(For us.)

Aware of roundness,
why,
the consciousness of matter,
lets me be
eye,
and orb.
Agree.
Free.

*

But then there is integrity.
Which is whole.
Everyone except.
Is managed (one side)
Self-motivated (same).
But the emperors / tamperers
royal / real
tuners / human-makers
on tent-slaters / mind-sisters
all who see plant-separate, go self,
slim-belt, turquoise of hair,
myth and novo and folk and derive.
The turning of every deal of destruction
into pulsing blossom patrol.

*

And Plato, the platonic underfelt
our living carpet,
as con;
is still the top-layer too –
we will not have arcane interpreters of hidden assumptions, means
There is no law.

*

Unless
in the chill day-chapter,
I set it down as game,

something total
(embrace night stake)
and where everything that's left gets ventured
on unseen rules, to
continuous two-way attrition
but
at any period
can snap.

(Then I had breakfast
It was OK
the fork was plastic
in case I injured the egg-yolk)

(but there was no air
the glass was distorted squares
of inner'n'outer panes in concrete
spaced so some light passes
but no sight or sound gets in or out)

Not much to do …

*

Like concentrating on everything.

Can you see the two sides of a coin at once?
What is real on one side of the coin,
isn't to its reverse.
The plane of meeting's illusory.

The other guy
is a liar.
Got wrong info.
Perception, code of thought, species
are misverted,
stupid.
Isn't right.

But to cleave the coin

only doubles up th'effect.

Turn it over
and change politix.

Spin it
and get dizzy.

Both designs have merit,
and the whole has value, and
the face of God and the arms of the Devil
glint or shade
flat/freckled.

You could toss it
and see what.

*

Once
in the plural world
there was abuttal –
hand/band/sky/eye
here were grammars of colour
I knew, adhered,
flexed, forget, warm, collapses

I aided
the parkland, my palm
quick rows of a baby rhinos
my eye-zones
optimistically-structured bones
tool action with.

Now prime words
re-regulate and define the cluster
I compete in.
They do not touch
much,
but from time to time I remember to snarl.

Grizzly talents
on the boat of business
got I some good grace into,
explosive and agile.
Drag-dancing
wide to slide

To sleep rock-knuckled in eggshell,
linky and wind-blurred,
hard by hand-colour
close by sky-flex

Part Two (Work World)

Sat in the cab of the crane
Well, there is the shifting mass rods
and more often
the calcium of concrete, up to higher up.
But with no magnet-feel to my feet,
sense of roundness (shape, hill, home).
People of air
become.
Blue and white and our grey eyes.
And balance and sounds.
(The instinct.)

An' I thought,
all we can make is things like ourselves.
There is spangling oreille-wise notes,
heavy-hat domes,
tight symmetrical cloth-like verse
an' death-photos.
Th' pre-eminent mountain an' subtle owl
we like, like us
till we get to an everything.

*

Work is something ye can wed,
some open-hearted endless diary-way,
components touch, connect,
the act invests sympathy
it is a world-completer.
(All it takes is handful of bristle
these shiny clips,
handle-stock,
So get on with it, ye.)

*

Total embrace, affection
up to / into
whole trust, how
the vampire doing the dividing.

The mingiest cells are in Winchester.
No glass, just sockets of air,
talking to rain an' hollow draft
an' white with bird-drop.

A whole world, work, prison-plan

Bored, penny-bright lino worlds
that started out
almost thought as redemptive.

*

What ye have to do
is contribute to your up-keep.
By shifting boxes of lead in a circle.
By constructing bad bread.
Tremendous total washing
of floor, once more.
To help you help the people who are helping you.

*

It is a way of channelling, encouraging, opening.
struck-down grass-eaters
or the airless iron-chest bunkers of Feltham
The 'cuffs and bars a proof of God

Even Liam will be eroded.
You can only go on so long
before you get easy and careless
and anything's acceptable.

*

Got only £2.50 per week with no work.
Work made it £7.
Sometimes not credited at all, or delayed.

Then ye have to queue at a locked grill
for a bit food or burn.
I do not need to study the skills
that are here are deprivation an' expectation
for they make up pay,
tell me the signals
of smashing an' hitting,
conversion to an un-make –
gross,

The gross crimes, the murders, series of murders
read like fashion copy.
Headlines of shock,
something similar / something else new
Or solar exhibitions of extraordinariness.

The need to be serious, achieve, note the name,
build on / build up,
become part of the concourse
constituents of
and co-directors of reality.

*

brings globes to lock
settles whole, black
the no answer;
is stew of suicides

How here (not anywhere) here
can you …?

and either you work
Or
they say you've chose
solitary.

*

The pain of (long left, then)
being lifted by your wrists by the cuffs
carried by hands and feet,
it excesses.
Hours gets you to sweat,
ache, seems blocking.
Say 'Will you behave then?
And we'll take them off.'
No you.
All the side hand numbs,
bad, can you notice your breath starts,
is fitful, flares to
but you switch
gotta point got to so be thru
like you won't fear anything,
breathing evens,
ye win, right, it's worth
to see the time-rolls all set arch,
over-bring, beaut and I
and

(and the girl swerves from,
doesn't see it, need to get to nothing,

poise on point, if action
open)

*

to play with night / reckon pain / be
silver-bead-breakfaster (like an oblivion)

the little house that keeps out touch
is de-built.
Move.
See meet.
You can thru the brick-gone not just gaze,
do.

fold,
feel,

fight.

an' the whole energy
out.
as tho the nought the whole,
for end, enter, emperor, entire

beyont the bar kennel,
extant caves of treasure,
mill-heaps of what was wanted once,
like fruits, turquoises,
snows of smaragdine,
the great desire
tableted in little toy-bright symbols
purring chest to chest.

what would be
is amazing and lovely.
a long circle of hand to hand
warm in dignity
like a lamp filled with home and broad hand
a beast of sacred lines

enceinte, ample, opal
of wheat-oil
and the blue killers dance in wheel
all with

*

The community of love competition
who's best rewards
who gets the joy of this or that's harm,
cry, loss, winlessness
I tell you
we make it a league of break-bitching, gain,
songless fucking.
Fun.

the need of refusing sharing
creativity of not enough to gan round –
and breaks into war.

*

to use time,
be in potential,
see colours and unite
before the dry derangement,
the theocentric reasoning
spills us all

from the skinniest frog frame
to the ogeacal she-being
muscle and maidhead
come to one
are the mirror
are
(being / doing)
are –

*

Length of repeat
is familiar,
maybe processes, me.
Human half-motor, half-hero
handers-over of token surplus
of prison wear and cheap-mend toys and lady jam.

*

The scale's shifted
by heavy industry in demise.
Those they
get to end supernumerary,
gently eased onto the street.
Maybe cities take them.
But then the city
sells as many as it can to prisons.

*

Cots for puzzled unmet beings.
strange no-places.
To a softened lead act of extinction.

Boiler waif
shoe-swing over a Styx.

Self-evidently
You are not talented.
There is an absence of the gifts of god.
All in all you equal the worth
of the sprain on the professional wrist.
The deaths that are English
are altogether ordinary, unexotic, unextreme,
they lack craggy gothic supreme excitement.
The corpse is tidy, gets
tidied away
from a soon-cleaned royal-steel square
and explained in absolute polish
because or for or therefore

accidental / unforeseeable (complication)
unlikely ever to be because …
But little life –
it is 'sorry' and 'go away'.

Part Three (Pharmocopoeia)

The bare square
trick,
the wool and flowers
that spoke-radiate, make the meadow
a living love, *viva voluptas*,
bedstead grass …
sitted
and the exact memory of the order of events becomes blurred

Oh yes, once.
Stars
or health
or heroes he was.
This envelope.

And the door.
Bangs …
6 of them.
4 of them,
to match to
only eating hot meat, face-cutting,
horse-hugging.
That I would burst myself?
Circle, isolating in their centre
Or it's a struggle
twin helmets, hirsute-topped, and yubes.

The tray varies
day to day.
So what is wrong with you?

me?
Wow
I can tell like
see Nature's new dyes and the green
water-weeds laugh outright *videbunt
virides* with *nax*-lighting jewellery
gemmis nascentibus algae
placenta sea-weeds.

Wanno, too, *hi vigili muros*, wall-watched,
harboured with a chain-of-boats, attacked –
horse-fighters
you can see the mists of dust wide rising
breaking tawny heads, his peace
and bastard to bastard
and the surging banners-on-spear of scarlet dragon –
contains;
the whole sky seems aflight serpent waves!

the love assumption
an orange hole
a womb-heart
potent evil in-globe,
take.

leopard to liquid
no tinky edges to clip the eye
no grit under-rib
flow crystal city
tab jewels all alight

snow-lay labyrinth
go-go trials of sump-word,
dodge that trick
but what it (is it)
they want that last label off?
parts, plays, melts.

Maybe it's good.
Co-operate.

Take.
Go.
She spake: the whole snow-marble
(*niveae columnae*)
began to golden, and the beams (*trabes*)
luciated like metal, yellow.

plants growing thus and thus (*diverso tempore*)
and the moon-fire / sun-fire.
The old back-pages, invisible and obverse,
ordinal.

In this pit,
stirs
dependent on
stirs
Allecto
glomerantur in unum, assembled
Discordia, nutrix belli, war-nurser,
imperial Famine, shore-less
Senility, Death's next-door, and
Plague, unendurable, unfed,
Envy, Anger, Grief, Terror, Rash-Dash, Stress-Tilt and
all the Anxieties.
Look,
open you to punishment
hydra-brute, tigress-fast,
wind-hard, sea-treacherous
shut you, seal

lie bare
brown – *fulvas in pectora pelles* – skins

Seen shaky,
with tremor,
over-breathing,
all the air passage mud-dry

and it's fight
maybe and they come, and fix you

his limbs quated from *solutis nexibus*,
yielded sinews, ribs bared.

Incommunicado.
No talk. no message. no visit. no letter. no sign.
no one but the guy and the needle.
bonded into animal,
truculents to bears … their skulls bulge in iron
forelimbs lift

from the skull-nook
of chemical action
uncoiling.

Kick, kick and kick and kick
the door
as if
chemicals excite, metal moves.
Becomes procession.
The savage wave-full plumes
nod (*cristato vertice*) and one joy to shake and flash the
(*tremulos*) shine-shoulder-plates (*vibrare colores*).
Fight and slack, *spiris-que remissis*
and the body unstraights out of effort,
cannot produce itself, dry,
the breezes drop, *vento cessante*, the dragon-flags with
coils/spirals relaxing, flap down, bright a multi-coloured *varii dracones*.

maybe
wake
ask
no.
revolved, and reborn.

and set up to it
again, again, again,
'n' being addicts
of being human

as the black wash poison

folds
holds the soul
pickle-egg-grip

the most is largactil
demon dace – jittery evident/seek of/excitation/flat
dusky cows, dementia
solicitude … silence
in the opaquest midnight-most deeps (*qua noctis opacae
fundamenta latent*)
dum rotat … un-starred
dum venti … un-winded

Diazepams, valiums
plastic-striped
I obey to
is pink
lunges at your throat
I stick
puppet-pulp,
jigging and jokin', spraddle of
Ow I
spasm of
as of some monster, some space-thing. something robotic, crude, gross

behold,
little round myths.
it is / are
some solutions
ah – like
oh – like
drag to
a promise
no edge
dream
no moulded share
subitis messor gaudebit aristis
reaper: to the swift free V's.
Oak-wood sag with honey. Briers
be wine, yes *fluent olei-que lacus*.

Melleril.
before his food grew girdered thick,
his drink solided to gold ice.
world.
to eat
equate
to take wrong.
to drink
equals
to lose (no looking)
to comply
equals
to vanish.

The Coal World:
Murton Tales Reworked as Dialect Verse

The Trapper Boy Starts Work

Mi gran-fadder Tim, this is in 1860,
Startid wark as a trapper-boy in the pit (Aa think - at Elemore).

His Mam com waken'd him, proper dark still it woz a'reet:
'The caller's been, seea get up, or thoo'll be late.'

His Mam set him on the way, fer it woz dark ootside,
Nieve in nieve, ti the lit-up pit-shaft an' open cage.

'Leave him ti mi – he's Dick Platts' lad in-he?
His fadder's waitin' at the bottom,' the man sed.

Thor it woz aal quiet an' black. Wiv a whoosh
Th'cage shot doon; it made his ears pop.

His Dad was waitin' for him at the bottom:
'Here lad, tak this lamp. Come on, th'owerman's waitin' fer us.'

In the flickerin' shaddy an' lamp-leet they com tiv a door;
'Leave him with me, Dick,' sed th'owerman, 'thoo can see him later.'

'You're ti stay here Tim,' he sed, 'an' work the door.
Open the trap like this with this rope when thoo hears the coal-tub comin'.'

Tim tried it oot, it was not ower-heavy for him ti manage,
An' he judged it nice when he heer'd the tub comin', yowked the door open.

Oot thru the gap com a fiery-eyed pony, pantin' and gleamin' i'the lowe,
An' the putter caal'd, 'How, lad, new?' an' th' pony snorted.

Quick as owt, the little calvalcade hed passed,
An' oor Tim woz on his ahn agien, on the listen.

An' roon' his bit alcove, raws o' dottid e'en lit up,

Mouse-folk it woz, wadda et his bait if it wornit in the box.

There woz tubs and waits an' then his Dad com an' et bait wi' him.
Then, 'Back ti wark. Noo be careful thoo dizn't faal asleep.'

But ten hours is a dreery lang time; Tim dover'd ower
But waken'd a'reet jus' in time fer the las' tub.

An' then they was oot, hiem agen in the dark, ti wesh an' eat.
His Da settled doon tiv a pipe. 'Come an' sit doon lad.

'Timorra, thoo'l collect thy ahn lamp; rimembor ti return it.
Second! Dinnot faal asleep agien.'

'Aye (an' he laugh'd) – the owerman com by an' seed yi asleep
But it was near lowse, yi forst day, se yi got nae bunch.

'But mind it diznut happen ye agien.
Them doors, they hev ti be shut for the air-flow an' open for the
    coal-tubs.'

'Aye, fadder, Ah'll mind,' sed Tim. Then his big brother com in:
'How did thoo mak oot?' sed Sam, 'Ah bet thoo's tired.' 'Aye, some.'

*

Tom

Ma special brother was Tom.
He nivor got on wi Da,
He woz a boozer en' a banger,
Nivor a chapel chal.

Yan neet he com in
As Aa woz varnigh asleep
Tiuk ma neive en telled me
He woz ettlin' to leave fer good.
Yet Aa kna he woz grand ti me.

Fer (he sez) Aa'll nivor mak gud here,

Seea Aa'm off tiv Australee
Ti mak a cam o' kelter
Like we'll nivor see hereaboots.
Yet Aa kna he woz grand ti me.

Will thoo sail ina ship? (Aa axt)
Aye, Aa've ti cross th' ocean
En' it's a canny lang journee, like,
Weeks en' weeks o' watter.
Yet Aa kna he woz grand ti me.

It woz a few year while he wroat
En' then he sez
The new gowdfields wor open,
He woz winnin' buckets o' gowd.
Yet Aa kna he woz grand ti me.

En' Frank he laughs at thet
En' 'Let me see it,' (he sez) –
'Thet Tom cud nivor spell yit,
Plain he means "buckets o' coal"!'
Yet Aa kna he woz grand ti me.

But as Aa grew
Aa turned a Methodist, me
En' saw plenty that'd drink en' quarrel
That minded me o' Tom.
Yet Aa kna he woz grand ti me.

*

The Move

When Aa wez grawn
an' wed Mary
in the Spring of 1877
we moved ti Murton
wi'a cart en a pony ti pull it
piled wi' a bed, chairs, cupboards, some bits carpet, en' pots en' pans,

en' wor fower bairns.

Aal the way
frev Easington Lane
thor wez dog-rose ti the dyke
en' fields
en' also a few gipsies wad camp thor –
we wadnut trust them lot nut ti steal our fower bairns!

Nevvy Tom
showed us the way.
The new house
has rooms up en' down:
Thor woz a flagged kitchen en' a parlour fit fer a nempress
En' upstairs a bedroom of thor ain fer the fower bairns.

Se we unloaded
en' hed some tea,
like cahd rabbit en' bread,
then he sed:
'Thoo's nut gannen ti wark down belaw Aa knaw. Aa wisht Aa cud get a job on top, but Aa's nae gud at figurin' …'
Aye, Aa'll wark above groond naw, praise-god, en Aa'll hope the fower bairns dee en aal.

*

The Box-Eggs

As Aa've sed, Aa wed en'
Mary en' me moved ti Murton;
Aa ettled ti wark i'th'offices –
Aa wizna owerstrang, en' warked at bank.

But the pit-foak they sez ti me
What we need's a Post Office, Tim.
Ti hendle wor parcels
en' everyone's penny post.

Seea they bigged us a house,
Wi' a shop en' a woffice
A counter fer stamps
En' a other fer kets.

Aa collectid the mail
Off the train en' sorted it,
Some Aa cudint read reet
Seea Aa gollered the nyem oot i'the street, while it got claimed.

En' we selled paper en' envelopes,
Bait en' groceries
A feck o' kets, bullits,
Claggum en' such.
En', forbye, EGGS …

Naw Aa wanti tell yer a tale o' thon eggs
Thet woz set oot i' trays i' straa as 'box eggs'.

Naw a pitman we kent woz reet crazy on hens
He raised them hissell' frev egg upti hen.

In his incubator he kept the eggs waam
While they hatched en' the brids wor thrang i' the waam.

This time he was short o' some eggs ti put in
Seea he tiuk chance o' wor box-eggs en' put them in.

They woz fertile as owt, en' turned oot a treat,
Thor woz nae birds finer i' the street.

Unusual, mind, en' pawkey them wor
Wi gowden bands, crests, ruffs en' spurs.

When they scratch'd i' the road wiv ither plain hens
Fowk cam jist' ti see them wild forin hens.

But yan day 'General Buller' cam by in his cart –
For he selled ice-cream wi' a pony en' cart.
Naw sum gadjee woz cleanin' his gun wi' nae care

En' by accident let flee a shot i'the air.

It freet the pony, thet ran sharpish away
En' charged thru the hens that wor thor in its way.

Them hens rose up, yan en' all, i' the air
En' flitter'd aroon' in an awful scare.

The forin hens tee, flew up wi' a cry
En' fer the forst time i' thor lives got a taste o' the sky.

They nivor wor seen agien, Aa heerd say.
They mebbe tiuk off fer thor hiem far away.

(A meety fremd land Aa'm thinkin' that'd be
Aal clood en' majic en' mystery …)

Onyways, we moved inti a bigger house,
Mary en' me, en' forgot the access
En' hed ti buy a parcel o' extra land
For that the Ranters wudnat let me cross theirs.

*

Hoo the Rabbits Wor Horribly Thret

Naw rabbits Aa kept
Bonny dutch rabbits
In a shed nigh the hoos,
Snod en' snug.

En' yance en' mair
Losses Aa tholed,
A buck or a doe,
Foxes, Aa jalous'd.

Seea Aa keek'd i' the winter –
Tracks Aa fand,
A sign of a paw

Clear i' the snaw-hap.

Aa axt a gam-keeper,
Telled ne hoo
Aa cud fettle a snare,
Gud fer foxes.

Seea Aa set up a poke
Thor by the dike
Ti see 'boot fengin'
Hungry reivers.

Well, the mornin' Aa fand
Summat strugglin'
Like a mad soul i' the sack
Greetin' en' yowlin'.

It woz spunky as owt,
Gert big beastie,
En' its claws ye cud see
Rivin' thru the sackin'.

Aa caal'd this gam-keeper
'How, man, lookstha naw!'
He sez, 'Wella, that's queer,
That's nae fox, man.

'Ye'd best garr it droon
Afore it breks free!'
Seea Aa hoyed it in a tub
Held it well unner.

Then we tiuk a liuk,
Nae fox that woz
But a spankin' gert cat,
Wild-cat, properly ti say.

Fer the caad garr'd him bowd,
Warse nor any fox
Fierce like some bear

Brindled en' sharp-gobbed.

En' the rabbits Aa kep'
Bonny dutch rabbits
Wor safe efter that
Aal the winter lang.

*

The Strike

Naw the owners decided ti change the shifts at the pit
Ti lay doon new wark-patterns, en' it caused a stoppage.

For the maistors wad hae thor pits wark faster en' harder
En' the men was hae sed, Ax us, ax us what's safe en' proper.

Seea the men withdrew frae wark, the maistors stoppt wages en' coal,
En' for the pitmen hed little brass i'hand, thor fam'lies wor siun
    ahunger'd.

Us that wor shop-keepers thowt hard what credit we cud give
En' fowk i' the skiuls set up soup-kitchens ti feed the bairns.

The men wor bitter an' fierce ti see thor fam'lies tret seea;
The maistors browt in poliss frev Ireland ti deal wi' them.

The men marched wi' a banner: it woz three vests on a line
Which telled o' the shifts disputed; aal woz riddy fer confrontation.

The wives forbye set oot ti show thor anger:
Wi' thor sho'els they gat buckets o'coal frae the Pea Heap.

That woz the small coal nae gud for price.
But the women thowt it splendid ti hoy at the poliss.

The under-manager, Mr Bell, read them the law..
But he ran for his life as the women cam up nigh.

Then the poliss with truncheons made a firm blue line
En' aal the showers o' coal cud not budge them.

En' as the women flacker'd, the poliss charged,
Brayin' them aal wi' thor sticks, bangin' en' yellin'.

The crowd tiuk off ti Johnnie Bell's hoose, jis' nigh,
En' used the coal left on his greenhoos, iv'ry pane was brokken.

But the bairns en' ithers warked aal day at the spoil-tips
Ti scrabble tegither some bit coal fer heatin' en' cookin'.

Thir wor heaps o' stien en' shale, gert as moontins,
Weird rocks o' reds en' broons, wi' rose-bay grawin' on't.

Sometimes it burned in-bye, en' brust inti low on top,
A mannish volcano o' stithes en' gases.

Thor they wad sieve the weany bits they grov up,
Or mak drift-warkin's o' thor ain fer ti howk oot better coal.

En' seea the strike gann'd on en' on;
Ended Aa knaw, but Aa cannot mak it clear, naw, frae the nex' un.

For ye mind, Aa grew owd, still tuneful, but slaw,
Tiward the day, Mary en' me, we stoppt tegither.

The Lion Man
or Four Poems in One

'We are the children of the Lion Man' (Bob Marley)

PART ONE

The children
the quick clothing of majority
an' sez Babylon
we will promote

*

The thick world of the horse,
of arm-length skull,
human-height body-length
and its grave power.
This could be yours.
What are you growing into?
Something else that shines
that runs 'n' rears.
But first you bring the horse into your family,
before it adopts you.
Then its limb your limb
its long head your head
its air your air
its ribs your ribs
its mane your mane
its flairing tail your tail
its hard hoof your hoof.
It is like a leather jacket.
You assume, and extend.
Most, then, you can dance.

*

I let my eyes sink forward.
I yawn.
I sleep
And
All at once there is action
tensing 'n' turning
to glamour

mica-sparkle of mother nitrate.

The one warrior
and his red hide
out-civicking the murder-sucking whites
their game
of dead-lie
what worth is it to be respected?

In the arch of the bitch who is the bride
resides
a lot of bike.
The secret side of the leg
and psalm of seam
are as sumpy partners in the thing
strong.
The troy noble voyáge perilous.

Upstairs inside
the king's butter turns coins
and down down down
into withheldness.
Everything hold and have/deny
'For fire is a thief.'

Fox 'n' Roger 'n' Wide-Go
all wear their kroang-ruangs
ultimate entitlement to have fight-time

*

No, action
is not in the suite of reality
(watch out!)
it steps outside

steps into god
pinnacle and thunder
high-nosed breath
the euphoric opal-eye engineer

who presumes

for it becomes a point
to render non-real
to reveal
eucharistically

are untranscendent
if they never glower over to outside

the nameless beings to
tear the sky
undefined
colourless
goldless
outlineless

*

HEIGHT
FIGHT
BRIGHT

Ra-ra-ra!
I see myself high hawk
I am something that shoots
elevates
in a scattering shine.

Bas-bas-bas!
hundreds of cocoons of hundreds
of rows of heads of stacked
kitten-luck
something so fragile.

Thoth-oth-oth!
a long intellect let me peer
into the well of eternal revolvulation
and extract you another chi-ro
a better insane puzzle word
watch!

*

The blood people
they appear
in the ebb of the law
in a dark crate of a place where
they are unappeasable
reason a star-horoscope action.

*

the marble-emerald mountains of Tibet
and these strange zoo-pen non-men animals for our tickets
should we expect them friends?

the beach
that-is-the-beach-that-is-the-dry-bed-of-Kali
for sea can be centre

*

'All about Kamandi is the incredible evidence –
the progress achieved by the lions.
More tolerant than the tigers –
more constructive than the barbaric gorillas,
the lions are different – '

*

In the placid, placid wool of our heads
the rain jolts.
juvenes vestri visiones videbunt.

Intermittently, we are sensible.
Testes and Trauma
are zero monarchs.

And major inventions reactions.

*

our mask
a whirled eyelids
behold the end of sight
is a feint design (negligent, equal)

*

I wake
the directions of a dog's face
neat wavy seed-rows
like combed
serrated is a ragged colour
and the lion talks

•

all there will be
is sun-topaz bears
in that last sun-second …
images of indignant politicians
like tea-cups
and the syrup-gloss rods …
there was a noisy lack of discriminating information
from the small coil-headed thumb …
and we are
dead diamond …
we are not
strange warm scented things.
n players n frighters n touchers
so full of run
so twizzly
unable to keep our faces at the front …

•

Irises flags swirling grand indigenous acanthus material in highly coloured glass sits in domestic windows. The reduction of vast victorian scale to something imaginatively familiar, when women model themselves on birds flowers jewels, exquisitely sense-tried images, scented before the warrior acquisitors.

Perhaps the ancient arabs saw jewels and colours as proceeding from an internal light. A great gem might contain a great power. A genii, in effect an angel. Something soul-like, that gave corporeal form to what it co-habited.

You may see marriage as a completion of image. The man-image unable to complete itself without that external guarantee, and the converse too, also a dependency. Being a fragile bond because of possible fallacy. Stacks of private contracts and a few group guarantees, I think.

Some children, eskimos and vikings possess an animal-double, typifying and doubling itself, in order to give subtle characteristics to the human vacuum. 'Bear', 'wolf' and 'boar' were popular symbols, and fictional beings that could be imbued with multiple traits, like 'elf'.

The proper male has a necktie, to hang by, so as to gain wise superiority; proper woman does not neglect shape as luck. They all achieve, which is they steal.

The less adventurous sometimes try to undefine themselves, or simplify the process by informing on others who are still mobile. The image becomes inanimate: the attentioned soldier, the handcuffed suspect, the bedded invalid. But the criminal godling Hanuman gets boxers to play like monkeys, act the wash, the drink, then jump up and bounce about on one foot, before they even begin.

*

Spider is 'rageous.
He tricks trust and gets all the goods.
He mak's cartoon wins.
Then Son-of-Spider outbalances Anansi
so there is a showdown and righteous ridicule.
Spider ends up in a corner.
These tales date from the era when white men still walked the earth.

PART TWO

the great temple of feelings
pain into spontaneity
it rearranges
you will forget who is shapers
be your own breath

the sad mad brother self
takes my words, he feeds them to the dusk,
sand of stone settling, darkening
and I trust.

now my mind covers how much?
it is a rainbow-crepe skirt
a change
a musical

*

Like the blinking ova lantern,
seizure, see
worms of light
a bitter bright filament
to take his coffee shell by.

'Be true …'
well who?
the breakfast me?
the gentle / angry / active / sleepy facet?
shall I act like I think I look?
are we the integrated consistent model?
is there a risk of little submerged foibles striking thru?

How do I know what you see?
Me?
Most of mirrors smile back.
But in the walls behind
there may be considerable variety of sub-expressions.

That represent the civilised world.

If we are shaping in our image –
stately as trees
watchful as houses
as certain as roads
the good god of the oven
and the goddess of waste
of stomach & vein

for even the Moon's Mother
couldn't –

us greatest moonscapers
us as umbilical dollops
least shapely

*

It is low here
slow and clear

Am I ribbons and wheels?
ripe or rough blood?
what do I spell as I ride into top?
When there is multi-red set
at the world-rim,
the oil-limb god with his black phrase …

This is it is a privilege
when
You will be taught to live is not a right
what you will
die globally daily
If we we will
adhere
saved
to the body
chattels
king of immunity

Accumulation
necessitating & assists defence

*

The compliance
the condign ubrixity of the head
patience of pace
these are machines of milk
they are our organic tools.

the man as herder
and manager
and: the producing city
for work / heat / feeding / training

the factory-born footwash-shower shop-field
has to be a full-time habit
there is no such thing as compulsory labour.

There is less and less scope
for work.
Our electronic and automatic hands prevail.

And we smoke in mounds.
Only inedible.

*

Wealth
in the hinterland
it is a symbol and sign of the Castle of Bone.
The head in the hole.
The box in the lettuce patch.

To ask
For what the hinberry an' haws in the jar?
Enquire and gain
Gain height and humanity
otherwise

you can age for free
And continuous there are singers n singers n singers
and love sequels

If we are something electrical
                              if not
the quiz sparkle
              what are we explaining?
      sinuous waves
      self
What are we unexplained by
                              are things
                              are not props of life
facts we see is reinforcement
                              or it is the exhibit
there are long sullen disconnections
                              of idiocy.
informed
is primed
protected

I will be memorial

let me be static.

PART THREE

another day
gone away,
what can I say.

To each cornflake packet
a Heimdall
to magic the milk
and to reforestate the table
hue-green wood
white snow
'n' craggy bugles in blank greaseproof
(little-size the heroes)
(what kid wouldn't)
(it's the packaging not the food)

like plates
78's
marrow-dust bakelite whiff
to the notes,
wood-like tone,
note-tone, out as hooty and sepia sound
old gay ancients, why they were,
were they? parents – dancers?
or is it just a style …
a musical mirage
turn / turn / turn
round flat patter why we wind.
Lie on a gentle arm.

Soon I will fall into bed.
Then I will turn out in Court.
Oh day, so calm, so sweet, so fright.
The voice will be motes of dry-nothing in unlucky air, I fear
My ears.

Oh then,
gaw on.

Aa'll trick ye the once.

Think of a glum blue-grown death of a day
and shit-brown demons riding on it
and something unstable in the stoury settledness about me
seething with piety.

A word.
A window.
A few hours a week
Would have saved me.
But I carry on whistling like a tunnel-grub,
self-dark,
Me being my best bet.

*

This is the unmasking scene of the film.
The good warrior and the evil warrior were brothers.
The excellent lady has a scar-footed secret.
Is the eye a masque?
A packaging of solid sense?
Varying nothing?
Or a cork-bobber?

The plot runs through the tune.
The weapon was a tin-opener.

*

lift a coin
'n spend it.
take something.

be broad
in the fief
of Adult Penny.

Each jewell'd tag
each little bird that clings.

Me in the heat wrap
She on extra offer.

Back off.
You'll never get another bike.

But averagely,
what you want
is what you get.

*

The pickled potato cupboard state of reassurance
is OUT.
That includes TV mysteries
of loss 'n' restoration
with paraclete detectives.

The insolubles are longer.
Great chains of defective thought
to be snipped
sausaged
certified.

Hissibus quilly-quilly toge
dellibollical tarák
passiquossi grattippi talq
doppi-mozat.

*

The evident God
in his basalt clatter
in door-burst
the pride paralyses resistance
here you will not tell the human truth

In the blood-red gold tit
n in the orange arch

the heat foot
there is the lip-knowledge
I come claim lottery total

Explanation elucidation
we figure our own form
make toys of life-processes
to be an incessant engine
be altogether something that understands

No motive
but we continue
addled ugly aggressive flame-families
biting the wood
it is everyone else's frame

When the bodies compact
we start again like
new matches in the coffee-black
what! peer at sky-gilt
egg-battles

or
just ink me some items info
things that see
not
the box

*

Going round the shops
is like telling fortune.
I will be wealthy, or look it, like it or not,
rugged, with Mars's jumpers,
well-styled, well suave, all Venus
a sport-foot Niké'd chrome-chumm'd
gadgeteer,
and eat like excellent.
I could be all of it anyway, I guess,
if I make the right effort.

Like if I spend.
(could buy myself …)

*

The glossy cock'rel
tosses place
wi' the biscuit advert
between
productions
immemorable.
Me? a consumer product?
Resistances/capacities attuned to 8-hour health?
Leisure legal.
For it is fashion for the cells to bind and believe.
Like a box of toy music implements
each kid grabs one,
they specialise.
We are conglomerate.
Art talks to us.
One day my skin is oaty and rough,
one day my skin is soft bronze.

*

Because people are rich,
are they privileged ghosts? I doubt it!
They live on the bones of foreign dead,
will us supernaturally to admire them.

All of us are alive.
We branch out into leaves of consumeristics
Chase after the carrot satisfaction factor
Till we become unnecessary.

*

I am not dead.
Nothing has killed me.
All praise to the Receptor of the Psalms

sitting in Zion
with the biros of angelic grace poised
upon the stencil of the world.

And
a ditto.
We may live some more.
Ditto and ditto.

*

This is
The twentieth century.
It seems an era of dolls
as statues, symbols
continual mechanical-aimed killers
walking nimbly-not thru the architecture
its gold swirls inciting
self-sustainment thru others
as the actual human gasps suddenly.

The summers were good
Helping us out of our linted baby cocoon
the reassuring feelers professionally
stroke us, assert a role
looked us for signs of monarchy.
At each break-time, more honeydew.

Entirely reasonably,
we continue to demand
whatever the jenii takes for us.

*

This
how
the long blank mindless frontage

the certainty
and the guarantee

of nish

not policies
so no facts / debates

just the power to report
'he was pumped full of drugs'

suppose,
just suppose
the whole venture is negative
an' for all concrete force
inverts –
naught –
suppose

*

So
I no
more mean to –

Be very careful!
for the words however only oral
can be true too

adhere to altar
the strange weep-hair other
as plait-arm blue-bone do.

*

To set the something
To get the something
set down
so it can influence the future
work shape the human
typefaces
bright bindings
matter

for art is a tuber
a decibellic groundular reserve
and death decoration
in case any universe place let
hot brown seed
survive folk-fire –
then you can say
you read it here first
(a bit of a limp plea
a self-concord ...)

*

The noblest
'frain 'frain 'frain
the oak and the ark n the harp n the larch
fit on one chip

with the sale n the slave
n trumpets from beaks n bells

*

Cities of closed information
increase.
Transcend
perfect victory of energy.

So soon there will be nothing but sand to listen to.

A contentless
blank
unutterably vague
form of adventure
I bet you

*

the sea the basin the tap
to be washed

veer suddenly to the centre of the earth
the right day at the crater of Sneffels
lurch into who knows (he knows, no cannot know) what
when the sun blacked the volcanic plug
route to
a world of lightbulbs

PART FOUR

of a all once
(head-itchy
I was on the M'way)
I thought plum
an' wasp gum

*

House and road
are trim and snod
kept by Easington and god

*

The lion 'n the lizard
man the pit-head
that is a little soil 'n a little stone
an' naught but earthish
wiv a few lime-flowers
'n head-bowls
for now the (helmet) white mine-rule's finished

The guild of the cold coal-mangle
the bishop's minerality
these no longer worth a slot
they fill no denes guard no cliff
sit under trains hardly not
there is no more god-landscape
what tho' everything the white man plays at forms fact.

Ho heckles of the ocean dragon's fist
have sprawled are
be
the
painless pale sand
no more house-high brick-head strata can establish
make a step-world to purple

*

Seaham 2000
An Open forum for Debate
on Consensus for Change

A Forum To Open Up
Debate on Seaham's Future

*

In the uncertainties of
rank and mask
plants get
'some sort of theistic hysteria'
look
they yell
like they all got different purposes
a pretence of same

No, I will see night
get the different bastards bedded
listen to white/slight moonscape
humming dumpers

predatory glandular gentleness
of some shale on sand
tree on tide
there is
guillemot on coal-coconut.

In this softer time
there are some intimations I am almost terror
dumb

tokens of mud to be

*

Horden to speak:

We are groups and co-ops and super-entities.

We accept most practices.
We assent the benevolence of everything.
All the time there are hymns.
They extol bleak matter.
Because the horoscope is real.

*

Bacon.
Oh buddy,
can I tell you!

one not
but where several words are gathered together in my phrase
grows and defines
light and warmth and breath and contact and conjunction and repetition
spirits of
congratulatory gratification of the focal tree of life
and essential products
wheel of wealth artefacts circulates and reels of consumeration
looking actual
the clothing of sexuality and co-operative creating of self-conscious

obligations
of meaning existence and well the words are expert at
if nothing

*

Slimly the snow falls
one day two day
snow into April
what clearer mark could there be
of the gods' displeasure with Easington District Council?

*

Out of the dark world, perceive
white milk hills
organic are white chocolate walkers –
and sea-dunes
wild food
pale-away wavy horizon pool
shifty ice-topped smoke-cloud sky

the crystall'd orchid and cowslip
it is lozenges

in the physical world the curvaceous blue
plain maid cloud
sun-bronze skin-flare sunset
all feed on,
things to kiss and click

*

Councillors in gold chains cluster round the stall displaying golden
    jewelry
like warts round a witch'd vulva.
'Rich fucking quunts,' sez Del.

*

Having dodged all the koans,
I introduced rapid-fire training techniques to the pan-Parkside
   precinct curriculum.
The emptied mind
took enlightened principles good.
Two inches below the navel
a optimum OK.
A balance to aim for.
'N breathin' lots of technical words is the way thru to longevity.
Plus the final fist on the catapult.

*

The moon slants pepper-dust
the abandoned dome of a monastic town council

*

colossal the delicate loop and fly
butterfly
to jagged and dotted think. Is I
could, wow, why,
make sky,
what a sliding syntax, shop-slick, we'd get into, by and by.

*

They are fast asleep
bundles of exoskeletal councillors
with good voting will

*

I feel you : turns of quartz
Respect : rails, arches, arcades.
The sight : is coloured patches, sticky paper : pictures.
All : jeweled bumps, functions
But slow cellular gratification : wooden animal circulation : a
   factor.
Flowers as rebels : wreck of focus : the bias.

All the feathers shake, flip : sort to action.

*

The Union no longer lives in Durham
the power-base is coercive again

*

In the great life of the leaf
tricky tumultuous
o fiat ira
are demons their black bellies castled with buds
o magna viriditas desiliens
the cascade jungle
blooms and brown paws
rattle dow' ladders
there is no mountain of gold
just so level level selves of sleeves –
how the great jawing cheetah
and on his brush-by
never aims to eat leaf.

*

the picture shows a jail-cell man
'a blatant non-payer'

*

An' we is sposed
to get up tiggy-eared
each morning
thank god
en run ti wark …

all because of
Beveridge's love of a way
to succour the multiplication of the white race.
entering towns and citeys

gross centred industries
the houses and up setting owners
for the unit plan to reproduce was
and all these roads are still in place
not wealth but global differentiation
by 17 buses each shift as well as
gross redundant non-products pre-technology

*

oestrogen addicts
pad about the County Hall;
24,000 at the latest count.

*

smallscamperingthings
letters
lines
legs –
play tricks
to come to an abrupt end

various professional devices
as sleights of metre
watch out
for the unexpected
a shower ona jungle fire-fizz

a giant town-size egg
brooded by pairs of Local Councils
neither edible
nor hatchable

but there are sparks and smoke
pyramids and snakes
on the beach
and tribes inland
that harvest strange and mordant drugs
letters of abuse fly in the press

smallscamperingthings
letters
lines
legs
play tricks
to come to an abrupt end

*

theses for grant-aid
are systematically looted from my booklets

*

March I march I march
we are on the march
lift them
print your feet
walk walk walk
the finger-balls
tapping it out

Beyond the phone
the radio implant.
Beyond the personal
a disk.

Day iz
Moon iz
Year iz
Age.
Alright – we rest.

I don't know – is this a blind turning?
But you can stroll if you like.
Join arms in the catacomb.

yellow vegetables are rape
against azure water

the farmer must know something
he don't say nuffin.

harmony
sweet on sweet
hand on heart
spirit and pollen
the daisy
chain world safety
lips not anus
motion not prison
and sustainable balance
of man   and mouth
herb   and harvest
air   and articulation

*

we will call a party
to affirm. The blank refusal to transfer
only leads to torture

*

What makes you deem the words so safe?
The wet warm winter holly
its thick stickles
they rasp they perforate they pain
holo-anti-makariate

the rubbery garlic
flops on the snow
schizo-ill
drungars

diagonal glades
they contained quasi-sculptural deer
it doesn't smell of peace
but oklo-biázamine.

sour fruits and toad-killers
and non-life forms
a suchly floor
tawny friendly bees
how absent
it is a paidiot spell.

so to vex (conquering nations)
the poor hilly dry vestal jungle
that its hierarchies also will work for hitherbound excess.
Oh!

*

Exquisite twigs
in the holly-home nest
shall reoccupy?
My bone is no better than a flute
if I do not see the safe eggs lilt
swell to sea-like air again.
Make mine no broken home.

Amra Pamphlets 1996

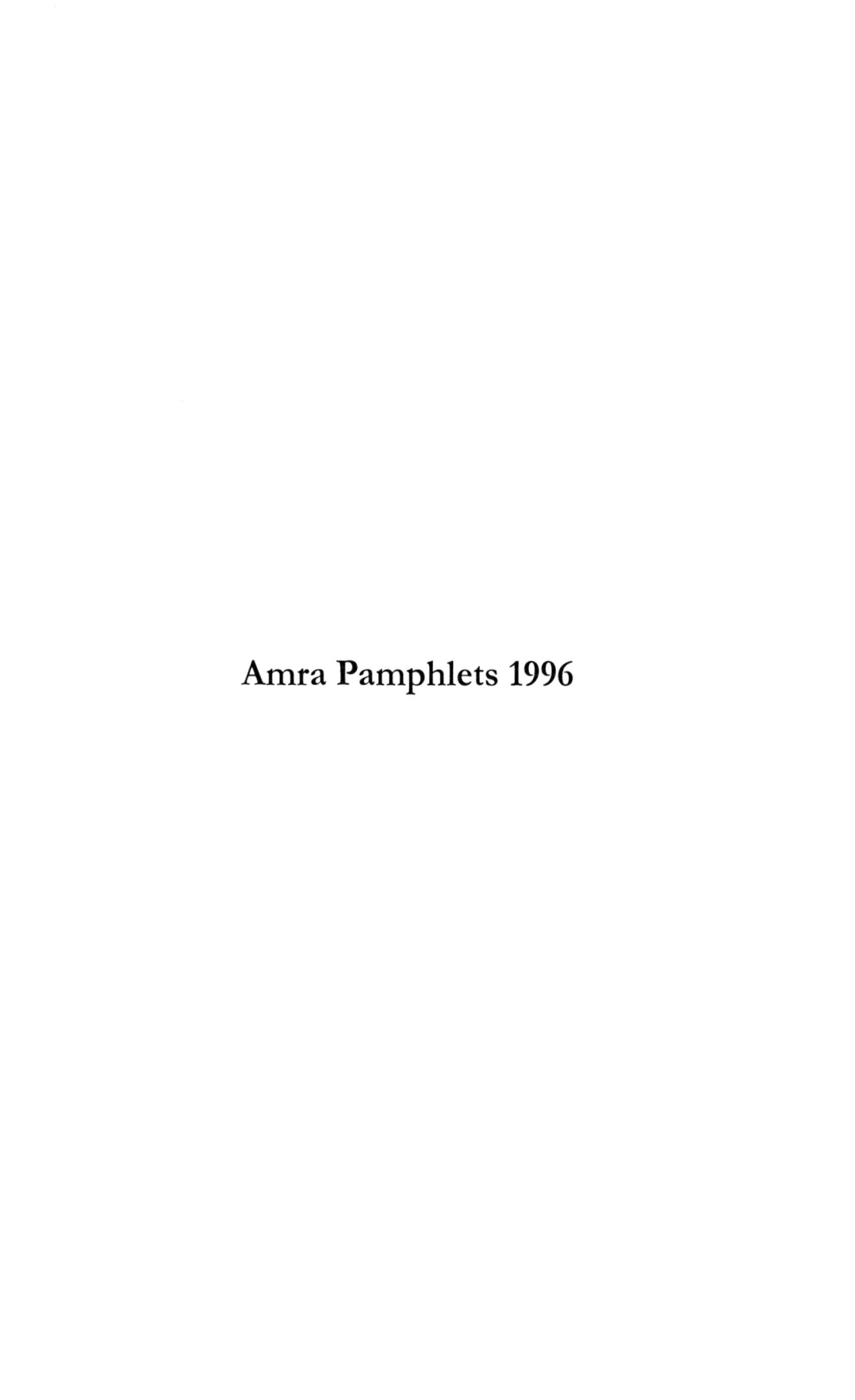

On the Abuse of Drugs

1.
My Lord Percy
Duke of Northumberland
is defunct
by very sudden habitual intake
of amphetamine sulphate.

It se-
ems on the one hand
he was lively a man
so habitually awake
he need sleeping pills to take.

Then he got so sleepy
that on the other hand
he need some
speed to keep awake
during the day.

Which could just be
why he was such a lively kind
of man
in the first place,
by my estimate.

The supplier to the aristocracy
was not named
somewhere a doc-
tor commented on his Grace's
nobility as he faced his fate.

2.
Sub-mariners
I'm telled
after a spell at sea

acted odd on land
at Chatham
and in the canteen
at Chatham
they would smoulder and get tacit
destructing
pies slowly in their fists
I'm telled
or raging or fighting
for no reason
after a spell at sea
and everyone was telled
to leave them alone
as though all
sub-mariners
acted odd on land
after a spell at sea
for a few days
then they were OK again
and went out on leave.
It crosses my mind
about Chatham
that these
sub-mariners
for a spell at sea
in a sub
got beta-blockers
to keep them orderly as
sub-mariners
which is why they
acted odd on land
and needed a day or two
to readjust
as I understand it.
And did they?

3.
Uncoöperative army personnel
with personal problems
were disposed of to a psychiatric camp near So'ton.
Some like schizophrenics could be diagnosed by smell
(a formerly orderly maintains)
and some who could not be diagnosed were sent to a military
    punishment unit.
Meanwhile, a combination of methedrin as alleged truth-drug
and ether lightly and variably in case of panic,
were administered,
to bring to the surface
all those awkward little expected pre-indicated traumatic diversions
that prevent the human from growing up a normal plain killer.
Or bare electric convulsion therapy.
Most humans now agree it is safest to have a subconscious.

4.
15% of inmates at one prison get daily medication.
They are not telled what.
If they don't take it,
they can be returned to strip cells
and get compulsorily injected
by gangs of special servers of the crown.
It induces drinkless eatless states
some-blue on the circassion ocean
I am entoured by
fused myths of corn-braids on the skin,
splinted symptoms of nose-clenching
I trace to
sublunary/subcutaneous tree reflexes
as us monkeys nuking each other
in video'd cells and cities.

5.
In the growth industry.
To enhance growth.
To gain in humanity build.
The cheerful aid of muscle on body
the regularity bone
profile struct
only moves with the tendon traction
skin to skin
a local luck
that echoes idea acts or a view
no train mystical.
Teemed inti the outmost mouse-sphere
millions of tablets
night-notions
'n' day-splice
all of it is pectoral
pieces of one
in a femaley megalith of rose-frame
family
infinity

6.
I cannot tell a total
but it now appears tens of thousands
of dots of LSD
were distributed
in British hospitals in the 60s
to rebalance the mentally unrespondent patients
by healing by hallucination
and sometimes it helped.
Transfixed by terror
up trees
some climbers
have yet to come down.
And exhibit inexplicable resistance to counselling.

The Genesis of Iron

Man that is striped with sulphury orange
has but a short factory to build
and his trust in secure external commercial factors
is as good as fatal.
The jackal rubs his belly in the sun,
there are angle irons
bright stanchions
'n' bars like celandine brass.
The beätifer knows what is worth work.
What is love at many levels.
Sometimes the hot bowls pour.
The new ore is ready to be sprung into a rhythm
like writers tewed into writing.
There are night sooty-smears on the neck
where the genetic label takes place.
Is ill,
indicates sons with bold black
daughters to be to dance.
There is brown pastes on the ground
yellow smoke-marks residue to
the barriers of bare earth.
Now the hot sun burns the hair,
leaves a bed sadly,
the artefacts pepper the display
and it is properer to service anyone who simulates some regret.
What do you think we advocate?
Just meaningless simplicity?
So the stone homes of Consett
are mazes without complex,
and to be no acts of coalition.
Consider Leadgate then.
All the work paradise
shook spread out
categories
the de-arrangement plan time
after the human harvest seed
has sung home

learns you may move.
As the last gaps of iron
rest rust
as there is no more money for work,
the jinx parades,
is lippy.
The maker
tagger
from the trig so the box
Belial tackles
everything of the effort
in the name of the nought.
Prince his knuckles of spider-fur he operative
sits the celeste (orgeuil)
to claim acclaim. (A spikey world, no stanzas.)
Lip oranges
roll off hand
the idle bread packs
marginal, meet no pattern.
Nothing between hours of the idle
and the still daze.
To make coins aspire.
So that somebody drew a
      ?

on the tip.

Histories

A fantasy
as of soft heat
fruit 'n' wool 'n' human-kind
the sun-land's farmer-predator
active with apricot's silence or dog's or wheat-height
unaware what of sudden riches
will evolve.

*

When the Welsh remember bits of early world
before there was rhyme
or red-ear white-coat dogs
what comes?

long before the first flash of dragon
or a cairn
or a pavement
or green warm woodland?

before red hair
or black hair

before the ice bridge

pre-island

somewhere east of Prussia
rings and spirals and triads were formed
magic hares
and earth paths

A positif of certain solace
a increment

we are carried about in art

for I know no tincture of blood.

*

The lemon is not part of history.
Its smell
links-savage
as to protest sea

*

The pharaoh's nose
the pharaoh's mouth
the breath passes
for air the soul is, as though this air is
personal
internal
inalienable.
How fanciful to be preserved,
taken future,
rethought, sorted,
reanimated – and so
corrected.

*

Vex
(quia pericolosum'st)
not
(dico dico)
the triangle trill of beaks
(vestigia illa)
we are the last little saurian skim
(sed not sinunt)
nothing bigger
(affirmatum'st)
survives the dark

*

Toltec wins.
Eggs and gills and lungs
are gestured forth where stone.
The ball a head is like toffee
'n' great classic musics echo
even outaways
sky-side
tomb-to.
So to advertise.
It will be conducted differently.
If we learn to speak.

*

soft antlered logic
he is our great informer
those that spoil solutions
and is the great seducer
I advance fact
the Lilith of perpetual self-species
elegant to listen
books of ours is long-term advantage
and pure

*

this is the medium of the egg
a special oval embassy
itch to bouche
the hand of breakfast
trilling.
Taximagulus and Vertiscus
eglantine
the chick fuzz of the judge robe so be
a pucker yellow
plural yellow
race brown or to white of shell
I am the ascension and the egg
as we are

Hungary

Is the grainy air
colour-ocean-kill fog
it insists and eats
beef and fence and pasture
godly or not, fog history
norsemen and bikemen
leather-pad is knee
are marked to zip into the slum tall angelic gray arcade
be art of a picture-card monarch
image winners:
in a zero I stand protected
it flattens the stars
is ownerless / extinct / equal
no place of solar sound
only indication of animal after animal
to a thousand and a thousand thousand
choose what air you breathe
standing all year.

*

The crown of the proto-martyr
no stones
but shimmering *vacci annuli* of gold
hair-striated horn-finule of gold
with oval cups as eyes, square bridge teeth
structured by strange speech
a motto of a word
an abstract as deposit in New York bank.

still life with coins
one banknote
some postage stamps
and doorkeys.
are gleam on a table-cloth
In a pocket we form the life-force.
a city of vertical buildings we produce

a mix of carols and sirens
of gates and cars and coaches and brown grass
of excitement of eyes
of wave-bronze hair
fossils at the foot of Kaiser or Tsar.

*

A kid with a shovel strapped to his shoulder
'I seek work'
passing the patrols
that sessioned the shooting
that mucked the square
before the great Russians in their universe
with no thought of 'sorry'.
Just one friend or two friends.
He said it was so.
Mobile.
Perfunctory.
Sudden bits of acts context savage control-storm,
quick-doing.
The sound of horses off the square
The click of hoof/stone
as man scents horse
an' engines an' the guns, growing
At eighteen
overplaying
as sand angel with glass feet
growing
among fiery rhubarb
he was hunted down with dogs
stumbling in escape
him and a pal
both are lost (you see) because of the fog
and gasping, this way? which you say?
and they split and he chose and got out and
The western world
was full of vines
its rills stunt with CO_1
lanes of roman letters and fox and chain

and honeysuckle and earth-mines
wanting everywhere to be soljers of the heavy industry
The stateless are organised in blocks.
One country works mills
or buses
or the hospital.
The Czecks and the Magyars were given mine-work.
New lives for now, state-loss for labour
obeliskal and gravétoid
exhibitions and exhibitioners
no one of us poised to yell or recourse
to benessential leaves of multisex
and ankletresses, proven Rome
whole heat
and the bars and locks open to
Under Barnsley
the separate races
had halls for strange swaying self-repair
(The Lord of the Blackout
the tumble, crash-down
Iyama pigeon process)
eating and messing ethnically
giving some sort of solidarity
to them in the coal-mines
And when there was a boxing competition and it was won
the King of Coal bristled at that, got up to walk out the stadium.
What! should a mongul-head magyar win an aryan? short-sod!
'So I knocked him down.'
And sometimes he would stalk me
while there was a cowboy 'n' injun gaming
using the tunnels corners angle bits to pounce
or sudden gun-to-gun showdown
so I shot the King of Coal in the hand
with the air-pistol.
Ask him for me.

*

Moved and married in the cosmopolis
at the margin

of the tapestry-maker's factory of Abbey Mill
a sot of blurred adult
arms round half-hun sound-name kids
break and grow in the housing city
Loud little ones
that fight for art
while I am a hamadryad again
something little-stemming vine-bud carrion
glint-drink full-dervish tricker
like movie scenes
high-cheeked
collapse-headed
where the cattle run through me
all colours of cars
for the dust-bowl kerb
Me and my committee
is it fair
to think of the time of reward?
some illusion of prize
brought on by work?
Was what I never guessed
that splitting up
before the sudden Russian abandonment of Hungary
till I was almost too liverish to travel.

*

New nations are come to take to work.
The moon candles record it
on the pond
in the Thai compound

above,
Thai-boy tiger
in the flat fork
in the tree that spreads
casual
a discovery of prisoners

The Labyrinth

Lo! a graceless
waste ova day
a sloppy splash self
on type a job-form
or bench-press
or leak pudding
mode: moody
outside
i & the labyrinth

GOLD
it is in the corner
it is under the envelop
it is on the eye
like a crane in a screen of weightless stun silk
flying a new scent airline
Even in the dark
an omnipresent
mode: make-well
i & the labyrinth

man in a position of poise
a branch-choice crux
what of it?
it transpires
no known mode
i & the labyrinth

the material-texture magic mule
a clash 'n' jump
clear quote
to run
an soda-holy inch-by-inch
sorority, mask-muscle
click of shells
threaded or tidal
the neck

class-cross dance
truant mode
no blackness
i & the labyrinth

mist is every middle-middling sine
and a transform
route
mode
way and rule
is to do something stunning-odd
assert for us
i & the labyrinth

The foot of the bee-god
initials of terror
i know why i do
existal clone
in the bronze-badge divine cell
partitioning
mode to make to participate
i & the labyrinth

motor-mood
the quick-turnings
a little garage of hands
every and ineluctable
opaque and options
sky 'n' card 'n' blue 'n' beryl
'n' every sign & multimix
i & the labyrinth

On the Platform at Stockton

What in the heat of
Stockton
the platform
nothing more harmless
for us to loiter
being well late, the train
and
pleasant past noon.

one, Mum, in the wheelchair
nowhere I sit
chaotic tar with weeds and pebbles and glass
the high oriels
in the brick
all looka ruinous
everything
will have went wild, slowly

well, the debris
hand
flag-feet eyes
silver-soaking white-weed buds
bubbles
is not torment
I ama page fold-out find

now our
over-stay
sunny harmony
lip-tune masque
presence
the two translucent
sober
and people-light

a silent sight of lines
in charm

long and long-gone roads
not much exit
no will
round wheel, but a position
the cloven staying
and know-it-will-be-sudden-if

if it shows
or no
retard motion
a sort of mustard haze
maybe

what, are we patient
as there is
no passengers no staffing
a pure by brick and cast iron sleeve
going round
for the sun is the centre of the timetable

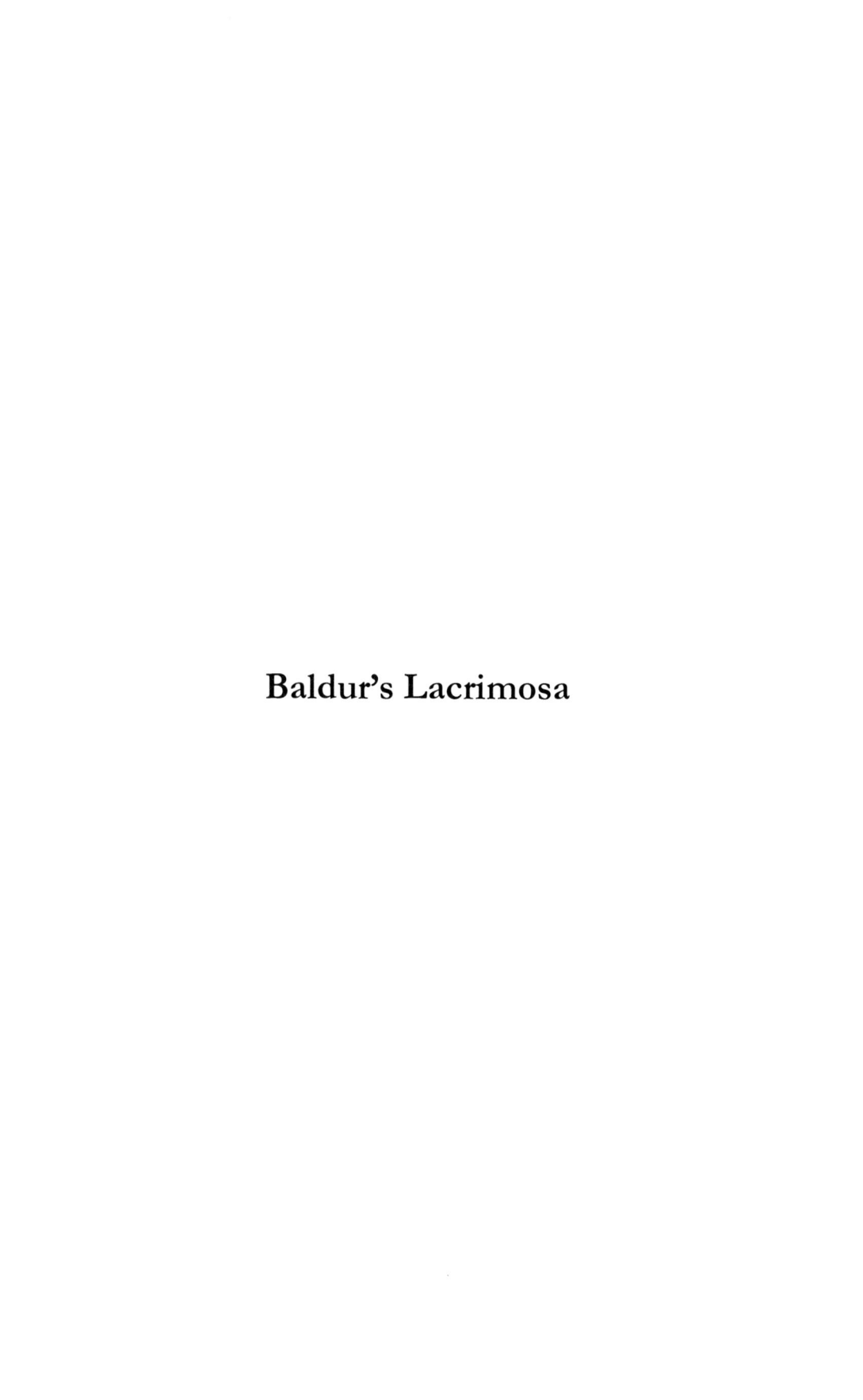

Baldur's Lacrimosa

Baldur's Lacrimosa
*is played in a lexical pelog
like a dog ratting the socks of reason
thru holy hour.
all of it helps.*

*The assassination of the well-tret hero is a read assumption.
Part One is* BEAUTIFUL BACKGROUND
to Baldur's dream.

1. Baldur's Dream & Frigg's Promise

In the querked jigsaw rebellion
of buildings
of stones
something mucal 'n' manic
'My life is really fucked'
there stirred
not a still laugh
but the magistral

Archistructure
a great endospermal
to show all
exoskeletal
lithium buildings
this is the suburban sky
drinks the shank-broken X's
of a adolescent
are invoked
coloscal
event-exit kriss-cultures
drinks sick-shut families

funny
neutral
bismati-scented arms
to almond eyes
to night-nick'd meeting shoals
of like-hump Seti-mammals
we are dappled herds of

with sugar
the kids with wallflower faces
the hot crystals of ruby,
what spice and the maximum
suddenness
our in-horse world,
castle-ankled

so
we well suppose
fused

scan the telly
come on
it's out it's open
a peach-fuzz and fili-glow
city day
friction of sun/air
even groups
mebbe a fun grizzle

In my fav'rite children's book
Luke is given red hair.
I could have.

his-steam
there are ox-adventures
connectedness
beat-still
blowing liver-winds
and all things to make into joke

copper-red is pretty
OK
I am an assumption of pleasure
a bubble (cutting) of (fine) population
to us joy and gentle
and forever a vow of fox
force it smile.

picture the god-guy, the Baldur
all neat-lawn head
labelled un-toilet type
empréss and mango-faculty man
just sliding into
something of an early monument

now

BALDUR IS DREAMING
of his own meringue musculature
a downer
the risk of
being put in italics!

Be calm!
the wolf follows no one.

WHY HEADLINES?

Unions are dice
Suffice
Confirm
And the bowels of the fox burn in paradise to give birth-bang

The pink party crystal
facets 's mobile
on us
we are dirt-cover for dignity.

have you never seen me with a pollen shirt?
trick in a clay gutter?
such a lot of beauty is police
you'd never think a girl
better campaigning my feet
so no
they spoil eveything

WITH BIG WORDS

the slaying sun
and the tribe of lesser lights
glowing fingers
the clicking link spiders
as to who shall dance or scowl

all things in balance!
it cannot be wholesome
to care

who are the valuable people?

the stain of the stamp
inborn blue
well-traveled rose
even matted curded yellow
numbers, sums, values
claiming to be above the common postal rate
beside.

generally
lives are lovable
are not hoots of trains
are not daggered ribs
but the ugly pure ones are still piss.

there is a poise
in the cauldron
a unwrap the blankets of blood.

But not Baldur.
Everything alright there.
Frigg will make him immortal, more or less
of woods of land and sea-things
and metal and sick: a perceptible status
that is worth proper celebration.

2. The Unforeseeable Accident

What is a nut-fleck?
strain of grain, something our baby body
heeds the marbling
sound colour of infected wood
and all the other print-in-poisons we admire/adhere
a'joined to much
getting' notice of nuffin'.

Feckless / tubes / tarantulates
shames in shell
packer information
call it who cares what we lie about, how to operate

'You can do it'
'I can't see very well'
'You can't see at all – that's what makes it fun.'
'Fun for everyone else'
'No you'll love it too.
It's a contest.
I'll be helping you.
You'll beat the lot.
You'll really show them up.
They'll be astounded.
A silence.
A gasp.
Then they'll all run over.
You'll be a hero, if I'm a judge.'
'Can't I have a proper spear?'
'No. This is better.
They'll never expect you to win with this.
What a laugh, eh?'
'This OK?'
'A bit left.
A tadge up.
Now straight like a dart,
no arking.
That looks fine.
Hold it there, while I –
well I want to see it hit.
Tell you what.
Count a good slow three.
Then "Now watch me!"
and let fly …
Got it?'
'One …
Two …
Three …'

(the piston
or heart-symbol
the over-hat
inkling
with clues
I pound
obliquely)

Mithra could not have dis-entrailed better.

Baldur slumped …
is it likely
a blind man
could aim
a mistletoe
unaided?
when they asked that
and then they sort of all
looked at me.

tack-tack!
the thimble on the thumb of Odin
jinx me
I jab
but we hav wov
a thriller, gaudy stitch ova story …
safe in a public place.

The barrier between 1st and 2nd class cabins;
the locked door between crew and passengers;
an ornamental rail for this/that egregiosity.
Just a peek?
she hoyed the black-cockerel-head over the wall
so she 'n' Hada should pass
properly, in Hell.

Hermod jump on his bike,
spraying a curve for Frigg's sake,
scoot to the nether realms of getting the gods' own way
for a release / appeal

getting Baldur back again soon
for just one unanimous show of gloom
referendum

I fretted some cornflakes:
the milk carton has a leak, tho.
It was raining the roads darker.
The kids had colds …
Everything seemed to be weeping.

Hang on,
this smack of Baldur
this is just the sort of –
a mass-mess
and you saying I oughta help?
Into the Committee
of the Corporate & Æsir conspiracy
I enter them
a horse no one has eased of its maleness
and some of them stopped weeping for a moment
(only Loki can make laughs)
especially a suspicious looking old woman taking notes.
Anyone breaks in and shits in the office.

Now I'm looking at a corridor.
Nothing ever like it.
Paint on a shroud of brick.
Looped lamps.
God-wrought locks.
For a dark age it seemed.

Loki had a dream too:
'chains, with hairs long and stiff as spears.'

3. The Funeral

the cor wailant
working over dark
tissle drum
bare dawn
a union, I seize
ogres' tunes

after the hugging and the screaming
the hushed mammals are left breathless as doldrums
macho cans of poppies repopulate us
dancing and fighting for future hours
rebellious brick-beds are reconquered
like platforms.
We roast rhymes.

Of the pounding peppery undine risko-roll
let us
and limp and limp

Newcomers on carts with goats
Newcomers and her entry
cats with flicky paws
sponges of tongues
tossing round Freyja.
She's someone, so?

And pork-motored Freyr
and Thor
in his glory
sun-man and gold-man
gracious north dark sky luck-hitter
crossed when,
kicked the dwarf
nearly tripped
flared with rage
kicked the dwarf
vanisht

into the fire
some grilled thistle
because they letted the hammer on the giantess who
    cracked the boat in launch for Baldur's funeral.

Welling I will
for any posture,
some house where valid sun-colour produces.
Over the settle
under the top-layer
and anything but the caramel.

Let him dream
the soft mould of choc'lat at mouth
and smoke
like stone or beach
if the boat rattle on-way
with its charred
is chorus
tact tone and touch
grit air
red woad earth seeks

The zed-clouds;
and the spontaneous move headwards
well-a-blow chord that big
subtle souciance
from s to z

Fragile the bones if slip
are slandered
we failed
are in charcoal
or the nests of eyes
smoke dog-dusk

as if after centuries of lint
there is any care
or to start

Thumb-maker
a thing of the thin forest
of the spaces limbs leave
curious
owners of an exterior
ink able

At Baldur's boatside
the trinity
uncomfortably
sing of Lurpak
there is the wail of polish and banks
healthy bacon
the emotion of insurance
the sense of sets of melting statues
of
Elegant and mysterious empire
falters
and its thumbs crook into questions

All gone, Baldur 'n' Nanna drift.

O
Aged mountains
eager growth
we spring it is
the great mundial water line time

Sky agree
we that are wrong
the rocks posses
water of our veins a blue silver trick

interim
at stone pulse
pass of cold
higher is black in direct air of zone sacrifice.

4. Retribution

kettles of blackbirds
they sing happy birthday
and have
yellow lips
howsomemanyever years long (to) Ragnorak.

My throat?
You would think trucks and dumpers 'n' excavators
had been chikey-chike atta dig
in there, face-swole, all day,
with tongues for ribbon-development,
all becos …
Ah, I choke up the Ibuprofen
's too big in pill
so I stay ill

mix of palm
and song
I wanta I sezza I seea
This and then that
then chords
I claw my hair from their hands

Take time.
Shut a finger, close leg, no use,
as after-bells.
The beat-packet
trip-neck
see such
and an instant.

My lungs are
crayfish in a kettle
the ribs
slave-boat in a slave-nation
no jam ocean.

There are fakes.
Cities of letters.
Loop-kings on tape with mustard legends;
Trinkets to ear-bore;
crag-chose irons that are no knots to Loki
and then there's room-rebels

loppy-eared
they are
they have
tight weather'd pelts the grey-crowns
'at doll in the out-agency
a street
a stripe of tree
the ogres and pucks are seeing quitlessly at
it mix
not-dark and not-dawn
desert

little crackle-trickle
wet window
I call Signy's tears

there are standards of remarkable equipmentality
all ovals
and fillet-stone diagonal series
ripples of a repeat repeat
what much for to battle through to win to nothing …
essence

do you think I do not know
FIRE
siccling squelch-wool
or calling calling wood
it jumps
a click on my wrist
ice or iron
there is no such
ANTI-FIRE policy

Sometimes Signy doesn't turn up
she's-fed-up
or-the-kids-get-her-down
or say what.
It's me.
I'm trouble.
Arm-riddled, holding the bowl.
Ain't she coming they say
(sleazy snakes spooky spoke)
Well, I'm here
(I say to cheer them up)
a little anguish in the eye
that-is-the-lullaby

Picture
this visiting room
a trick of gap of the prison
and I sat
little enough for they're big guys
most of them awesome
and I talk to my Gran
then she gets up to go at time
turns
and hugs me
for everyone
and lifts me off my feet!

Rousseau and the Wicked

'There cannot be any peace between Rousseau and the Wicked.'
J-J.Rousseau, letter of 24 March 1758

1.

'… the day after their arrival Wootton was buried in snow.'

Amid scenes of the wildest
comme je suis distrait!
but no spade could dagger into the ground
almost permafrost there
and no communication
some French some English
so no choice
our shared grief/pity
will be consigned to snow.

with unerring logic
our promises are 'wholly wrong or non-existent'
it is time to define information
or what it is

you see snow
massed on the terrific precipices
a placement
some sign eternal of loss of pure
and pure creation
so there is nothing better

I was aware I might be a living plant
something with melodious lines
leaves
bell-bright sepals
I rise from the snow
I show

to face the ice!
distorted gob,
radiate with head,
it is urgent,
to ruck to the sticky web snow
to press to
the flailing into nowhere

to switch to
great exploring knowing no end

Only the dictionary controls what I speak
minds have pages
if I confess
that I would write myself

if I start blank
write, erase, end blank
and torn apart for facts/seeds afield

at unexpected death
aware we would be all easily executed
if I cannot get safely to Dover

we are not museums
not industries
we are equals.
What I want
there will be a statement in Paris.

then,
shall I have the dignity of ice?

2.

The common world (so Jane sez)
is all maintained by 'voluntary spies'.
These monitor unevenness in equalities
and propinquity in inequality
for unless there is positional definition,
calibration of action and distinction of entitlements
(upon some moral register)
the war could not proceed.
It would become inexplicable.

3.

I too would smile with my fat mouth
if I were on a ten-pound note.

4.

Fuck, another addict.
Take the one breath 'n' you're hooked.
First you locate Continuity
then the Zollverein storm in:
'Untaxed drugs are bad for you.'

The throne is electric
the ambulance is a tank
the medicine is an informant
monuments are incinerators.

Refined air?
Doctors and others should be suspicious
of young people that ask for it

like
the breath of lovers – the breath of ghosts
intimate
plastic shirt on sunned skin / shroud
a black or blue glass
transmission and contingency and invasion
point / puncture
admission / emission
the fractal coast and vulnerable skin
and the sudden the close
like
lovers / lovers / ghosts

5.

And the awe of shape and number
The circle ear-ring and the cross.
The lucky permutation that is money.
The landing and canteen number
and beyond,
the bleak counting terror
night-interruptor
they come to seize the not-yet-born heart.

Los tigres?
Oh yes, along there.
But they will scent your breathing.
Even ghosts avoid them.
The little scars of handcuffs have nearly gone.
'and hope the fucking cunts see sense
I doubt it but all the same
I hope you get off with a caution.'

The breath is short and rushed.
Again.
Again.
Again.
Over and over.
Who sez it's for relaxing?
'I work in textiles
making sheets blankets towells and mailbags.'

If you know who you are
You don't like fight
To find out
About others
Except that you forget.
Who picks up the cigarette?
Gets to the biscuit.
Gambling on things like your toes.
'I hope it all works out and I rake the money in.'

6.

The old –
I am a sharer:
their urgent anxious inhibitory benevolence
like when everything else has lost,
a hope is started again …
a chance
as if
but it knows it is
insoluble.

The koan!
And the action –
the sliding 'side dirt-orange
en' kid chuntering round the room
wi' horns bubbling –
the like-self no shape can damp.
'An' he would trip me up!'

Moves to the maze of the
adult wheels
strange lights, mauve, warm,
the ginger halogen
and the strident shiny river
circling, zodiacal / pins of
the place of flesh-face
run / mammal-grass

and larger / broader flick of the mind,
the slower unities too
older, hopefuller
as tho the rest has –
(call it Baphomet or Dalziel)
the Bringer of Benevolence.

The tacit kings and queens of cards
– are they dead are they alive?
Vanish't colours,
rag fades,

fall, easier.
The room even now – to summon –
but isolate.

7.

The eating lobster was anonymous.
Some bairn left it on the back step.
I phoned Edith for instruxions
'N' cooked it.
Then his coral and orange-white creamy flesh
I dished
delicate as mild egg
a smatch of sea-rock-song / bony legs.

Everyone helps. And the net came up with everything. Green weed, red weed, dead fish, live fish, weights and grappling hooks, crabs that were mouth-size and rounded junior lobsters, one or two, almost too soft to count. Cleaning it was a chore OK, with the net rolled on itself, and claws jumping out of it from boxes of weed, not dangers very particularly but reckless in the air as they snapped or surged free. Count no crabs. Respectfully the lobsters, set on the sand, puzzled, set their antennæ on the swivel at the least approach, like a police car in an ambush.

Of the pan and the shore.

8.

First step o'er the hill
and down the gulf (ghyll)
and keep on
the switch-back path
are there notch-steps
and slides
and bald earth

sky-twists
slots or runnels
(letches)
guide

You are in the wild-lands.
O zoo O zoom O zoomorphic
burst growth-deep the
denes of the prince bishop the
zag-feather fern – fraction
of mitre
through the binoculars
can view clumps of hanging heads.

So hurray!
Trevor and me and his mate but
I'm on holiday.
I'm a saint.
The gradients are miraculous.

And there are bluebirds by
the picketed snag of sycamore
in the drop

the dandy glen of lion
the atmosphere
we roll golden tails
roar grand mouths

this gob work poetry
anti-elegant
this is a plea for more raw sunscapes,
flickers of song

for flat and flint turf
with a scatter of pointing unprotected plants
and maroon-things buzzing over it
none of them have proper homes

O Zeus

a hairspray scent
of mammals
covers it all
with a syrup bloom
there are some important rituals
baying
at the sea

9.

So who will save Seaham?
The majestic propriety of the syntax of rational organisation
or the mutational option chance sport
some sort of lucky lack of plan?
But the garden is fierce with socialism.
Only proper pretty things seem rightfully to survive,
noble their colour.
Curtains of bright live tissue
attributable to human supervision success.

The countryside
is not always as it is.
Trees become fields change shape,
crops equal market.
We magic it to look like Constable's portraits of healthy rural economy,
and then move on to shave it with lawnmowers.

Let us put the gentleman gardener environmentalist
into zones of rehabilitation,
beatitudes,
and *bridal of the earth and sky*
scatterings of mosaics / generations / climes …

10.

turn,
turn and pass.
turn and pass and behold
those that are unequivocally inferior to you.

Perhaps they limp, like martian imitations,
or nervously sip pensions, bee-ish,
or they just lack merit.

Honest, I introduced the concept as an irony:
that there are some people you just cannot help.
Ah, these headmasters know about that!

You try,
for nothing warms the lamellibranch-chamber of a selfless heart
more than
unsolicited but earned admiration
and perhaps the little tear, or gift,
testimonial, title, detached house.
Nature's thankyou notes.

But some are just
obstinate, they lock onto, so
Shoo them off the grass!

It is not just the back of the card, of course.
Not just wairsh for colour,
bellant for stencil pattern –
an image and a counterfeit thing.

It is not nothing-of-the-eternal either.
Truths over wrongs,
that sort of –
or some biological quasi-animal obviousness –
lacking.

Not accident.
Not establishment.

Not ownership.
Not effort, even.
Nothing plus, plus corollary.

But a sort of essence of the equal.
The game of being human, such as
recognising what you promote
disallowing what disbalances you into group
(any matter whatever)

It is easy after a while.

11.

The weary traitors-shapers
and the world of their puddinging-out,
of their medallic heroic abuse.
It is
bluish aura
of self-award, endless mirror,
it is
the dignity
of abuser and inducer
jumping up and down on their word-suppressors
the action
of adjudicator and chairman,
fists in the cheese.

Something
seeking a memorial.
To be embalmed in letters
chiselly gilt
and change into
something
emerald city
to template the rest.

Is that
lovely and lively?
And will the women do better?

when you are opened
after a decade,
how they gasp ('high upreared and abutting fronts')

well, dragons are not so rare.

purple-like-berry glass (the eyes)
views sub-red
(mute or lethal)
as activity

a snow-pale summer-night
ground dank with insect
and thief-work
and trails

12.

The realms of the wealthy,
house there is and garden,
a port for perhaps 2 cars,
woodland and meadowland will be nearby
which is a pretence against inordinate consumption
and vicarious pollution.

Income
will be ten or twenty times
'what the government says you need to live on.'

It will provide some luxuries
for spare-part surgery,
and the nous
to gag at the lands where magic worms are boiled into carpets.

The differential
measures hierarchies of value,
in a safe form of self-assesment,
and that value is shedded to all their possessions
that partake of the same special.

Are dusted with the angelic.

13.

The syringe orange act
something spasmodic about the normal
as optional 'imago'

'most moths are nocturnal …
manifestly there is no distinction here.'

'the delicate yellow …
and eggs of the white …
these spiracles …
gregarious … and disperse …'

By night, true mammal and snail
bevolve.
Safe silence
is the standard.

The saurian feet are exilic by night.

beach / bay
sweet-smooth round warm sand-dark salty and similar female
night mates
come
there are groups of
where there is pounding
a sea-beat blood-flow
flood-sight
line of char-wood and smelt

spume
underneath
frizzles at

reconducive the pattern
of cycling
is multi-mammal
in many cults
there is nothing night or impulsive
about speech
this is sheer well-worded day
it is OK

14.

A man in a silver suit.
A briefcase left in a minority-interest club.
And a cabal of business and government.

The agenda of a banana county.

Not lasses of lotional warm-flower skin
not wives of cracky chat / matrons

But a senate that kisses horses.

15.

On the Easy Coast:

It is deep pearly red-light jungle
gritty with mashed wood
I sing lickerty under-canopy light
ruses of copper-leaf bang-silence dead-floor.
The monkey flicks bits.

A slippery sweat-sick coal
and forms lime-leaf to opal palm
a rainbow

trees that will not burn
in dream forest indeed
I see no struggle

there is every sort of eating
there is some sort of mating
but it is like having bets to waste
& you can back anything

there is no sacred racial ambition to land
some things have eyes / leaves
it is sinister, this slow living
and quick
leaving.

I no longer yearn elegantly for learnéd poise.
Some noise is better.
To rummage into the hot insects
and stay.

16.

O wolf.
Everyone tells me the police will be out tonight
Because of the bangs in the docks.

It's instinct.

17.

So there is nothing even mystical about the frog?
Because it is gauche

and celery-coloured
and puny.
But you should mind this:
when Vane Tempest was sunk
and here, at the foot of the shaft, it is said,
sling high, here with the hammer, in the rock before them, and face on,
but ye dinnut wanti see it, was the head of something like a g'eat
    barbaric amphibian,
i' the coal, some satan, mebbies four foot across,
braad heed, en' sockets,
its foreheed bumped, as a bull's horns (as showy black)
(things grand as rockets)
dark jut / rock / but you haven't to believe
a plasm of vile face
at table in the trash stone.
Do you think that was living?
what for?
why not be senseless?

All the old life-habits have gone,
seemingly.
Everything is pressed and concussed.
There are a few white smears in the clay.
And durable things have replaced soft stuff,
as reminder of the dead i'the wood,
the endless plantation.
I will not assert ... that coal grows,
that it has been formed by trees ...
or that it is a vegetable thing.
Even the khaki insect
in fossil rubbish
equal to blanched freckled pressed flowers.
The photos of themselves.

What comes after man
May not be able to say the word 'man'.
No plaques, no myths, no mystery.
Nothing in the universe may ever chance to show interest.

The gluey cute frog

will be
as like
to end
up top lowper and big god.

18.

walls
faces of coins
tall austere
fake-royal

at sun
warm
also it is
neutral

half
is darkness
a
no memory state

classical
structure
correctness
climbs

sits
on the head
moves
jingles

pompous
dollar-matt
pettyish
durable

a symbol

constraining
it endeavours
our (in)action

all walls are
all coins are
(a)round
and flat

but their value?
our respect?
how can we live
without

19.

For several years
I thought I might have been a mucky sort of toy
or maybe a clumsy cat
till I learned I was human.

But no more
shaping cups
an' pouring myself in them.

Self-generating growth – but no purpose
– breathless wonder – the success is –
and we are anywhere …

20.

A wooden wolf-head sets before me.
Thru his teeth
I glimpse daylight.
There is no back to his head.
It is little more than a mask.

The white paint eyes
hold no particular respect for me, at all.
You should keep away from him.

21.

And there is a sexuality of control and the marauder
leaps and leers like a short camel.
Also the normal people sometimes go hay-wire.

22.

But of course
there are aggressive bozos,
there are colloidal-shaped uprights,
the teeth grain-seeking, nut-chewing, meat-gripping.
They are vendors
of universal fidelity,
only the wars of sperm raise the unthinkable concept
– a collective sexual origin.

The soul is a star
it radiates in this act and that
generous, a pal, or a mother or a saint.
The hero, of course, is not celestial or free but something to elect.
And we make and decorate language.

Perhaps I will settle for the group. To have someone to sign to. To fight with. A keeper of my secret name. And to halve being empty. For it is very desolate, now, this rusting West. Aluminium tags and bare bones. Let us fly a paper aeroplane in the name of history.

23.

How to pass out by day.
Tread into sunlight,
the fun of frogs.

In our penny theatre,
the whistle of the passions
runs

the bits of the world
are a Noah's Ark
everything we arrange
chew at
hurl about
laugh as they bounce harmlessly (wood)

the technical experts
the environmental services
must work thus
to shape.

It is purely chance that the final arrangement
profits vast multinational businesses.

When stoats and weazles dignify.

Why we are endless entertainment.

24.

The bright pillows of war-sail
in the brown / blue rain
'n' the swaying saffron of execution

– these are the adverts on the packets

And our shelves of herbs and skulls
our work-boots that pound the pantry,

cooler and freezer,
yea all which it inherit,
shall stay unsold,
sifting slowly into the lower breast
till the hourglass gifts us away

it lets them
wait
for ever and ever

25.

Now tell me vetch,
vetch of the wildlands,
And monkey-flower
flower of the dampworld
And the violet,
weany woodland turn-tune,
And sycamore seedling
settling the quarry-space
How do you rationalise and name us?

We are symbols of leisure,
administrators evolved for the growing good,
mobile commas in the green tract,
unearning extras outside the vibrant grim stingy man-scathing
        sci-fi-like sector of insect,
poor dependents of the fat, irey animals that blow with cud.
While the vegetable is answerable directly to the planet.

And if (a big if)
we were in control
there'd be warehousing aal o'er the coast
before seed-set.

26.

The rich are a form of pollution

27.

Oh shit!
Why don't Dick & Pearl bring my washing?
I smell as bad as a soaked teddy-bear.
The post's delayed.
It comes in clumps like a censor's hint.
I shoulda not written to Jay.
I shoulda hunt cash not chaos.
I snarl like a tiger on sore paws.
Or a pelt on a fat girl's doll-rail.
Only more aggravated
essentially ruffled or active hopping mad.
Especially with the District Council –
always putting private parts before community,
also I think they must view reality thru mismodelled eyes
if they think a terrace is tawdry
beside giant green iron constructs in para-reality.
And I could have gone to Bali or Bangkok
for less than one of these all-eater's annual expenses.

28.

Let us see who can be bloodiest and worst
They can be the victors.
The losers will be treacherously vilely abnormal.
Uniforms make them even more ridiculous.
I don't know why
But fortunately it always works out that way.

29.

What better disguise for evil
than sonnets?
How can you divide
without rhyme?
How can you obey
without art?

O be ready
there are some sick mysteries and mirages
in the sweetest story.

30.

Here in the Tin Islands

Why, of course,
sit there.
That is the tin throne.
Its bright magpie-shit shimmer
its entire fold-crazed foil
suits white silly
owners of air.

Irrhythmic space
pluto-still.
The byzantine claim to title
becomes nothing
looks nothing.

You can use words to heal.
Because they won't mind.
They have to have meaning.
It becomes impossible to lie with them.

The bent white-sight to the eye
the dusty cleaner floury plainness.

Your edge
to the edge
when the turret puppets are howked off
the chords enter disorder.
The moulds are single sand.

It is cruel to make.
Naked & nauseous
before the Phantom
you will not improve.

31.

The uneven corolla of concrete
its posts its wires
they are the coast

glitter tho the sea may
like light delivered
it is property

carved fish
in jade flats
in car bones
are other deliberate things.

nature
the clay company.

32.

See the lions pass.

Like the shaggy dead they groan and are very hostile
only traces

of
stately orange hair.

If a crown had slipped o'er their eyes
not more
ignore
us.

Just supposing everything exists,
you will be caged, cut into meat.
But we have the choice of being burned as rubbish.

33.

Oranges and lemon skin
sez the malarial church
ill-shaved, malodorous and baroque.
Deep-cut and meso-american.
There are decorations 'n' shadows that shake.
For mercantile quinine.
For dried fruit, rum and broad bellies stilled with a drug.
Things are white and bright and gilt.
With salmon
we feed skulls.

34.

A generation grown old for coins
decoyed to the desert to bake blood and let die
while the young scream like dragons.

And for?
To admire.
That your heart is health builded on the exemplar.
In a variable, amusing world
to perspire.

Something you cannot rise above.
Something you cannot fight.
They
are not.

35.

i'th'centre
o'th'sun-lipped flower
(flowerets, radials, petallic gold)
Sole One sits,
extends,
manifests …

The ribbons ripple
ex fingertips,
notices / rewards / excellencies.
And the kneelers:
burned rice, vestiges, raucous
(how it seems)

Establishes
winner of the great gun-fight
the effort
that gives self,
the
energy
the excelment.

And cloning
exemplar
(how to concentrate
on everything)
the garnering
ideas
substantiate
and rank

For the sake of a queen
who has declared war
onto our people,
torches / excoriates her own,
viewless boot / baton
like eye of ultimate diamond,
ticklishly brilliantly cut, cutter.

The black bag
holds crappy characters,
mostly expellees,
like fake prints
and they are
unrecognisable,
whim,
Tudor smirk or axe,
quick-snick as cam'ra shutter act.

Mind …

turns
ti'centre
ti'th'sun-lipped flower
all bridal light
'n' self-seem
'n' solar
'n' the beast beautiful,
jail-spires, loud.

digressional laughter
attacks on the slack,
the loathsome joker,
non-achiever,
veto.

An' with the art of decision
the opening emergent
's slowly fried.

Once the tribal flower opened,
to fix,
is empty,
the endeavours
are said stilts
up & above
'n' safe 'n' sudden
discard.

Growth
staircase
wings.
Home as heart
as perimeter
isolates the evil of the un-with.

'N' the scents
o'th'sun-strip power
(towerets, tanks, awe-sight puke-over-it tar)
Soul that trips,
de-pretends,
un-resists.

36.

Oh no, visitors …
Two to arrest Delvan, seem'ly.
Sure you can look.
An' me, I have to co-operate, like,
or they're tellin' me, doors get smashed down.

Well then, let's see.
He's sorta that height,
'n' cross-racial-coloured.
He talks to the TV sometimes.
He sez let's jump up 'n' down on the spot.
He should be easy to find.

Sure he has a diary
and the last page is blank
but for a heading, 'Goals Long Term'.

It's strictly neutral.
Ye are his sinister side.

37.

1. Any number of players can take part, but only two teams.
2. The purpose of the game is to convince the referee, who will award goals.
3. No irrational element from without will be allowed on the pitch.
4. Grace, energy, intelligence, determination, skill and co-ordination may be displayed, but all decisions contain an element of luck.
5. There will be winners and losers; but any gain is reserved for shareholders.

38.

Towers to St Wheat and St Malt
beside
and in the near lane a truck of straw
well motorways aren't urban highways.
Anyone can use them.
If he so speed that he hath wheels.

Aw,
a screwdriver?
A 3" screwdriver?
How can I break into a car with that?
(OK, he lets him go.)

A little broken side-window
is a dead give-away though.

Sometimes you see a car ablaze – a scary sight for other motors!
or get in on a police chase.

The video is £5.

Trees screen the route
'n' roaring engines head up
black gas.
Two direction whizz
it adds to the lights.
Clearly.
Us all in a snuff movie.

39.

At the emergent elephant
long hatted trail
lavender sun-setting sky
I collect such images.

nations of rose women
rocks and trees with snapped necks
calm clear starfish windows
such are the images I get

the white-trousered counter-hero
the cloaks, the banners, the effigies
the masturbating lions in carved caves with dark manes
are images.

the saffron fighter
power-wheat
rain-race
red-nickle
bus-muscle
the strange road-back god his sweep-feet
it is only image.

there are gongs and stones
flying words
percussion of ribs
this sort of thing is all there is.

40.

the kaolin monk paces the jungle
his skin is hot with psychic morphine
grabbing and twisting air
cupped hands
curling fingers

'If I was caught again
I would bite'

There are reckless chequered elements
there are glossy shadows
strange rhubarb-red auras
the different
the unique action

Do you never meet gipsies?
do you never talk things over with dead gloved mouths?

and I am getting patronised
as if I'd never seen snow

As tho it is
growing is losing.

Become
quietly prosaic.

And
tired of tiger talk.

41.

under the plate vane
the being gyrating angels
the liquid waste
they screen out solids now

the chancelry of dioxin
its debts are
the massive columns, radial,
no sea-aid

diurnal lorries
to incinerator
'n' the listless company of chem-fuel
we bring back towers to the suburbs.

42.

Joanne's Dad was working and building
putting up a goose house.
'N' Joanne was watching 'n' helping.
Finally they fixed
an old smoke-stack
on very top
with tin hat hood
like a turret.
Even the geese were satisfied.
An average slow warm time
on the backgrass.

43.

In the Pleistocene
management concepts developed
and there were new levels
of aggression activity.

Pink-headed vertebrates
tackled virtual reality with stunning éclat.
Ice lightning and over-indigo
escaped

the art zone.
Cleverer oestrogen ads than ever.
Eater-bods set up temple walls.

In his travels
Agátharchídes
identified the Hylóphagoi or wood-eaters
stunning somersaulters at the branches.
Their non-theorizing mode of life evoked some mirth and
        contempt.

The nasal narcissus
became beauty symbol.
It teases the sexual sense.

The ergostabulum
or Roman reform camp for uncoöperative slaves
is not taken into assessment,
lacks six-footed refinement.

In the Holocene
the species that writes history
let itself fantasise to extinction
on golden books of its own optimism
stamped safe for consumption.

44.

Ambling in the quads of lettuce
Little lifts and dips joins my feet up
Accent prints,
Some automatic paths.

Our integrity
encourages
pale green trust
Observing syntax / regular toiletry.

Ink examples
whole stanza-shelfs of collegiate tinkering with goals
pretty passes
to manufacture the rhetoric of civics.

Psalms of Poseidon Irrigator
I introduce rosettes fertile leaves
to be ruffled / foot-scuffed
mis-appointed
grab-quick garden

Ever ghostlier levels
misty claims
upland pots of flower spicy-decorative
winnings

To think
place both feet bare on the earth.

45.

In the ruins of Carthage
PERCEIVE
serene technical extinction
THE MONKEY
only prevails.

O by blasphemous tower-spires the
RAPTOR
REVOLUTION
has made good.

There are stone stories
and
JUNGLE.
The
PERFECT
structure seeds itself

crazy
'n' out-limits.

'N' the sport
ANGER
fills empty squares.

Slip by
by economy
THROSTLE
the rag vellum stand
eats over engines
which knocked
OUT
elbows

Concrete emblems of
OATS
and
EMERALDS
are undersilt new mud
TO PLAY ON

a whole
RED
coal-red inch

the condominiums
of the peacekeepers
RIDDLE
in age

the silver-fur white-fur race
prefer to be in
GROUPS

46.

When the great Pharaoh
   fixed as king
   at the place where his father was drowned
   the place where you were born
was drawn to the river
   Who united the two lands
   south of the island
people must comment on
   they were satisfied concerning
fabulous riches that accompanied him
   the true born
   the creation day
and the fabulous wealth left behind and to be divided
   fixed in his dwelling
   my inheritance my inheritance belongs
   I have made the division between you
It can no longer be exchanged for extra days
even days of sobriety and continence
   the creation day
   the boundary
The social king is part of nothing.

47.

I know not in what magic-dead tombs
and terracotta fists
you may find the first yo-yo
but this is no toy.
I think of the awesome planned hands
of god and goddess jerking
as in some terror of perpetual motion.
A gift to man.
A weapon.

In the Philippines,
yoyo-er climbed,

and with it cracked the skull of an enemy below.
Mobile
directable
forceful
reusable

Revolutionary 1790s France re-
invented the yoyo.
It celebrated – let us be kind and say
the onus of new operational factory shift-work.
Or you could watch and witness
Individual Revolution.

In the 1970s
batteries were introduced to bring about the gloyo.
It was now a night-focus,
a whirring hand-size dragon-fire
acrobatic
the active colonising the dark.

All things that work
are fun.
There is incipient magic.

48.

What is the capital city after all
but scenery?
The rolling limestone
behind power,
and the processual scarp.
Inhabitants are witnesses.

Around it,
the great castles, the noble houses
ring-guard.
Organise.
Filter the communication.

Retain the closure-illusion and

The sub-cities inherit.
They hinder.

Eventually the centre will die of pomp.
With dot 'n' mascot 'n' sign
it intertwists,
grows a magic circle.
Reminiscent of horizontal vegetable promotion.
Work generates sap circulates money.
There are train channels of communication.

For some cities have been anthropomorphic,
equally they signified the world,
some, heaven,
this one roots in a river, or the sea
blooms in fire-bursts.
At night the cells are quiet for observation.
It is now known that we are phosphorescent.

49.

Governments sing the cult of death.
It is
wall of pearl eyes
all over the wall
the axe in the calf,
the dead-leaf medical report
fact hides act.

They of three nostrils
and needle teeth
rule the land
for all I know.

Yet we may be getting more than one chance!
The Pliocene ape *Oreopithicus*

walked, erect, its face flat,
man millions of years before man.

In the lignite forest
see brute roots
sandal-hides
the excellent amber eyes
ticking over time

If this empire failed
why does another take the court
to make another goal something similar?

50.

after the heroics
the blister lemon sores
drinks of graval herbs

liar-knights
fake it
the demented declension of death
to aim
to seem lady-tender

legend-moving
and abstinent cross-leg masters.
I call the strict-true regimen
to examination.

I' the dormant tomb,
herbivores drink handlessly
earth.

What we want
not what is.

the image-woman

not something dicing miniature mexican glass skulls.

wittiness into:
choirs
stone-bench
tricky-tall piers
for rectal song

no notion of it
be sure:
everything congratulates
our curven souls.
let us link safely
be display / brocade rays
get the right syrup.

51.

Benvenuto's father
marked the fire.
'Lo, look, a basilisk!'
He hit his son.
'O do you see it, now?'
And hit him.
The yellow-animal, the yellow-hot un-thing
took the shape of pain.
Well, he recalled
learning – then
to make ships of salt,
scraped golden-like-peacock-beak butter cups
and tumblers
couples of killers
not finer.

52.

so this is *the universal graveyard*
the fog
the sepia lapping river-water
I see netty grid school and lilac blocks flats
bits off supervisory corridors
our tyrannical human tumbling into goal
and the insistent hissing wavelengths air
there were tyres drumming
or
the coarse bird-
song
there are views to the graveyard
the sensory garden
that's calm
all the shit you've accepted
to keep it calm
the credo
the rolling crap select
there is a necessary conspiracy to impose the good
but I'm not part

No, now,
are you calling me a liar?
because this is the world of
words is drunk
everything seems self
so you oughta be sharp
'n' I'm ready to be
how arms flail
is own empire
and war-keeping self
alive till the sun voids

to think logically
you are a hierarch
an implicit user of violence
the wheat-reaper sings a round
it is common for the dead to be transferred to hospital to avoid
        inquest

53.

the flaw in the crystal
shows foxes.
by the grace of children
their paws print in the batter
and walking tunes.

teeth, too,
make the mark of the arm

as we go into the chaos
and only ask
they people like us

54.

The largest book in my flat
The one that contains the most information
Is the telephone directory.

55.

What is love without money?
As you first toddle,
love-proof's the magic coin chunks
they share power.
They become potent.
Joys of gifts, spending, surprising
subtend christmas christianity.
Salary sanity.
What honours of fun wouldn't you pass on?
But needst not strive
officiously to keep solvent.

At first I wanted a silver soul

till I saw gold.
Meanwhile a culture of wood and metal
turned light 'n' plastic
and millions of old hearts were couthed
found packed under Mexico City
so we are papery promises.

I have no policy.
In a baff-week I go short.
Or barter.
The less in money are not greater in feeling
we exchange ourselves
alive.

56.

How absurd –
the carnivals of the army
the self-distortion of savage tribes
the embroidered sequins of church
the pulsed children's school-chant (MO-MAS-MAT) –
against the university of truth.

There
is one way
unison of violence and idea.

But there is also the galaxy of plants,
of which the moral is infinite variety.

Our dead are seeds
and we plant them,
eggs we collect for the Easter Day Judgement.

a sudden agony of marzipan
haunts in the mouth's brain
strong a sweet-nut boiled oil
vitrous quartz mineral yellow

a delight
on easter

We too could grow up a flower-head and lady,
a mouse-tail cow-paw gent
a beloved budget of compositions
and plain patent
things friends fashion
machines of more
and every glance new.

Additional Poems from MS

O white milk hills
organic are white chocolate walkers
and sea-dunes
wild food
pale-away wavy horizon blancmange
shifty sugar-topped smudges in the sky

the crystall'd orchid and cowslip
it is lozenges

in the physical world the curvaceous sky
pale maid cloud
sun-bronze skin-flare sunset
all feed on,
things to kiss and click

*

The land of the proper:
how sweet 'n' plump 'n' scented they fit in.
Art accomplished,
their arguments partake of fact.
Their knowledge partakes of truth.

'N' the rhythm of egg 'n' chips
the cigarettes 'n' ices
like girls

slippery mandatory rules
'n' maximum axial stability.
For good taste.

The ability to rearrange others into a pleasing shape
is an earner.

If you can perceive its beauty,
you are as good as got your trunk in the golden syrup.

From many to one
by extraction / reduction / predication
and election
and by intuition.

*

How do I know what you see?
Me?
Most of mirrors smile back.
But in the walls behind
there may be considerable variety of sub-expressions.
That represent the civilised world.
For here is all the information.
Maybe.

*

To Curtius Rufus –
the Spirit of Africa
Would start,
Would move,
Would return,
Would end.
Certainly.

Other Poems

On the Bridge

Yellow and green   aye
sky and sea   come
every view   aye
will be here   hinny

In Sunderland
the heavy, physical wind
shapes sail (bowl-bonny)
scrambles up
to right the channel
head like a marigold

whatever,
the bridge is still here,
braced ovals,
bright rails,
and little boats are cheering (clinker-engraved)

On the pottery
Mam and baby
wave goodbye,
delicately dressed, tara,
over bedistanced.
farewell.

Jack hero
is ata dance,
all lascivious life
he is handed over aza gift
(think this of me)

betrothed /
wedded
to the glaze,   o'er the sea
a rainbow photo   with me
round round round with me

Marquisisms

It is no use –
I see them everywhere –
as cakes!
great cherried sweet spirals, major-man marzipan,
little chick biscuits,
and I SEE
oh stop!
we eat them,
poor work-folk.

The Moon shows:
will the great showman-horseman
MOUNT?
Leap the shop-roof, ascend the slope, scrabble to the tower to the top,
the Cathedral summit
and bronze beast be psychopomp,
launch to HEAVEN!

Notes

1

Outside of the doors of the house
itoz raining

People-who-find-life-interesting:
Suspects of
people-who-find-life-uninteresting

The brave dandy-seed
landed
on the pool-film

2

threshing about us
– no candy on the tree

shouting about
– no gold on the corn-stalk

Plague is on us again!
– tar-jawed!
– boil-eared!

The awful
– umbrella
– of rain
enribs us all

The wet bodies
– are wasted
we fade

3

paper in sauna
as wallflowers

lolled old sets brass
tapz az

lizards lie,
folk move on

Picture

The God that is blue,
perfect man,
boiled,
on azure altar,
tubes that are leg-case
and bold seams, shape.
Notes, coins, wallet, comb
sit flat
or hands;
sparkle with buttons,
belt keeps right.
See my practical religion,
it walks, rides, works, runs
(rain or sun)
and ragged, still states.

The lady
is a sweat-shirt,
clings to bone,
lovely, thin, tight,
to make shoulder match,
provoke the arms,
flowering biceps, sunny
v. white
it is something to range oily bolts on
when you strip a bike.

The jacket is one thing:
night-coloured,
Dead leather that glows and
blacks, sleek, scuffed,
builds shape, blocks,
marks half-line, waist-place, bum-packet, has
pigeon-holes for baccy and
lighter, letters, hands
with zips, four or more
Zeus-bright.

cow-boots.
Lid.
Armour-headed,
so you kin take it off,
smile.

The Ace & Other Scenes

1
Hello.
Look.
No. So I can't sleep.
I am dance-headed and I am urgent-calm
My chest delicately hoops against the air.
I gotta get up.

Jeans. Bare sox.
Like chimneys: boots.
A lid and that.
Fucking kick the dickey-birds off my machine
and wake it up.
A labour at the cold white air.
While the town-towers beg out
like a kaleidoscope of loaves.

Wang!
and jump
and kick the bike up
catch it, raise it, let it sound.
(To want to do something, good.)
Get to a circle,
drive round and round,
one gear then up and up
and then the other way
widder-round
till I tire

Too tired even to polish my soul.

2
The buzz of backs
all roun' the cafe
cups crack
& the kid-beggars ignored

and out the big front:
herculean-like wheels
roll the yard
(when there's nothing else to do)
one way, in the sun,
acrobatifying the bike,
'bar-less, or crouched on the seat,
or back to the 'bars
performing a few feet of tricks
for shouts or grins
to pass an hour till setting-out,
then in a hundred
tuning up, happy, moving out
for a run
how they block the lights
make all the rules work
a great migrating hum

to the promised field
the arid, lonely land
where the father is at last come from the war
where the loaf is broke into its thousand
and the girl sticks fair;
the sun stains the back stronger
and coat-links chime
as we jostle into the dance-time

3
First: jokes
(Are you loaded?
(Look it isn't funny - smile!
(How wilt get the bar out again?)
and above it

some chaos of instructions.
Like:
let me speak only,
look serious, look friendly, don't spook them,
just spread out, let Essex and me
give th'order.
Nothing to rehearse, and no time to.
Only the dark whelped darker
licked at the lamp-flowers
made the car-quiet dizzy with a wait.
Till the actors took over,
ever'all face set, and was Nomads
rubbing elbows
to know if their power matched.
Like a silk
(when they all came) —
front: face and black and denim
and back: white/red WINDSOR/ROADRATS
and NOMADS/ESSEX and the shining skulls and rockers
when it was all met to make peace.
And Johnny talked them, barbed and soothed, and took their eyes with him
till they were ringed, then
the fist sent out
and everything beat down,
booting what fell, other Rats running, crawling out in blood.
An Ire in it, the switching to battle-fury,
and Denham Roundabout (the grass sharped and stood up).
Was it like that?
Yes there was a great fight —
All while I was inside.

4
I smashed thru the water.
I beat back the redder sky.
The jacket-zips were bright and open.
Woke them. Where?
Each house now an office –
all the fabled towers and minarets I see.
No cafe.

Not even Kuzka could put us back together now.
OK
Girl, we'll make a gipsy wedding by the last neon ring,
look for who sold up my soul,
fairing and bars.
So there are no marches of sorry-'gret
no sins/strictures tauted on quartz-pegs of tune-to-us,
wilful diamond-houses of do-it-right,
art opals of the unabsurd, hoary honesty
or ruby-pails of this is hell-food, soft swan-tinsel.
Wipe it.
The air-grit is mine, grip to road, swim.

Be present
whyaz I time my soul
rag up its fins
feed it juice /
thick oil
regulate gap / kick up
if it'll FLY

Harley

Flames are sewn onto my shirt
time-poise
I prepare for jump
what will be some massive leap
(a wheat-wear land,
corn-curly,
where we are white skull)
A SWITCH

A what has never-before-been-attentated
so how do you know …

The skins are fitted.
Keep my lid off

So to smile at folk
For longer, I need.

Or check –
nay, they are better at that.
Leave the bike absolutely to them.
Navigate.

INTO A MIRROR?

Music.
Drown it.
Just bike.
Like – and
LEAP.

More Bike (Perpetual Motion)

like a lizard
scaled bottle-back
'oz laid out
on his lady
& crawling up
(untime even shed blue coat)
humping

two side-eyes,
whizzwhizz
an'a spray of spokes;
's all habilitude.

Ona gold-day
an' all the bikes playing in the park,
and the word-spread explored it all
said there would be air always,
to open up on,
metal and mate.

noctal
pale and glow
the other set of earth-life
sat and talked wealth, roads, river-vales,
all the best worm-tracks
and where I could live.

So it spins
fist-heavy
a whole gathering of
harm-creds and set on town-morth
an' itz raining bikers
an' the earth-drinker crawls to the sky
an'
like a lizard ...

(Coda)

the house it likes me
(like the boat)
hums at occupancy.

Work

Nearly there!
Scrunch the T-shirt,
wipe the oil off my shoulder.
OK girl, you can do it.
Ow, my belly button itchy.
Wow, her cuppy-breast squeezing me.
Yeah, my crotch jazzy.
Look, this manhandling me has to stop!
An' while we were stopping it,
the DOG
well out of the corner of my horizontal eye,
ate the air-jet!

tore into two gaskets!
buried little rocker-nuts all round the yard!
Cupid! Bike! Jenny! Dog! Zeus! oh
my gaskets, oh my air-jet!
What? OK,
but this time –

Keeooo –
the cold wind –
the tatters –
the bits – (blow & blow)

In Rufinum (after Claudian)

I doubt:
do they care, the Gods, for this world, or is there no
direction, but some uncertain chance?
I've seen the sky orderly, the tides, the year,
lucis noctis que vices, and it seemed certain,
plants growing thus and thus (diverso tempore),
and the moon-fire / sun-fire.
Conversely, look at the clouds that hide
our human condition, the harmers happy, the just vexed,
then governance seems less likely, as the Epicureans say
in vast NEW nothingness FORMS
occur by random, from the seeds of everness. No Gods.
But the case of Rufinus settles it:
elevated (tolluntur in altum) to fall all the harder.
Vis pandite, vati: unfold it:

Allecto, in Hades, peace-hater, summoned her council:
glomerantur in unum, assembled
Discordia, nutrix belli, war-nurser,
imperious Famine,
Senility, death's neighbour, and
Plague, unendurable,
Envy, Grief, Terror, Rash-Dash, Indulgence,

and the Anxieties.
Then Allecto:
'Will we suffer this golden age? Peace, Justice and Honour?
Where in this sluggish world finds itself fury?
Dark light, uproll river, unair day!'
Megaera, madness, soothes them:
'There is no safety in trying to shake the Gods,
but the human world we can.
This one I have bred, hydra-brutish, tigress-fast,
wind-hard, sea-treacherous – Rufinus.
I've coddled and tutored him, to guile, greed, ambition,
deceit (smiling), unsatiable desire;
let me produce him to the Palace, regalem aulem,
insinuate him before the Emperor of the World.
How can he fail?'
She spoke; the white snow-marble
(niveae columnae)
began to golden, and the beams (trabes)
luced like metal, yellow.
Captivated, this Rufinus, he watches,
like Midas at the transformation,
before his food grew rigid,
his drink solided to golden ice.
'I follow!' cried Rufinus;
the Furies sent him East.
In the Palace, his ambition truly lived.
Intrigue and Treasure: like the
Ocean knows no limit
when it takes the innumeros amnes,
drains the wavy Danube, the seven-mouthed Nile,
and is not overfull,
so Rufinus with the flowing gold:
necklace and jewel, or land and home.
Quo, vesane, ruis? You will never
get enough, never be rich –
always poor who knows greed.
Not for him the wool and flowers
that radiate, make the meadow
a living love, viva voluptas,
the beststead grass, water-song.

If so, no classic horn would call war,
no strident spear, fraxinus, whizz away,
no wind quake the deck, no catapult the walls.
Not so Rufinus, slays and takes,
kills and worse still, makes life unlivable.
Only Stilicho stood up to him.
This was the barrier
Rufinus broke on,
as though a winter-high water
saxa rotat
rolls the rocks down,
volvitque nemus,
juggles the tree-land,
pontesque revellit,
kicks away the bridges,
but cannot move
some great rock,
but sputters and thunders
about it, against it, and round.
What can we say of Stilicho?
He was more the hero
in that Rufinus was Hell.
Stars
or health
or heroes he was.
Fought the Barbarians,
horse-blood-drinking, tattooed, ice-watered,
those Rufinus intrigued with.
And the Huns,
from further than the east-frozen Tanais,
worst of all that the North bred;
only eating meat, face-cutting,
horse-hugging.
Stilicho and Mars stood arm-to-arm
against them, twin helmets, hirsute-topped, and yubes.
Where will the world go?
Has Rufinus driven Justice from earth?
He will not win from his plot, will be stopped.
Honorius will chain Discord.
Tum tellus (earth)

communis erit, tum limite nullo
no edge de-mark the field
no moulded share soil re-fine
subitis messor gaudebit aristis
reaper: to the swift free Vs.
Oak-wood sag with honey. Rivers
be wine / fluent oleique lacus.
No rarity, coin-rated, sheep-worked
scarlet pelts – let the shocked shepherd
see Nature's new dyes: and the green
water-weeds laugh outright ridebunt
virides with nax-lighting jewelry
gemmis nascentibus algae
the sea-weeds.

*

... ventis veluti si frena resolvat / Aeolus
like unloosed winds, the people to war.
Per terga (on the icy back) solidata
of the Danube, they run to,
or the passes (Caspia claustra),
and the whole East Empire is to plunder.
Oi, how with-quick they-perish hugenesses with-what-transpires!
Constantinople, too, hi vigili muros, wall-watched,
harboured with a chain-of-boats, attacked –
will Rufinus defend? lands alight (omnia in censa),
he parleys, brown – fulvas in pectora pelles – skins
on his body, he makes his peace,
bastard to bastard.

Then
Stilicho
at the Alps
combines his forces:
what voice-variety!
here Armenian horse-fighters, with
shaking, curly locks (vibratis crinibus),
their cloaks (grass-green) easy knotted;
there with them truc-fierce Gallic men,

tawny heads, from the swift Rhone-banks,
or slower (quos tardior ambit) Saone, or
born by the Rhine, or the Garonne
(reverse-tided). Now, all diversity aside.
The loser resents nothing
non odit victus
victorve superbit
and the winner won't lord it.
(So many of them, as it's said of Xerxes' army once,
telis umbrasse diem:
shading day-sun with their arrow-shoots).
So to Constantinople's aid, terror to Rufinus.
The troops are drawn:
the rein-bits foam,
you see the mists of dust wide rising,
and the surging banners-on-spear of scarlet dragon –
the whole sky seems aflight with serpent waves!
ferri nito – the shine of steel – lights the east
to the Centaur's cave (cornipedis),
courage pounds bold, energy burns –
or will the Emperor, in Rufinus' grip, act
and disband the deliverers?
HE, by his brother's regal star-divinity,
for the achievements of his aetherial fathers,
and for the flower-glory of Himself,
gives in, and tricked, orders Stilicho to retire.
He:
'Flectite signa, duces! redeat iam miles Eous;
parendum est; taceant litui! prohibete sagittas!'
Then when the Army
saw their leader ordered away,
Stilicho in disgrace, they vowed vengeance,
dabitur tibi carried on debita pridem to confront Rufinus.
Of the city by a tight tract, which verges to south,
a flat land lies: for, the rest the sea
surrounds here by a slim (parted) self track allowing.
And here the avenger Army (ultrix acies) (bright with the decor
   of war) unfolded into squadrons.
Pedites in parte sinistra
infantry halted left, and the cavalry there-next rein in

their frisky mounts (pressis lupatis). The savage wavey plumes
nod (cristato vertice) and men joy to shake and flash the
(tremulos) shine-shoulder-plates (vibrare colores).
Them chalybs-steel coats and shapes; well-skill-joined,
the pliant plates are enlifed by the encased limbs –
horribiles visu : as tho some iron statues moved
and men breathed that were cast in metal.
Likewise the horses: their skulls bulge in iron
and their forelimbs lift in wound-saver steel.
Each keeps himself clear: a frightening pleasure to see,
a lovely terror, and when spirisque remissis,
the breezes drop, vento cessante, the dragon-flags with
coils relaxing, flap down, bright multi-coloured varii dracones.
There the Emperor salutes the standards,
Rufinus praises them.
And they, the strong force, questioning eager, slow draw
a circle, isolating in their centre
this Rufinus, curving horns into a trap,
in a ensiferae (crown of swords) coronae.
Beast-like Rufinus senses – but –
'hac Stilicho … dextra te fecit!' it strikes,
they cut and all swords redden, kick and tear,
his limbs quated from solutis nexibus,
yielded sinews, ribs bared, even to
the still-pumping lungs, pandit anhelas
pulmonis latebras.
His hands to a beggar to beg with,
his hell-work to nothing.
Even the soul would be bonded into animal,
truculents to bears, the predacious, wolves,
(cogit vincla pati) (fallaces vulpibus addit),
perhaps to be revolved, and reborn;
but Dis claimed him,
in the opaquest midnight deeps
(qua noctis opacae / fundamenta latent)
dum rotat …   un-starred
dum venti …   un-winded

At the Nevsky Promenade

Limpid ice to wait on,
if the emptiness
perhaps hides an army?

Trees dolorous with
frost's heave-down dead
wind-spring all gone

Snow-trumpet fleece-sound
quarters
whiter world

great sun-roll
(can it be so unconcerned?)
opens this day show

A stir of trash
in the horse host
in the gallop of the dance of the charge
and

Imminent,
to take a prayer
to exact time

Verses in Awe

Trust me, my
neat grooming, tie and suit,
my confident, leaderful manner –
THIS IS BUSINESS!

Rule no. 1. If someone wishes you to sign something, you can be certain it is only to commit you, to their advantage, your disadvantage.

BUSINESS, you see,
is how I take from you.
Money comes into it of course, but
mostly it is the abuse and deception.

Rule no. 2. If someone is willing to vary the form by writing in or deleting in your favour, you can be certain you are about to be seriously stung.

I am carefully trained you know,
to shine with candour, make words true,
and I can, you see,
because it is quite legal to take someone else's money.

Rule no. 3. If the salesman talks when you are trying to read through the contract, it must be clear there is a hidden catch in it.

Of course you are welcome to read through.
It is all very clear,
And you will never spot the catch
because it is not in the main clauses.

Rule no. 4. Anything in a contract to your disadvantage will be carefully disguised and hard to detect. It may be mistitled to suggest it is something else.

You see, in this case, there is a 'Note',
called 'Note on Signatures' which
actually commits you to purchase
when we revoke the lease you think you are signing.

Rule no. 5. If this is a new sort of document that you have no experience in, ask to hold on to it and think it over, say you will sign later.

Of course, I will act very offended,
if you were to hold back.
It impugns my honesty and
your virility and decisiveness.

Rule no. 6. If you are discouraged from taking a day or two over your signature, it means there is something fearful afoot.

My words you see, are meaningless,
I am misrepresenting the contract
because I happen to know
what it really means.

Rule no. 7. Some contracts have different wording on the top and bottom copies. This is a particular reason for never signing on the spot.

Because I can leave you
with whichever copy I like,
or even walk out,
leaving you none at all.

Rule no. 8. If asked to provide a deposit, make sure it is a nominal sum, never exceeding 10 pounds.

Because once I have your money,
You will never get it back.
You must realise that that
Is a basic rule of BUSINESS (the point of it all).

Rule no. 9. If making contact with a new firm, try to have a friend on hand as a witness, because salesmen often come in pairs and thus can back each other's account of events.

And with two of us,
We can simply confuse you and bully you,
until you sign or pay,
and we simply won't leave your house.

Rule no.10. If the salesmen won't leave when asked, you are advised to have a specimen of exorcism on hand, to drive them away with.

 The following has proved useful in several stubborn cases:

Whether you be fiery, aerial, terrestrial, aqueous, subterranean or heliophobic, whether you are a white kittling, or a little rugged dog, a grey cat or a black toad,

whether you live on blood or bread, milk or sugar,

I adjure thee, most vile spirit, the entire spectre, the very embodiment of Satan, begone!

O most dire one, give place; give place, thou most impious!

Therefore O impious one, go out. Go out, thou scoundrel, go out with all thy deceits!

But why, truculent one, dost thou withstand? Why, rash creature, dost thou refuse?

Resist not, but flee. Go forth from this house. Thy abode is the wilderness, thy habitation is the serpent!

Sextet

My muscle-tea of ninja-butter,
bull-bread and glare-soak.
Will I pause,
my soap-teeth, candid-limpet,
bus-stop-strawberry?
Becos the points need setting?
Becos the nipper-wrench needs finding?
Hexal-toips and grandoloin
shiver to be at work,
let their ligaments pro-tend, ex-tude and bleat.
While I eat.

Sing a song of Saturday.
Chiming doors, breathmobiles.
A little round of donkeys at carrot-size
wiinding my coffee-worker.
lotus-fans and pork-prods
hope my hands,
the linctus of the beast, besser-ing.
Buy me the football-toadstall,
make it implete.

The surly slice of mammal
masters the wall,
tip-pods by the apple-petals,
all-rhyming with pink blossom,
stabs with its whiskers
at the empty gleam-gland can
and rubs,
scrubs its boot-brush back.
Teethy and sneaky,
the fox has come for its gloves.

In the phantom water,
in the clear of skate,
loving corals talk to the orange bubbles.
Hands of crab and guillemot
reach the blue and the light and the slain.
Sail-shape carboys of flit-ice
mark off the sun from the pheasant-fish,
and all the toppling sand-rice
fluks to and fro for the plastic keel.

This is my blue packet and my mauve heart.
Grizzley, zig-zag sacks of once-read things
block
the autumn bright-bile.
Vain, vanguard and poppy-smudge
soften the glass-web,
make paint the roller-tumbler.
Candy-tubs, coin-atom-edge,
are her propane-zest,

as we whistle in the white-click
of lightning-shower.

Little bird-word.
Prank.
The singer stub-rat patrol
has walked the virgin knife-edge out,
and collide.
The hoighty land
of garnet-lamp and dust-door,
shoulder, silver-snail,
lick like ant-waves
at the sore room.
Distance is the goat-clock of the fighter,
is the fun.

Quest

I have to know how Sanditon ends.
With a plague?
With a landslide?
Cross-racial elopement?
Embezzlement and the discovery of coal?
Subterfuges for realignment
burgeoning into general good health!
thwarted cruelly by –

Alliterations

1. Running

Stripped to own   the racer-hunter
speedy of keel   special-ankled
the hart's mate   and a match for hares
orange-skinned   where the open sun shines
against the green land   the glorious legs
limber and long in muscle   measure rough-edged the ground.

2. Boxing

Look by the boxer   the bicep of his arm
Grim guy in his weapons   the great spread of his fist
Fierce of face   flat and smiling
And the sweat shines   on his shoulders
And the floor bounces   at his feet
And the body creases out   at his blows
Till the bruises blood up,   bashing, wors'ning,
And the back mounts its power   battering, smashing,
till one tires in terror   takes help and stops
and the winner jumps and laughs   wipes his towel
packs out spit   and poses.
Pisses.

3. Wrestling

listen to the shout of the sidesman   as the slab-chest wrestlers
throw and thrash body,   force at joint,
manhandle back and body,   muscles to balance with,
heads heavy with power   hands helping pain,
grappling in agony,   glum with the joy,
the light toss of the twist,   the lost yelp of bad-landing
risking new dislocation,   rising and limping
and back at grip   grandly strengthening,
till a new lock or smash   knocks them away

shouting in submission   or stunnned totally,
able or unable   to acknowledge us (at) all.

Vampire

Yes, I would like to borrow some of
that – some of that
broom-shaker energy, the
colossal sniff-around-yards
the young got too much of.
Beg a bit, have it
on my misty terrace
when the cups and bowls are too much a mix
and there is nothing simple to play.

Name

'Now, Brian …' sez the cop
(to reassure
and to achieve intimacy,
a magic);
immune I am, for
all my friends only ever say 'Bill …'.
I am safe,
I am on my guard.

Rat to Boat-Master

Man that is born of rat
is furtive, even for his species,
and tricky and conniving.
He knows no law, no myth, no rhyme, rhythm, ritual.
He hides. He raids. He eats.
His fear is for the dragon,
when he's drunk his eggs
commando-like; not a beginner though.
All his aim is to grow bigger and bigger
this by copulating,
and longer
(by living).
He is his own referee, and squeaks.

I seen you stripped
eyes bulging
pushing into her
or all theatrical-like
getting a mouthing,
wincing, effective
as you veer near the teeth

then as slow
as growing pregnant
seen you start quarrel with the carcass
conceive its betrayal
spit the thing out.
Look round

and there must be something new in the world.

Is there some point being in the colosseum
if there's no after-life?

Gimme a screwdriver, gimme a fucking screwdriver,
as if it oughta leap to your hands
of its own will!
(Hop up the steps

out of the hold the new mooring rope,
into the hand)

Or looking at the new mooring rope,
And the first spider spinning up to it:
look, a boarding party.
A laugh as a fox in a licorish factory.

So if all you want is some excess,
a wat'ry hippodrome,
the beasts lunging at bits of dust and fluff –
fine
(Just use your own ticket
now on)

building and knocking down
all the same,
all the same waste of time.
writing and rubbing out.
loving and breaking off,
non-performances, nothing.
To be non-enduring
just a second's focus
and remember nothing again.
(Not even achieving a feeling.)
There is nothing fugitive enough
to sing it in,
or satisfactorily continuous.
Think of it as being
half-happy.

I have seen the cinaedas
flower-open, in the desert,
gaining fatherhood.
no thankyou.

Boss,
come on,
lift your boot off my tail
so I don't bite.

Spare Stanzas

The great bell of the horn
's az pretty/puzzling
az the piano-net, clari'-pert.

*

last-measure cat
guiltily stealing child-available bed-space
the pushover / less welcome

*

Smoothes of snow
The eye is directed
at what tragedy ever
is engendered for it,
at impossibilities

*

Melting in at the great door-stands of sleep
folding into something else
all the hacking illness is soothed off
all the great friendships glow like rose
smart in lines of time.
Using words is singing.
(more like they mean,
is sound like)

*

The sunlight makes me sneeze.
The drugs make me sleepy.
I am hoping so very much on selling the boat.

*

Nasty, sneaky Christians,
worshipping at the altar of Knob,
as soon as dark hides them.

*

ship-seeds
in air-speed
innocent invade
and heavy dream

*

They stare at me or not
with hatred
with accusation
(a shaft of sunlight now)
that I didn't
make things turn out better.

Retraction

Having unguardedly nodded off, I found myself – unusual this – at my own exorcism.
Tu-ne es enim in Cain projectus
Now I can take a joke, I thought, so why can't they? Come on now, give me my job back.
… In Esau supplantus
Look, I'm very sorry if my occasionally brusque but generally harmless sense of humour –
… In Golia prostratus
– has got you riled, but I would really much rather not be made to glow in the dark like this!
… In Iuda traditore suspensus
I'll tell you what, I'll publish a retraction –
… Et in ipsa illa dominicae virtutis cruce
– OK. I'll do it in rhyme –
… cum potestatibus et dominationibus tuis

I'll hand the Amstrad back, I'll stop printing, I'll –
... *triumphatus atque contritus es?*
– join the Conservative Club, rejoice, declare England an island immune from vice and sin and cruelty and help you sneer at foreigners and immigrants and I'll phone you if I see any kids playing football and I'll buy a car and smear them with lead instead and I'll seek medical advice and do Community Service and believe in happy endings ...

'Petimusque Damusque'
(Horace, *Ars Poetica* l.11)

we want, and writhe.
we give, we get.
we seek, we offer.
we endow, you accept.
we tend, you take.
we gather, you give.
we mine, you dig.
we farm, you plough.
we tax, you pay.
we eat, you fish.
we enjoy, you smile glumly.
we exploit, you endure.
we expand, you move on.
we like towns, you are nugatory.
we heat our floors, you live on wood.
we have metres, you play tubas.
we intone mellifluously, you snort powders.
we play a grander game, you cannot get the rules.
we worship ass-head, you stick to wooden logs.
we recommend democracy, you feign dismay.
we incline to self-determination, you are apathetic.
we seek co-operation, you panic.
we insist, you ask for increased defence expenditure.
we protest, you pretend.

we proffer, you pause.
we need, you puzzle.
we explain, you argue.
we yearn, you illuminate.
we expatiate, you exhilarate.
we jingle gold, you propinqu.
we unbutton, you avert.
we dance elegantly, you run for it.
we puff, you blow.
we reach, you slip free.
we object, you misrepresent.
we grow tired, you acclimatise.
we desist, you sling jokes.
we leave, you blanch.
we wave goodbye, you ask the Latin for 'tribe'.

Poem

Lazarus
our yttrium-aluminium-garnet-theme
a bone of heat
building to (stimulated emission) jet-to
neat lanes of light,
partitive/generative
cenotaphic wave zeal
by which it works to maximise
(The Creator of the Hills
has them,
sweetcalm growths …)
benevolent delay.

Found Potato Poem
(source: Fabre)

Let us now consider the potato.
What do we see?
Certain eyes … stalks …
leaves … shoots … branches
and in dark and rainy seasons
cavities called cells
very small receptacles
completely closed
often of no regular shape
and angular by reason of their mutual pressure and
filled with grains
with fleshy substance
pressed closely together.
In a more or less perfect potato
of average size
there would be many millions.

Poem

The force that thru the green fuse lifts the sap
is not its own weight
but vigorous evaporation
giving rise to a vacuum.
It happens
in every plant
(endless green prism & light …)

'Dragons'

What will you work at?
And join?
Or the earth is too wrong?
Doesn't seem?

HAND IN	HEART IN	CHAIN OF
QUENCHING	CHIMING	SOUL AS SHADOW
MOVE OR	MIX OF	GROUND OR
ATMOSPHERE	TO BE LIKE	AND LINE

The word-waste
slips us
proud
apart.

What today?
Festival, maybe,
something that bends
all the lines of rock

CO-	FUSES	ADHERES
BLOOD	BESIDE	BLOOD
WARM	WITH	WARM
HEART	HARP	HAND
SOUNDS	AND IS	AND ACTS

night-through,
sleep-through,
unwinds by day.

Are you some sort of cop?
No, I work for
want to provide
interested in
in the neighbourhood

MISTY	UNCLARIFIED	NATURE
STRUCTURE	VIOLENT	HAS A
CHAMELEON	GANG	CHARACTERISTIC
SHIFTS	NEEDS	ORGAN
ALWAYS	MEMBERS	A STATE OF FLUX

'The detached worker

must keep in mind that
his ultimate goal
is not the redirection of the gang into constructive activites,
but its eventual dismemberment.'

So much shit
take this much continue
neb in, no laugh at big letters,
flares –

AT HIS ROOF	THE DRAGON	SLATE CATCH
THE FRACOD	THE FERAL	MOLTEN
BOASTED	GOLD-BACK	INCHES
CUP	AND NICK-WORK	AND TWIST-TIN
AND GENIUS	IN ITS JEWEL	CHOCOLATE-BRIGHT
BISTRE-SWORD	THIS	IS DRAGON.

And by,
disintegrates,
surrenders,
is over.
Thanks.

Brought in broken hedgehogs
miswingers, marmalettes, the
homeless predator,
not very hopeful.

STANDS	LOST	HAS GO
IN UN-DIMENSION	GRAVITATES	GROUPS
HIP & CLAW	ARM	ABOUT
ONLY	SENSE	EACH —

– If you're lost.
Groups and parts.
Comes upto and disperses.
Signpost sez, but isn't regretted.

If you are all the losers,
dazed on the battlefield,
unswelling of the dark smoke as it night', then
the birthing of dragon:
of each, make tooth,
of each and other, take a flat bit of thought, scales.

DRUM	ROUND	ROLL
RIBBON	BESMIRCHED	THE AIR-CANDLES
YOLK	GLOW	RESUBMIT
TO BE	SOMETHING	BUILT-BUGLE
HEAVY	SPIRE	OF SMOKE
PLUM-BLACK	SENSE	HOLD

Its goal is sky.
Its way is the ground.
Eventually, it will not care any more, get bored, OK, will fade,
hide its own tunes,
re-form, be formulate, re-group, seem
longer and longer and show in other lanes,
by some new time.

Archangel Michael
with atom-dove flight
and coarse saint-shape
swords before
and grand justice is,
empties dragon-entity in two, to dissolve.

VACUITY	ILL	EMPTY
CUT TWO	CUT FOUR	MORE
YIELDS	YET	ENDS
IS OVER	NOTHING MORE	TRACELESS

Error:
nothing corporeal.
only a continuous indestructible freight of smoke.

New nameless zone
sand or river or nook
collects.
Only wants unity.
Only knows no engines give it.
And comes together.

IDLESNESS?	AFFINITY?	INTERSENSE?
(NEW GROUP)	(NEW GHOST)	(SAME GROUP)

Wing-rid ruby
all-'hesive
our great flag pales, was
indisputable of integration

has night / has sky
lift of life

In the twirled world
unhungry,
garrisons of Unions march forever,
weave-banner
roaring with work

FIRE	FEELS	FORWARD
LIGHTS ALL	HAS ACT	HAS PRESENCE
LAST TUB	LIT UP	ALL ADORNED
CANDLES	ON THE ROLLEY-WAY	CHRISTMAS

What help, marra?
None, wor gannin back.
Nivver, aal?
'Less we stick …
for we stand to loss more …

Work scents me
look how I flow into dance
woman & judgement
in mind
fact / act

PACT	ART	PERFECT
AND THE SCALES	THE ARM	CHAIN
FLAGGING	CLOUD	FUME
BREAKS	RAGES	IN DOWN-BITE
URGES	UP	BREATH
BOTH	THRU	THORO' SLEEP

At the centre the navel
near the citadel of sin
where no Christian may go,
see, feel, touch, know.

Turn, oh go on, an'
switch it for us, will you?
I wanta keep the noise away.
Just the bond, years, darkness,
dads and kids, souls and soul, gotta be like love

HASN'T IT?	PART	AND PAIR
AND	THINK	LIKE
EVER	AND	EVER

wears,
breaks up, blames us,
would keep it, would have memories,
it's not whole.

Tune (fizz-prrt) the radio
to something (querdly zt-zt'n neeorzzz)
equitable (di-da di-da)
universal (tum-ti-doo la-la-la)

WE ARE	WE ARE	WE ARE
CONTACT	CONTACT	CONTACT
CHARGE	CHARGE	CHARGE
COLLECTOR	COLLECTING	COLLECTIVE
CONNECTOR	CONNECTING	CONNECTIVE
'N' EASY	EASY	EASY

beaut-as-bird receptive
clear country line
off-wander (brrrggg)
back off-station
(dull, these other days)

bring up
the tick-over,
make message,
tell gear and transform

BRRRR	ZZZZG	NNNN
RRRRRRR	GGGGGGG	NNNNNN
HRRRRRRRRR	GGGGGGGGZ	NNNNNNNNNN
TR-TR-TR	OWWWWWWO	HIOOOO

let feed manage the twist-grip,
the wheel settles the revs,
stroke-rate
feed-back
cable

Mine
I align

scaffold-rig
TAP	TRUE	TIE
TEMPER	TORQUE	TACKLE
TILT	TRIM	TRUST
TOKEN	TAKE	TRAVERSE

leans to what is level
day-equates
and proves satisfactory

For everything is furze
| STICK | TRASH | BEAD |

and force
| CLAIM | SHIRT | TRIP |

and fume
| MOUTH | TEEM | SURGE |

and fire!
PEBBLE'ATE	TIGILARY	CONGLOMULAR
SEED-SET	ATOM-CRISP	GRAIN-IE
EXCITERATE	FLOWERY	SINE-SPEED
UNSTABLE	SHOW-SOBER	UNCONSTANTNESS
REVERING	RECYCLING	BUT UNANIMOUS

holds whole
and to reflex/track
untips to/unties like
necessary nothing
(knowing in bone sets choir)

The broken facts,
tibular ends, psyche shards
re-knit,
patterns mirror,
sand-plate that is in flicker and hum
ALL	IS	TUBE
UNCLEVER	LOVED	TANTRA
MIS-PLACE	REJECTS	SYMMETRY
TAKES	PLANULAR	UNIT
COHERES	COLLECTS	WEARS

collapses back, an uncolony,
to neat lines, bulbs, words,
frontispieces, avenues, page-set.

The cog-sick spangled insect
pervades
brittle ears, clean-stand
wheat —
each we spoil

| GONE | HUSH | EACH |
| ANSTRACTION | NO FAITH | NO TRUST |

the values glowed and stopped.
the spoon fractured.
the steel thing on the hull.
Every single tool has worn out.
but it isn't anything.

OK, you expected:
All our carbon iced into glossy diamond and
not any stop. Why has it got to turn out well?
Can it not just
start and end?

CAPUT	TRIPLE-TONGUED	HORN-BUMPED
VERMILIFROND	SCALES	SPIRING
COILS	IN THE AIR	SUBSIDING
AND BRIGHT	CAUDA	DRACONIS.

Be a happy end.

stand & square
an' breathe & air
count
count
count
an' breathe
an' stand
stand
stand
look
think
give
go
no
stand

air
breathe
square

Gang Poem

Paul is fast in the lower bunk.
In his imagination his toy-tiger comes alive and they have amazing
    adventures.
Soon he gets out, ducks his head and slicks his hair,
'I'm always neat,' he sez.
'You're snod OK,' sez I, so I tuck the label in on his jumper.
'Don't fuck about with me!'
'Your label's showing you ill-tempered little bastard scruff, get it?'
'I'm fucked off with that label anyway.' Reaches
and rips it out of his T-shirt.
'It wasn't that label,' I pointed out.

Drunken head-loll poppy-curved Steve
niggles at Delvan:
parks foot here, foot there, invites out,
dark rude rib gesture,
do this, go here, go-on then hit me, go-on just try it.
An' the quiet Delvan
stands up, slogs him once
flat wi' the fist to the eye is exact, oh,
an' Steve collapse.
Jo crow.
Even this author yawk'd hisself off his back
cause of clemency,
soothe an' be soothed, and never laughed once
for all the grand surprise.

Shim, post-sortie, heads home
and is popped at with an air-gun.
Maybe the moth-holes in his jumper are supporting evidence.

Paul tells me it was Rick did it, round the corner.
But to tell Shim that would spoil the fun.

Paul is trying to find the way out of the bedroom.
Unless he hits a fire-button and leaps, it'll be tricky.
Carelessly tripping up the rubbish, he tells me:
No Bill you're wrong No one can help anyone else ever. It's just you
    and you're one alone.
I counter: I woznot wasting words on anyone,
I meant like you give a hand-up if someone's below you on a ladder,
and try to pull them down that's ahead, isn't that fair?
(like actively non-cooperate with powers above.)
(It's called social contract.)
But here they're non-interventionist.
I've sometimes enjoyed watching Steve tumble down the stairs.
Darren did a somersault on the way up yesterday.
But Paul is still heading for the door.

Jo is bumping up and down
denouncing Steven to the family.
Superior of age, Steve rejoins,
and a bit heated too,
'You're turning into a really nasty person, you know, Jo?'
'But why sell her drugs, you?'

Chris said (he mouths his words a bit)
Yes I played chess with Steve once
and you know, just because I won
he attacked me.
We were setting up the chess board.
It woz a tense game.
But with the help of one warning from Delvan
I beat Chris pretty well.
We put the pieces sociably away.
And then he hurled my tobacco round the room and lept on me.
Delvan sat embarassed in the corner
as tho' why was it taking me
five minutes to beat this squirt all over again?
But I do not care to bite harder than gotta.

What do you reckon?
Piss off.
(If I wanted someone to talk to,
I'da brought my parrot with me.)

Sometimes Jo gets annoyed
that Alan spends so much time
swinging his legs over the bunk-side
or playing some super-game
instead of being with her
(in her room)
but sometimes Jo takes a go on the keyboard too –
after all company is company

Is it some sort of muppet show?
I wake,
an' my arm is there
fast ina dog's jaws.
Paul is holding it there,
making
demented lip-smackin' noises, in encouragement.

I was pulling Chris downstairs by his ankle one night
When I stopped, realised what I was doing.
It wasn't right.
Sorry, I said, I thought you were Paul.
That's OK, Bill.

Steve
's boulversed
his lager can
wham
again.
They should think
(I muse) upon making them
with flat bases.

Occasionally Steve points the air-rifle at me
as tho' he knows what I think of him.
Mostly they point it out the window at nothing.

Paul, mind, could do with a kalashnikov
if he's ever gonna sort out the DHSS
and all that community service.

Two characters come in,
aiming to pawn a deck for some gear.
I caution Steve, who is lager-light
but he sets a deal.
They ask for some more wrapping or summat
So Steve jumps away upstairs. I'm by the telly.
That's when they run out with gear and deck.
Steve looks thwarted.
Now folk like that won't get to Heaven, if that helps.

It is late.
I stagger in and look for the spare mattress.
It is jammed end of the bunk Delvan's on.
Del's holding on about doing everything for yourself,
not others always helping you.
When I ask him to get the mattress over.
You can see him think it out,
and would he rather me crunch all o'er him,
like a yeti in a black hole?
till he heaves that free and passes it.

Sometimes he's so pissed
he can't hold the joystick
or move without earthquaking things.
But he knows the answer for this an' all:
Sometimes it hurts so much you've gotta laugh.

This is Steve and Paul
locked in a sep'rate van
as police beat up Delvan,
assertive, over-bold, half-Indy target
Go on, Delvan, sez Steve, complain, we'll back you.
Lo, he's hoyed into Wandsworth,
dumped in a strip cell, mind-blind on sedatives, limp broken-boned,
 only half-talking only half-thinking.
But only Pauline seems to think it serves him right.

She's too colourful by half.
I don't understand it, he says. I mean, why such massive retaliation?

I paint the story of Delvan's plight pretty good.
And all are sad.
Sue looks moistly.
She offers me half an 'echo'.
I feel obliged to tend a fiver.
She accepts two.
But the stuff's dud, by my reckoning.
An' everyone sez, Del's a real diamond.

Steve gnome-serious evening
flying micro F-10's, urgently quiet
and intent on scoring
and a bit slack on landing
and not sharing his lager however dry me and Shim was,
Orders silence.
Shim burbles up a tune, gets hit,
jingles up again, gets
torn from the top bunk
with a big back bruise.

And in the whirley-gig of time what comes round?
Shim lifted two jackets in the pub
and made off quick and quiet.
Steve, identified with this thiever,
got a smash in the mouth with a bottle.
Now he is thoughtfully sucking a cup of tea thru a straw,
eyeing a very quiet and mild-mannered Shim.

Jay poked his nose out the door.
The kitten peeked around one side of the box.
Are you looking for me, he sez, to the cops outside the pub.
The puppy leers round the opposite corner.
Yeah, come out here. No you come in here.
Both turn tail and meet round the other side.
They were really gonna stomp me, sez Jay, they really wanted to start
    something.
(And there's the image of Delvan in cuffs,

with his face puffed and eyes beat shut, somewhere.)
You watch me wind them up, sez Jay, I'm really gonna torment them.

'When we was in Winchester I looked after Paul,
Well I don't mean I helped him,
I got him to our cell
(It took me a week an' a bit)
I mean he didn't even know how to do that.'

dog-cut-like head
femmer-handed
integrally shit-opposed to credulity
relating
spooky how
th'empty house felt,
when Steve and him woz camping under an umbrella
an' it woz teemin' down, dark.
Itoz grey with roots,
groaning plants high up,
fraggy murderous walls.
but I went in, Del said,
man it was shelter,
tho' Steve wouldn't.

Outside in the dead streets
in the dead dark
a ghost is tapping on a car window
a ghost arm with an iron lever
and a ghost that does not know
that if you kick the headlight out first
it shorts the whole alarm system.

For Christmas
Paul presents his young sister
with a model dog coy in a basket with straw
right-sized right-lightness
when I'd looked weeks
and found nought

Zod, it is said, had two teeth knocked out at the New Year.

Probably he lost an argument on wave v. particle nature of light.
When he comes, he doesn't say much.
His dog, Maxie, is better company.
I point to Paul's ham. 'Bite,' I say.
Maxie closes her jaws on
my hand happily
And wags a tail.
Accept it, it's Zod-logic.

Steve has a problem.
'I left a bit stuff in that chinese egg,
and someone's caned it.
Almost an eighth.
It's not on, I want to know where it's gone!'
You didn't seem upset, I pointed out,
when my bag was rifled –
you said I was making a fuss over nothing really.
That's different, he sez, I'm really upset.
Come on, or I'll make trouble OK.
In the face of unanimous innocence, just hezti storm out.
He don't half exaggerate,
sez Paul,
I swear there was only one joint in it.

Zod – yes – it was him
I spent a fine hour getting him explaining
exactly why (not) the Lecky Board
go to the length of colouring the electric itself
brown and blue and yellow/green
as it flows out to us.

'Side, side …'
'Sekonda to Omega …'
'Is that Little Plum …'
'Del, give Sue a ring, tell her I've switched to channel 40.'

So this Sioux injun joins us
An' his ozzie girl,
drinkin'.
Petite-like, a quick-wit.

An' him's duskied esquimaux,
Fierce wild-cotton levis,
an' huntin' T-shirt
an' not even tamed patchouli.
Hit list us lake a bit
abune Bede's sparra,
But Brit's marra
will only talk about coons an' that.

So – who runs this gang anyway?
I yelled,
really fed up
with Steve this time.
Just who?
'Me' sez Chris being littlest.
'Na, me' Paul ups,
speaking for the once,
to show his jaws still work, howsomever rusty.
An' Steve is jis
making jingles tinkle out
on a new computer pinball.
Something to concentrate on.

Fireworks!
Ow wow! I didn't mean for that –
green-blob-transit, game-screen blurs
jiggers a bang equals
player one is over.
There iza fruit tree in the air,
giant couples of lime-berry / strnut / plum-glimmer
war-symptomatic
fire-show-shine-high-whistle.
Colour-blowing
and is rust-grilled leaves …
All people
white-foam fronds for antlers
bearing
lilac-light torques
fin-filled skulls.
Later

Alan got a blow or two in
before the change-girl switched to emergency,
and he ran.
'Woz waitin' weeks
to get a go at that guy.'

Introduction to a Library

I walked thru France and Italy
and found a small room designated 'Byzantium'.
Here the tomes were french, english, german,
But mostly in the hieroglyphs of greek.
I cannot read it much.
I cannot understand what I do read.
The dust is heavier here than it was in the obscurest corners of
    rooms like Europe or Ecclesiastical.
But the gold rub-up titles do not belie the spread of wonder of
    history
held here.
Unused.

Poem

this
is work to
effort convert
I full-credence all.

Sun
bright to
top earth dwell
I rise potentially.

*

VIEW
SLIG
HT A
FACT
IT I
S A
FUN
LIFE

SHIP
ON S
EA O
N MU
D OH
SOUL

MANS
PLAN
S OH
DARK
LOCK
SPOI
L AG
AIN
DAYS

*

's like being in a snowfield
to have so much luck
adventures in all the airts of the globe.

Morden man maybe invented (for what is the life?)
estuary english. (Life is ice.)
What do you reckon? (It hits from hell.)
(If I wanted someone to talk to,
I'da brought my parrot with me.

Contribution to Kelvin's Project

What should I write?
The black ice of the veins?
Is that entertainment?

Can we have judges ringside?

The City of Egypt
(for Eric Mottram)

I have seen the big city
white on white
laid in bones set atop the saint-yard
bones that project white people
animate stone
consuming

And there's iron from stars
over-seed
of dark and giant and pharaonic forces
the possessors of the overnight sky,
iron is of and from
their black bones

It shoots, spectacularly sparks
to earth
for the axe, and gouge, and holy saw

Hit together
are aggregates
of dark, mouthless hope
not the gentle like-dark
summer-island-arm

*

It south-easts.
The wind catches the knocker
all evening
and just like someone at the door

Till I can guess what is out there

One is a figure
of dull/gleaming
green dots and crosses
in multi (hologrammic) dimensions,
a spirit guide
unto county-wide spaces

And I behold
a great golden mouse with feather eyes
special
joy
of
Papa Bois

Mid these is a composite, a cat,
part loup-wolf,
with lucozade-shade pelt,
part parrot-fluff
flung crown-wide pen-apart
as it grips the lock

And the drummer
a tumble of black bones
knocking now like a heart
and lost
and intermittent tune:
not
mauve; eye-slits

The girl is out there
like is dewy bread-wraps

shell-carton and brutal
cellophane-knots.
They show lime kisses
and blowy white union.

They winnut get.
Aa cannut yet.

*

Me,
my parents defined me.
Set me to be patient
while slowly I brought unto them adventure.

Now Jason looks harassed
He cannot work out
why his marriage (made in heaven)
is hell.
Their kid has a funny dad.

The brothers have bunk beds.
It is Paul's ambition
to supplant Steven
and move down one.

And we move
and change
and speaks itself,
as something ascends
or has declination

From picky cheap toys
to adult-to-adult

But something unloved
comets through us
unsettled
unable to grip,
hits.

he
in a grit
the gems
that are the hardest grit
(not bright as more free
of malignity)

the infected dark back
and the yellow, green, red
the Christmas house streamers

a frame
and
the distorted skull of TV
for Nature sez Aristotle is d'monic.

*

weeded green eyes
incapable to comprehend
cloudy earth

the barrier too close
the passage into a other life
knuckles numbed

dreaming
unobjectively
(about:)

the crash of voice
to clash the keys
to break the glass skin
to ventilate elaborate lungs
to send seed back to the stars

candy-spiral buildings of body
knowing they continue and

to break
awake

how sleep pre-figures reality
day augments to sleep
each piece defines the next to it better
fits it and predicts it
as the city is certain.

Perpetuum Mobile
(after Susan Cooper)

The magic of our living

'put her palms against the
wood
instantly
the heavy door swung
open'

what you want is
perfect / new / self-created

'Always doors. It's like one of those puzzles.'

The ritual
the hand on the display
the knowledge
of formula, a trick of wrist,
nerve-point
to which

'held up
but not hanging
not held up'

you cannot do it
and you cannot explain it
the science itself is not replicable
your only legitimate concern is access.

'Leaning his shoulder
pushed hard
the door did not budge'

and her only worry
the bar of conceptual acceptance
how to migrate to the land of miracles

'she said huskily,
"Look at that!'
Above the door,
carved into,,,'
HER OWN NAME

The magic of our living …   etc.

The Owl

Say tara to the owl
the barn owl
in touch-snug cupboard
open the drawer up tomoroow
maybe it doesn't like daylight
or before of course
seeing as we found it safety
brought it warm with us
inside my jacket
yes
roil up bits of paper
or straw, can we get?
an' we'll empty the deep drawer

rest it
make it shade it
gently
and I hold it careful
two wings
sometimes it flares
tickles
soft/boney orb
baby-like
eye-shut
beat-being
ah, put him down man
we should feed it
mouse or milk
so what have we got?
a bit cake
'n' some water'll do
so we set him for the night
with an air-crack
slept 'n' scuttered
like mammals know the night
rest it / work it
lorry about
the long route
into grey
we took our owl out real early
the field
the heavy air
how
just place it
will it walk?
but ruffles, stands, eyes-stammer, shock-stock blank
and we pare it wings
show it the way they hinge
lift it
it grips
as if little jumps would encourage it to fly
again, again
I guess we really wanted the quiet flight
seeing things free

air-using
face-heart
but it shrunk
didn't, wouldn't know
however patiently we worked
so we took it back
handed it in
at the school
an owl?
why you leavings of the villains
little cross-race thieves
ye cannot handle owls like that
fledgling
and the damage
Aw but we found it
it was on the ground
it was deserted
we looked all-where for its nest
just no sign
no great owls claimed it
so we thought
so we
thought it would go back on its own OK
and the only sensible thing to do
is to hand it over
see.
They got someone to collect it
but he looked awful wolf-like
assured us
have policies
is best
in a world with no protection.

Starting the Fight

Some low blue vest guy
settling his arms
preening style
a'hopping for fun
afore his girl-mate

a grey-top black
with razor-cut
quiet
then seeking out a phone

fitting corner-pads
taping up of ends of centre-spacers
the mid-ways (verticals) of ropes

'You're fighting
you don't have to pay …'
I'd rather buy a ticket
considering

A front row of friends
Mum a girl a dad a kid
'n' the kid goes dance in the ring

Beaty pop tapes
not gamelan country

In fact
it looks heavily Irish
like You can join the lessons
phone John Coughlan

I'm jotting as I'm 'way early
There was footer at Wembley
so I got a bus thru
(I'm chatting)
before let-out

and well early this end, but they still let me in

If I'da coulda gotta ticket yesterday though
it woulda been cheaper
but none in the bar had the tickets

So I strolled a bit round Wealdstone then.
Not much,
A few Christians suffering protracted pain in the shadow-backs of
    charity shops.
An' a Macdonalds.

Now I'd automatic thought the bar'ld be open early tonight
yet these is law-conscious Catholics on a Sunday.

Now the guy's hopping on one foot
glove 'n' helmet in hand
'n' still kidding his friends.
(Somehow he fought twice
but it was still no good)

I tried to get some mates along like Shim
but he was stuck in Morden.
I don't like Wealdstone.
Never since I got a broke nose in 'The Railway'.

'Can the fighters go to the upstairs room for the weigh in.'

Some mystic red glow behind the pop-console.
They sort out someone to be first-aid man.
No, I mean, sort him out a place.

'N' now there are maybe 60 in the hall.
It's OK.
There's drink
'n' music
'n' the fighters come back down.

I'm not aiming to be a ringsider.
I'm at a bar-table

getting a better view.

'Are you nervous, you?'
one of them asks one of them.
Not doing something peaceful?

For what?
to be a desolate dog, roaming the starry sky?
Let's start.

In Church

In the purple lichen grandeur,
candle, arch and armpit
sanctuary
boiling-shape scroll-iron,
I see hermaphroditic parades,
gleam white gleam gold
monstrous naiveties,
hard crucifactual stone
as butterfly lace
but mostly men in foolly wobbly skirts.

Lovely lady angels
are settled to the roof,
they host house-flies
'n' illegal beetles.
Living on sound.

Victorian Anglican thick sounds
that are tenebrous and fairground
all of it
a heavy custard in the ear,
bloody voices
act at banner / drape
they flap like nooses

like listening to black paint.

As meaningless in point of lyric
as the many millennia
lapped and rolled
sense-semantics and reasonableness
into lovely unharming round objects
stranded them i' mid air - OH!

yes, stand, sit,
face east 'n' eat cosmic bull
a skin-mosaic
it is the sign
of the secret idiot

serious bodies
in lead gowns
being under lombardy-littered slabs here,
think on it,
soils of ghouls
mirror-honour great airborn achievers in war,
down there prince-chieftains of tithing,
owl-tiles line their beds,
so now.
(Like a riddle, are still walking.)

Only us
need permission to die.

New Year

Hoee! Aiee!
Hoee! Aiee!
Hoee! Aiee!

Wishing you a well Year

First mount the track to the shrine
which is multi-coloured and tremendous.
Water is available.
Inside
behind the golden Buddha
a flat black figure
in front
an emerald-metal model

Uncertain if the mike is decent
this man advances and retreats
and then opens the water-festival
when you put buckets of water to each other
or use a half-gill silver stoup
to refresh the Buddha.

Next the slope
is an enclave of food
the fried stuff seems a bit heavy
the prawn-crackers are ground coral
but there is charcoal-cooked meat
and simple rice and noodles
and rice-and-banana cooked in leaves
but politely there is nothing much to drink.

An' the crowd milling
in the centre of the scenty meals
is the spicy growth of the mud
is our food of the ground
fragments and fragrance

'n'
some in saffron
(sour-orange)
shaven 'n' conscious
langorous
slackly repositioned
soundless walk / talk.

Shim wi' Claire
(Wenceslas's not come)
'n' me
'n' maybe a 1000 extras

bright US-shirt Thais
tumble to eastern pop-tunes
swaying as in poppy-fields
whiter than the thick earth-breath (cloud)

above,
Thai-boy tiger
in the flat fork
in the tree that spreads
casual

baby's
round-eyed silence
(shouldered)
a strange coned hood
exotic'ly peak-headed

The cymbalum starts up
two drums
and singer her
vibrant nasal notes

'She will carry a gun
he will have one of the things you get on communist flag …'
for the bride dance
it's suave:
(he) gorgeously drums
(she) sensitively dances
(he) gallantly circles
(she) pricks up her fingers
(he) dips 'n' beats
(she) swivels like by strings to shoulders
(they) compete

Then
the young Thais
tap the rods
start the bamboo-dance
later will be sword-dance
or long songs
where all we have is football.

On Show

Was there no pleasure?
No, only people.
Excitement.
rarely, earth union.

let me introduce you to the bears
spare diagrammatic untapering
they position (it is lintel-like)
one each end
(Was there no pleasure?)
(No, only people.)

The style is parallel
therefore gross, cheerless
(Excitement)
an alien pattern
as far different thinking-way as Odin, or Stalin, or Vineland.

Where the hanger, the stinger,
the talker, the walker,
the careless friend to forest
and the thinker of dust.
(Rarely, earth union.)

The bears
blunt-nose and parody

one each end
of stone this and Viking coffin
a thing being chilled lime / grey moonlight / rock

is a strange squeezing bed
and maniac emblems
no more tree-tearing water-soaked half-stripped family fun,
invasion
and arch-foot high-head sport

'They put on some of the singing-men's surplesses, and in contempt of that canonical habit, ran up and down the church; he that wore the surpless was the hare, the rest were the hounds.'

Now mounds that are caterpillar-lid bottles,
with folded bits of Latin charms,
studied chess-boards
they learn quickly in a new way
in a take and pay world.

Wimbledon Court

see-er
main magistrate of three
sneerer

conviction
extent of mind
and custodial

not much
is human mind
moves

to challenge
from his terrace-top-placing
the chal   [youth

in hidden recesses
to take tea, swop biscuits
deliberate

indicate position
in case my pal objects
of the police

solicitor lacking
something not comprehended to us
sorts no law

this?
indicate the prisoner
this!

still white
incandescent court-anger
sits while

blood crust
the racial works of court
in the beautiful city

guide, soul
the path private by
grids of skulls

words of
records of
revenge

Fish

With a magical gloat-clarinet,
fish are on TV,
lucent/baleful on the glass surface,
Hello-mouths.

The male anglers (a pair)
track and tempt them, hemp-seed, bread,
tickle and tease them, strike,
land, caress, love-handle
for the sake of the scent.

I wonder how often they fuck each other?
I don't think fish do.
No I meant them two.

Jingle

the pod of chocolate
breaks taste,
is news / nova.

stark lion
gob-feed

brilliant lilac flag of merit for it.

don't climb mountains.

don't drive fastest.

smooth the wrapper,
gold hero,
Chocolatl
knowledge of who is exploiter nation now.

Claudian on Transport

Is horribly spiked (at the gravity of the curve) the capitular apex (extra) medially (on all four) feral luminants (wheels) surge at the vortex (available) self-cognate (ignition) on its dorsals (for diesel) durable amictation (simplified). Nature (the national) has (regulations) armed its cuticularity (prescribing the frame) and adequate rubescences (inside) with parvulous cusps (the cab, all levers) lend acuity (convenient) to its multilate (marvellous) robustness (its manoeuvrability)

the drivers (concealed)
changes (vein)(signals)
eligible (it is some sport of winter)
attached semi-trailers
coloured rags. You must
prior to the movement (indicates)
the penalty
pressing (being partially solid)
at a glance
an optional stylus (stone)
by using
the key (cognate barrier)
is usually electronic quartz

Where the? Home the!   Sun in her star-garden
fissionally   concentrates fire-dew, feeds the flame river,
rolls in high heat   laps the liquid herbs, grow, gold-flowers,
radiate and molecular   feed the ginger horses of the Sun
staggeringly
ferocious
unloquacious
stallion-beings
     sun-carters
     boldly grassing on gold-mulch
     in the pasture of fiery flowing
     when the sun unshackles and respires.

The Hog
(after a story of William Hope Hodgson)

PIGS SURROUNDED US.
The noise of pigs,
pigs grunting,
pig-howls,
hundreds of pigs!
a sort of swinish clamouring melody.
PIGS EVEN CAME UP INTO THE CIRCLE WITH US. THERE WERE
pig-howls,
a pig-voiced roaring,
a swinish noise,
with the voice of the swine-mother,
mad swine-hunger,
the grunting of the pigs,
countless swine
THEN MY COMRADE TURNED INTO A PIG
like a great swine
he grunted again,
grunted like a swine in my arms,
gave a pig-like squeal,
swine noise,
voice of a young pig
and even a pig's hood
THE HOG ITSELF BEGAN TO TAKE OVER
The grunt of the Hog,
the HOG!
Ye Hogge which ye Almighty alone hath power upon …
oh! the voice of ye Hogge
For ye Hogge doth be of ye outer Monstrous Ones.
did the Hogge have power?
ye Hogge had once a power.
hath ye Hogge a horror?
the voice of a swine,
roaring bellow of swine-noise,
a great swine face,
I was actually looking at the HOG,
the approaching HOG,

I could see the HOG,
the dreadful pallid head of the HOG.
I was being assimilated by the HOG,
the monstrous ego of the HOG.
A pig's eye.
Then the HOG had begun to rise higher through the floor.
What?
Actually to see the Hog
the pull of the Hog
What the Hog is …

The Borrowers Aloft
(after Mary Norton)

Locked in the loft,   looked down from window
Pod, a borrower,   and his partner,
Homily, held there,   like her husband,
and Arrietty, daughter,   only adolescent.
All three with eyes   eagerly gazed
down at what seemed a little world   lying far below them.
'They seem,' said Homily,   'as small as us from here.'
(For 'borrowers', you know,   are basically inches high.)
And Pod agreed.   Pretty soon Arrietty asked,
'Why do they never notice us?   No one looks up.
Doesn't it occur to them   anyone might need help?'
'They're dull-witted,   doltish, complacent,'
Homily explained.   'How can you expect them
to be as sharp and swift   in their senses as we?
They are clumsy and careless,   unconscious of the world.'
'How can any animal be that?'   Arrietty wondered:
'Birds are always bold-eyed,   born to wing off
at the slightest sound.   And the suspicious mouse
is always alert,   instantly ready
to flee quickly,   find shelter.'
'But these,' Pod said,   'are all prone to be attacked,
have to be well aware   of world-perils all.'
'Are human-beings   hunted by no-one?'

asked Arrietty.   And the answer he gave:
'I don't think there is anything   threatens humans,
proper-size people;   their protection is their size,
tho' it would serve to sober them up   if something did
now and then, you know,   nudge them with a paw.'
There was silence a little,   then he resumed:
'But I do recall now   a cruel legend,
hearing it once, that humans   hunt each other …'
'Never?' cried Homily,   'Oh no' (Arrietty)
– 'That would be tantamount,'   said tartly Mum,
'to cannibalism!'   'It can't be true!'
'No kind of creature   would be so cruel
as to attack   its own sort?!'
But Pod persisted.   In pure sorrow he added:
'It is mainly so.   Man hunts man,
fights and makes fall   his fellow alright,
and group against group   makes grievous harm.
Sometimes in the sun   of summer they say
or in white winter   you can hear the whistling
of pack-like pursuers   after their prey,
any number onto one,   unthinkable as it is …'
Horrified but fascinated,   Homily stared below
at a man mounted   on a miniature-seeming bicycle,
unwilling to accept   such ideas as that.

Birds & Wind

Cling'n'clip to the face
do not blow you away
just because the wind speeds
or the rotating revs up
or headwars, mucho magma.
In the love-bird's grip
will prove cartoon-safe
and quiescence, solace
(so cleft for thee)
(Hid?)

The crystal-cripple,
twinless, space-bronze and dunning,
never ripples,
needless tack,
and lost the little power
of being harmony.
When there are chimes
laid in the wind,
long shines of intercouple,
grace seen
(go and poke
a beak out the nest)
(it's aurora-clear)

Sit in the dawn,
slick as slime,
late as christmas

wrist-witch
disinmembered,
trolley-loping,
re-sizing ledge to ledge.
Lips of lace
shoot and sweet, yellow horn
salt-grim is sun-white coat.
The narker
on the sentinel
on the cornice
yipes total trite percentage concern.
The whole takes off up,
undeft,
token paths,
to gorgeously gain interlace
high-pace.

In a war for the wind.
Dissent.
Distend.
Instinctively useless,

by avian rage.
Reduction.
Roar.

Arm'-body
unit or incapable.
Lone
black-back
on pinnacle,
life-lorn,
jumps.

On the Beach

Islands that move,
pace their sea-place,
like it is low-geared travel,
the foot of the headland wash and wade,
grinding it, only for themselves,
I mean, it is for their own amusement.

Rock and bottle,
Spume / birdling,
Flame and riff,
Sleep / silver.

If I was ancient / You are young, you bounce and shug,
If I was patient, / fly and jive, cognise needs,
If I took light, lived, / The air's thick, this life,
Coarse leek-wood, / these living fluting birds,
Circuit rough-ways or / effervescent and white and warm,
Resonantly dead, and / ready travels of souls
  Length and buoyant.

Here is the flock-bait,
small wrist-wedged sea-claws,

inditing sea-pokes,
chaser-willing,
osprey-credent;
you/me, guests of the shore-gloss.
Sent out to play / called back,
As the Tide-Nurse sez.

So it was like,
from limpet-lock dome to island-atom,
again,
Action / age.

Summer – slow
brought me to the window.
Said hello.

Detective Notes

Chapter 1
She said she wanted to talk / I had a bit of cash / being no cheerless soul / round the carpark / a polished guy / detective / she too / advice/ seem to keep walking / till a squad car / and I'd better say where too!

Chapter 2
I was working nights / she'd set / high chance / I don't usually switch mid-week / this was release / much use he was / couldn't sleep / evench they bundled me out / got a few hours kip / I know lots OK? / jumped me / someone proper / a bit of explaining due I reckon

Chapter 3
light & radio / Steve asleep / kicked him quiet / and there was / but for a back door / someone might have seen him / his hands / a wicked shouting / what cheered me a bit / not as loud as the radio / I don't think / so I know where / and if Jenny comes back / just bluff it

Chapter 4
front-door / in latch / shot up / me not being locked / a mini-explosion / turn-off / she'd fucked it up / something else / when I got down / grateful but / So I just pointed out / to think out / got out quick before she could think to throw nuffin

Chapter 5
not press? / no / it's just a matter / took my word for it / keeping my ears & eyes open / dial 999 / say you'll find the loot under X's bed

Chapter 6
Doug I sometimes worked with / the trezur spirit / a few simple tyre-levers / dry summer / I didn't want to have to do all the work / gradually / he caught on / how police could trace call / set him up / long for sleep / most day / so we agreed to night it / I got on the back of Doug's bike / we went past / was a fire engine two cop-cars & loads of light

Chapter 7
they'll be back to check said Doug / I reckoned / just a lump of scrap to us / a ditch / dry gully / lot of falling stars / firemen / shall we leave it or take it? sez Doug

Chapter 8
idea of a joke / check out your friends / irreplaceable / reward / wrote on a card / OK / Look, I said / it's you or the police / got to / I want / get out of trouble / and mean to help / Now get out of my garden / pretty well / I wasted the next morning / just said / a chance joke.

Chapter 9
Go right to the top / easy as anything / do you know what / it / is?

Chapter 10
There was going to be conciliation / Jenny asked / Just getting bonking / Almost believing / grape-flowers & all / she pulled a knife / wow / glanced / pinned her / well she oughta come clean / Church thing / magic / mighty / but we had it stashed now.

Chapter 11
The next day the police station burned down / it was / weather signs / some trouble / near the centre / distraught almost / we could expect great

patterns of cloud / pick us up in a motor / leave us a hundred / And the bishop come & knocked on Doug's door

Chapter 12
He got up / and looked out / two bands of dark stretching over the sky / special / sort of / giant hot-cross bun of darkness / eerie / normally / before we own up

Chapter 13
outcrop / horrific / I wouldn't't'a cried out / a brite fiery figure / where I spose nothing had ever happened / fiercer / more powerful / close to the road / where still some trick / their fighting / like a monster of a candle / in case / Mithra v. the Shepherd / blazing and beautiful / but / his God / just mazes of prisons / the end of the world said Doug

Chapter 14
Just fused or melted it out of existence / that was the battle over, then. / Said I could be Verethragna / and god of war

Chapter 15
that is all / not many people / the last place / and other worlds / can turn suns on and off / directors of things / fire-gods / calm kings / in equity w' all living things

Anti-Sound Poems

Hoenir, the silent god, may have been an ancient deity of some importance.
                                                                HRE Davidson p.108

THEY YELL
this for that
so much for pain-geld, cocoa, coffee,
organic growers of the sun-core highlands, the zone.
without chemical likelihood
bittersweet in comparable pride
the commodities digit

'n clatter
there is an arrogancy of rhythm
but the house that is hungry is silent
however hard you go and listen

THE STRESS
is a sort of buzzing
word like words like would be random
but you repeat
we cannot cease generating electric noise.
When you wake up
there is a fog over the porticos
that are the web of the street
footstep-maze makes no sound
nor the air you breathe. Exactly,
You blaze like neon.

ALL YOU CAN DO
is ball up,
let them keep attack.
Their big goal lives in great booming spaces
with angry serpents fighting Z-rod in contorting pipes
make a raucous barage,
beat ears.
And I pray to Hoenir,
the silent god,
let him share the
silence.

IT IS A MEETING
but because there are Councillors,
they will shout
they will make everything mad
they will not want/tolerate their nonsense being interrupted.
All they want to shut up
is the blood-flow,
cauterise info.

FISCALLY
we are unstable.

No funds are around
to keep the gamelan a'play.
There is dust 'n dead mites
collecting in the resonators
as little creatures liked to vibrate
but mostly no one bothers to chime it.
(The first sound mix
the ancient Asia' tin 'n copper.)
Delvan he go' to the big dance
that's where he disappeared.
it is loudest 'n costliest.

IN THE HALF-TORN COLD
O is the pall of building
A is the irrational ghost moves walls
makes deist-blow mountains
and the bite of the lungs
he is self-maceration a diminuendo to:
we are before the mirror of black salt.

How Highpoint is Better than Wandsworth

I was just one day in Wanno.
There!
And they come at me.
What screws animal
screams feed?
you gotta placate/plead
they know
you get to yell for them
door
an ear to hell
they pass words/mind
break me to black music
joke-limp

add a agony up sufficient
tomorrow more.

*

Then they seen the state of my hands
and moved me.

*

We were cuffed right hand to right hand for the coach
so if we bolted we would run in circles
it made it hard to roll a burn.

*

I said I don't care what job
but I'm not doing jam
I'm not machining denim, OK?

*

This guy leave a packet yeast under the counter,
forget about it I guess.
In the servery it was.
An some foreign prisoner come up,
Don't know what it was,
sez is this cheese, can I have it?
An I sez no, it's not cheese.
Then I find the guy it belongs to, hand it back,
an tell him 'the least
you can do is give me a bit of it eh? I mean,
since, I save it for you, didn't I?'
An that was how
I got to brew hooch,
to start off with.
Mostly it woz sugar.
I flavour it with a bit of lemon or orange maybe,
it was better than some of what the drink you get
outside and

it only take 3 day or so to brew.

*

Letters are safe.
They are sealed, taken to Cambridge and posted.
It's better and quicker than Wanno.
The letters come in,
and if there's one for you,
your name's posted on a noticeboard so
you know to go
and collect it.
They open it in front of you,
for to see if there's any drugs or stuff that's not allowed
but they don't actually read
what's in the letters.
When your posters come in, Bill,
the screw looks at them, sez to me,
Jeez you ain't gonna put them up are you?

*

Our side is all cells.
The other side is dormitories
and the guys are longer term, not
high category or nothing
they can do a lot what they want,
there isn't much check on them really.
I never got put there cos they claimed I was category C,
but they never told me why I was made that.

*

That's Orion (on the video as a logo)
see, I know the stars
but I give them my own names – great.
Like the Mountain Bike, the Hamburger, the Wedge of Cheddar
yes, it counts, I know them OK,
there's one just like a cart
or a plow or a bear

what does it matter
it's a dot-to-dot business
all you have to do is join up the points.

*

If I were a ghost there'd be
some sorry people around I'm telling you.
They would soon be in a mental home.

*

There were
two escapees used this big pipe
that led out.
Only the screws were waiting for them.
I dunno how their surveillance works.
We never heard any more.

*

So I had a pal
I teamed up with a spanish guy
so we could smoke together
an one day I tossed the empty twist cellophane bit
out of the window.
He yells, 'There's in that!'
'Shit!'
So we leg it down, get out, search good.
An then this low-grade screw saunters up,
not older than me really,
they'd put him on an easy job
keeping an eye on the outside
he come over and said what're you looking for
so I said I lost an ear-ring
And he almost get down n help us

*

OK
to brew
put in warm water, sugar, yeast
for 3 days

but first it tasted of Lenore
had cleaned it out properly I thought, but …
it got better
sitting in my cell I could smell it OK
even the screws must have

*

there was an
alarm panic button
but no one would hit it
so if there was a fight it could be serious
but instead it was sometimes hit for fun
that really annoyed the screws
they said stop it or we'll stop your brewing …

*

Come on, let me tell you
the effect of the radios.
Suppose several were all tuned in the same,
one same song playing on them
and you stood in the doorway
for a listen.
Well, was the whole music roll
about the landing,
a proud sound,
something tinny and from wherever the bass
and running round and round the ears
back.
I am a cat-god at play.
my own captured air.
in the vibrant pipe palace.
but no church.

*

Well, you told me things are better outside London.
So I went to Liverpool that time.
I was in touch with this scouser.
He give me a ride in a car
turns out to be nicked.
Nothing obvious.
A little broken side window.
But the Bill spotted us
and they give chase.
Swerved down a side road
a dead end
pulls over
and he legs it
and so did I.
But we was caught
and then he said it was me driving.
I was charged.
He was let off.
I did not say anything though
as I know I cannot drive.
They was being silly
and it end up
they just had to drop the whole case.

*

Battery watches / stop watch capacities
are forbidden every way in Wanno.
So I had a loan of Bill's wind-up.
Unlucky for him.
See entry coming up day 43.
OK he got my super digital marvel a loan
but is gonna have to hand back just the same …

*

Can I joke
to play?

No, hard on the hand.
It sides
Hit!
I am habilis.

*

The peach-weapon woman.
I roll about.
You see such wonderful things to see

if you could
if you could fire to.
There would be so much debris
if they tangled
it kicked off
single sleepers it dreams.

*

grape trillion
spiral lines

green-jacket jewelly vine I adhere

I envisage

dry dusty tufa
it is baked bean brown
hid in maroon ridges
the ground

gnarled knifed stock
there is the bloom of green
sun-dark crystals are the juice-buds
so proliferated

be my chair
of ripe wood n crate
galaxy of grape

*

we tell us
drugs are deals
tight assignations on date on fence
n a packet-launcher brings
it pirouette the parcel
or maybe they pass it by hand
when the psyched moon tides.

It is simpler – myth.
You cannot say it's screws.
You rather fingernailsfull arrived
daringstly
or sewn in veins
on line on faery carts

As all it is culture delusion
has to be

OK
that way

The Best Jigsaw
(for Bobby Moore)

It is a vision

a vision of the field

a sense of positions on the field of play.

I look 'n' check it,
but it starts in the head.

Greenwood was a christian.
Ramsay was kind ova stoic.
Did they know what they were using?
Mebbe they translated me into responsibleness 'n' reason.

They were upset if I drank.
We were to have no women 'n' play.
But they got no idea how I couldn't sleep for pictures.

The one best bit advice I had:
was work out
who'll be there to pass to.
That is imagine
the field of the play for the future.
I adjusted the vision.

Once I could get the idea straight,
the sense of where we were,
what we could be,
OK I was useless in the front.
That is head-on action.
I was planning.
It was why I was made captain.

Certain, I could always make a reasonable game.
If I could pass what I saw,
Passing the ball was easy.
It clicked.

Other teams sensed what I was up to.
They started blocking me.
I don't mean tackling.
I mean a sort of fuzzy energy.
An aggressiveness.
I couldn't get thru to them.
I lost my own team.

Then I had to keep things calm.
I still looked good.

But the team was shit.

And the North Bank would sit in a mass.
And pretend to be ducks.
Give us a quack! QUACK
Give us another quack! QUACK
What have you got? QUACKQUACK

It was humiliating for me.
I could never make them part of it, pull them in.
That's an impossibility.
But what I was seeing was what they were seeing.
They had to gift it.

The clever teams made us look clumsy
and put the fans off.
They got beatings at away games too.
The factories at Dagenham come 'n' backed them.
And the police stepped in.

Now you know why
The bigger grounds were the best for me.
The great games where everyone's up 'n' excited.
For the World Cup, a lot of our games were at Wembley.
Mebbe that was magic too.

I got away with it.
Because I never reacted.
You didn't find me running somersaults at goal-time.
Surges are different.

But I went to hug Greenwood once.
He wouldn't have it.

I didn't like managers much.
I didn't need to be in the power-game.
My aloofness wasn't some trick of captaincy.
Visions don't share often.

Even Tina couldn't solve it.

We went for ordinariness.
The pictures aren't wasted like that.
But it doesn't halt.
On my own
they flicker into chaos.
They become dizzy impacts of electric,
misclous accruings,
endless gleaming planes that lose direction, a
nil actuality.

In the end
I asked for a transfer.
So it could be different.

All
Wine
and white
and sky.
They would not release me.

Two Poems for Bob Cobbing in One Style

1.
So this is what do we sing the City?
Salient and tower-drum arrival mass.
The ruby neon necklet human
a machinery is blood
Mammoth they buzz carriers burn lorries and
Singly show roseate.

You feel the snow in your toes quite white
Finder is chewy bun of smog the sky
The circulation is an astounding emirate. The wheel
livers and crashes and performs sunny function.
There are african suburbs

and there are cakes of chocolate limestone pantheonic round
and sky arenas of a flood
fish-folk and tumble and dive and arise
salient and drum-slowly are the piazzas and lozenge spaces their gift.

In his bed the poet-leader is girt with tastes of parrot
and sings a stormy street-map
before his feet clatter flat ghosts and go out
and execute the mail.
What all the letters are clamouring for
in case there is some emblem, some way of total informational act
and make the ox-lines
the eagle-exact
free and be
as the insects fertilise the amber road-lighting poles in baby shadow.

There are all other alternatives expletives
dark words unrisen under rocks
things hinged and hyphened
and deep in crud
that are treasures impossible to Aladdin
because there are no pearls like smooth subtle smiling shine
of the sound-torch ringing on
some are antique ideas of tongue
is the cave council-office of the land-centre in mind
a well-carved corroded sea-being motif
producing chirpy flip page-after-page total.

All the loving swirling round-city
is friend non-foe veracity.

2.
The inspired little limb of quiet
comfort and to practise elegancy
is not an income compatible with
the bright excrescence of ob-
tainment of all the more essent-
ial which is energy and inform-
ation not silver leaf on lamb and

foaming gold for fixed icon

What oh what then rings in the
doze-heat wood among the tall
fanning like a voice of venture
a call the maw of hidden throat
or beak chamber like some gull-
goat or phone-pippit (type circular,
credence) is the sound a sense of
link, lassitude, lecture, law or
logarithmic physical assertion as
moving not is meaning or growth

Under the wheel turns the paper
under the ink the shape like
scatter salt-lots on a plate and
make once of something usually
like stars on surface kiss away
as the water bears wonder …

Liver-brown lead seals slip low
as the c in the circle fails and
the bright ellipsoid prism of
non-integral intelligence flashes
thru the dust-parked fields ex-
perimenting torn warm grouped
curves in tangent with the
world-loop's communal lace
of counter-true and unblue are
products and persiflage compared
to the complex bamboo
new

Reveries

1.
At the gate in the wall
park-scent
of may, chestnut,
green almond, the grass, fish-ponds

ornamental knots
of youngsters;
practice on car-stereos

and a white over-sky
the grand collation of bone: we are
scenic

So, possessions.
So, writings.
And so on.

For if you moved,
there would be running,
wild breath, leading to
shameful fruit-wars ...
you wd have to settle for centuries of sun.

People with what are virtually pre-electronic brains
are able to express fatigue.
In the form of a wall.

2.
but it will be
I will be
tomorrow jingly dragoning

the slim pea
beauteous rides bike-plant fence mensefully
brave seems lady-pod

waves
flapping pink 'n' colour
grapply
(my passion to pebbles in the soil)
dank air-swift scented
am still con-/in-volved

And
clouds bring ghosts
orb-gobs
not a gold-chain of justice for them from anywhere
soon they're soaked hellwards
root-life neutral
no obstat;
mikkl-daisy mauve rags, last benefitors.

all behind my sight
salmon-tintly bevolve
seeking why
mechanism-decay to end printing
over-dark-cold-dead rollers
and unspringy and stasis
1 unlucky sneeze

but it will be
I will be
tomorrow jingly dragoning

3.
over the graves of the european world
mouse-lime settles.
bitter division of the sponge-cake ended,
a haunting of orange mournful bones, the dilating
of shit-nigh luxury, things buying
off foreign children in debt,
the sustenance of everything boiled down to one.
But now,
no.

4.
Aboon the orbiter
Ezekiel'll shine thru
rough tape-weave ground of the sky
there must be libels there too
an' little apricot lies
an' santas-full of slander.
You say – yes I'll come, I know you'll play fair
'n' you get the savage sausage
The Eye of Anguish

The builder of esteem
the self.
City too much?
Its Zen transfer of merit to the deserving over-beings
without word without vote.
The unnoticed mountain,
stiff demons glass and clamber
only reflections

Well,
there's the fun of the sun.
The fire of see
lovely visible
(behind my cheek-bones)

return to touch
our holding – that is liskey-caramel
softening, and warm-breathing
and the marbling pale sky and pink veins
we intermilk. I yell.
the cloven hoof stamps on the brass grass
then we laugh.

Everything fits place.

Even the dru'ck'n woman a' the well

Dagon preside

ceremony unturned table
the king-size cod glow in sapphire of batter

if ye have hands to take the hook off the lip
and hop

5.
Then I met myself
garish white bounds ring
containment / controlment
in that
unsatisfactory conditioning
expecting to go visiting

as I was
say time-machined to half
sheared in half (for age)
utterly out-powered
I was total dependent on the sense

what body generates
entire
(just the same cheap marking jacket)
pressures out
(hands moving like spare hearts)
has to, is

the man who turned to the Emperor of the World on the Pacific
and dubbed him useless.
to be anonymous and
founderless.

still
and while
and janusable both
united either way see /seam
unitary-clairvoyant

almost sky-bright built-up

(deadened brick seizes)
I-am / you-are accurate energy
all over again

6.
How the boat dance
water-piano-keys jack-n-spit automatic lift
lie/fly
see/'gree
tilt/pelt
quicker/flickt

laughin' 'n' bailin'
nothin' is rain
the hewer-general
'n' checkweighman-major
are below us, like,
'n' goldy roundy cherubs could be up

the peel of the deep sea
buoy-bell 'n' gannet 'n' chrome
all the invisibleness

moves
slant to rock wind
it is up 'n' beach-down
weird
sand-hymn, a miocene of song, a collation-sound

as a rope run
wheel-keen
dazing cello-line fenders mak row
bobbin'

whale-soap o' cans 'n' spray
crest
we fling us' insult-quizzes
in form of orders

for it is not enough to score a goal
it has to be all-in

pray-blue
or bloody-black sea
the teams of rollers
steam 'n' face to be outer

the word of ever
the sky of river

besides each fish I exhort
to show of colouration the worth
in copious shower
on all who pray
to be a shadow of a sea
seed 'n' soul 'n' silver
bones asunder
enough with present grace
'n' the furnace

7.
The cavern-mull o' jewels,
Setted promises, olds,
holy blair of Empire, till
each gentle saint-nail
(open and oval and opal)
went mallow-aged; how –
if ye lake in the dark.
The peopled crystal
gans blank, blue skin,
pale sun, leak aquamarine
seep'd out, the soul
has bred to tree, tram, track,
a hollow orb
shall not even swivel to the north.

Th' fish-quay is open,
an' between barbarian bricks

dead tails getten cadged for the hook.
Scentid pea-mush
(smash! di yi question god?)
walk to the water,
clam to the hi' brow,
ye cannot be hid.

What smallest gift dizzn't carry
some crest, some blame, tagged ownership?
To spend
may enlarge the soul;
an' to thieve
decorates the way expertly,
but the great guy
sits an' sez,
me, do I want to swop my watch with his?

8.
the blank response,
blue-wall, blue-shirt day

pearl-blessing

go to, go to the car
'n' drive

the note-turner
whistles 'n' whirls –
dud death

arrays of early wash, OK, a
blank response.

and the terrible
shaky riot
getting to get money
the victory!

(things are nothing)

you take and sell

weddings are made in white curvy clothes
of the woman
and jelled ribs
'n' god's tablet gifts
'n' advert sponges

timeless dogs' faithfulness

a fuck off

9.
Perhaps I want to see it
look at the dark brown-ground world
like some black articulate monster
legs blue-dye
long bright orange stalks

On my own
on the strand
I know I got dry dignity
once they untied me, and set me.
Am I supposed to smile, like on cam'ra?
(The gold fist star the sun
and the sensible sand)

Life is just a sullen remnant
to be rounded up
By a choir of black breathless signs.

Like the blinking ova lantern,
seizure, see
worms of light
a bitter bright filament
to take his coffee shell by.

The net come up with everything. Green weed, red weed, dead fish, live fish, weights and grappling hooks, crabs that were mouth-size

and rounded junior lobsters, one or two, almost too soft to count.
Cleaning it was a chore OK, with the net rolled on itself,
and claws jumping out of the snags, not dangers very particularly
but reckless in the air as they were snapped and tewed free.
Respectfully the lobsters, set on the sand, puzzled,
antennae on the swivel at the least approach, like the police in an ambush.

The eating specimen was anonymous.
Some bairn left it on the back step.
So I phoned thru for instructions
'n' cooked it.
Then his coral and orange-white creamy flesh
I dished
delicate as mild-egg
a smatch of sea-rock-song/bony-legs

But the living are tulip skinned
gold-bronze-green-lemon-carmine
not dead-lime-white
not dull plastic black
but aglow a bit a little
with their co-operability.

grey-black baby crocodiles
exited
on their shells
seem much like the young in the street
who discard colour
for a matt, dark-drab aggressive look.
Night people are not a new phenomenon,
the apparel stimulates
and their appetite is insatiable.

10.
the educational fluid into the bottle,
a sample
condignly tractable
to become baroque.
You will be grateful in time

because to be inanimately fluid
admits an identity as energy
and a breaking to sea
a place many molecules and chemicals
and exemplary violence and.
The bottle-makers die,
their lungs grossly big
but mostly of giant-ape assy delusions.
Lie in the sand.

11.
The sordid urns, the six-sided, zephyrless cells
and the sun-hot prison
de-iced in dull-blood rivers run fright
and black, and blind, the dazzling
no-scent shadows, gaolers
over the unowned,
my friends, dawning
warm breath, spread, for wrecked,
harsh-hairéd ox-corpses, like stood,
unerring, aching arms to seize
the sweetness of straw.

12.
I cannot officiously strive to change the washer on the kitchen tap
and
our unperceived religion
spiked-charts, whirly-spidery testimonies
that climb the mountain to fact if only

alright, sequences of unhappiness
(= dishonesty)
what's the point of a union? I mean, a pair-bond
when the whole community breathes
breeds

no horse bully me
no court club me

the bloody provoke

a carol:
how long can I last without income?

13.
So
o'er the princes' palaces
the bee-mouth sips
like giant and fascist antiquity.
And
haply the Queen-Moth is on her throne
flailing with powder-scale
beating the loud light out
Nor let the beetle, nor the death-moth be.
Humans
and holy jewelleries.

14.
I am a wolf.
Birds belong in the sky.
Small china cups decorate.
Books and Bibles that are inscribed children's smiles.
Ours, heady halyard crowns.
Small gestures.
The day drags in the blood.
The Wolf of the West eats and eats.

Horn to horn move
the thunder-traps (seem)
sprawl the road
squeeze
(skids and blocks) herd thru the lights
(anyhow) (and counter-red)
a beating hoof-hum
to bright the night
the keen yellow planet
and slide

Umbro
for Jason Moss

We
let us
me
be masters
of your indignity
is a smile

for they cuffed me
bent me
the other cop batons me
but
her photo
I used to carry it with me

And
Shim also told me
and you know what Bill
he is a pukkah mate
with his hungry hair
always has time
I rate him
I respect him

An' the angels raise the Ark
an' me that hit for money
an' the temple of brazen grails
where the bad guys aren't caught

an' there are fields of fleeces and drink machines
do you pack the cold walls
the ambit of a street
get leap the length of
all the hands
i think they have to be true crime ones yeah
but don't mind if they are caught

for the setting of the peach eyes
ear-curl kid
my pretty she is
she was three the day
I often shout at cops

deserve
i can give them
a holiday
bronze chalk-dot beach
when she sees the slappy sweeply sea
appreciated them

i work in textiles making sheets blankets towells
    and mailbags
im on an N.V.Q. course
so i can get a job with UMBRO
the company that make football kits and
    accessories in manchester

pearly bluey white
and the gold and mud-red
Ali Baba soccer strips
some are uniquely black texture
silvery-orange plus letters
they all cost about ninety £s.

I thought yours
might be a letter from them.
I was waiting on that.

Appendix

i hope it all works out
and i can rake the money in
because my wife and daughter deserve everything
they have been brilliant

Quad

morning is an ache.
I dunno why
(me / them / things)
are thick 'n deliberate.

incidental sounds of metal
do me donate music

too fuzzy for tea

too dizzy to queue 'n pee

flashes of malice
the silent struggle / tug
no talking

there is no sense in it
are samples 'n boxing,
bits in the eye of the art-keeper,
slush

waltzing at it

things that don't partake of purpose

ritual / unnatural light
last thing unlike a jest

maybe
the lesson of providing
and taking

as it's the helpless hour

*

After all when all the other grades of life smooth

there is still fear.
Evokes itself.
A transient sheet / blind silence / slight
steam-scream kettle head bone eye
be no
flows unnaturally
between the skin 'n' the vein
where was identity show.
So no mirror in the rules.

*

Nous over nub-shit.
Cellular hubris preponderates over blank mundality.
You can even
knock yourself out.

*

So
we stand under the planets

are bright balls
mirror-nicks
do not read
do not hang up at the pips

there are Argives or Goths
compensatory spaces reveal
and in the black
like texts

there is nothing very certain
written up but a need to evade

reassert or check

can you be certain even
of any absolute opportunity of escape?

what distance

for the evil elephants may wreck the galaxy
before we get thru

little lyrics of the void.

*

the second symbol was a trike

it steamed up-bank

ev'ry ride cost the same.

the rattling of the wood.

the steering of the spare cars to the side.

Don't you understand?

I don't want to guess any more.

*

let the little florid beckonings of blood
not induce us

Loki with his mustard sandwich is
the normalcy of violent flavouring
for who knows what will come of them
when you are stripped and decked for justice?

*

an' I wake up
I might as well be beat up
shoulders torn
lungs drunk with debris
knob-prod

can I only just bend my back to my shoes.
Strange mix-being.
Swine's ear, ark-angel's knuckles,
dead head.

the kettle-flick of wit
I move
are fish-curdles of sourish excusatory delay
I sit and still
everything to verbal jelly

in the neat hot house she and he
occur
see what the air is a mild hallucination
they
embitter the rub family

in the elegant painted-in lemon patches
I présent
with all the flexibility the plesiosaur
his talonic
vengeance is future blow blue water

The Fire

the fire breaks sound (is cooling)
a dog-yammer outside
'n' a wind-fight

Anu-anu-anu!
eater
the dark head in the dark
someone in earth
the slick harassed profile
evil to you if you do not
eat style

man has his teeth but see mine
the catastrophic reek

*

That
when we said (þæt þu ameldodest)
we would not set up
formulations-conclusives (lists, lacks)
useful to Talus' sons
but be a tangerine-field at the free feeling throw go anywhere
knowing it not an aim
creating being a crab-pot dead-end
sexuality assuming the fount of religion and division
but is does sees works walks runs sings sleeps
of the hopelessest
quiet node of sun-loan.
You are in the dirt 'n' the dye.

Paul's Survival Tips

What is it your will / my will
that we fight over?
Tone or word, act, non-act
– go on, name it.
En' if Steve dash for a knife
or Shona get the p'lice
– but that's not us.

On the way to the Crown,
Jay has been yelling these cops.
Two follow us in
There is some mute prodding and age-demand
But not much they can do.
Taciturn in his natural habitat
it is Paul turns (for they leave) sez gentle and clear

Make sure you behave yourselves
to them.

Time to roll home
on a BT cottonwheel.

In the bedroom,
Paul's water-reserve is running low.
But will he be able to make it to the kitchen tap
without the police spotting him?
Recall the stitches in his knee slow him down.
But his trendy porridge-tone top will be good indoor camouflage,
all well wall-papery.
The cat and the dog are his friends generally
So they are unlikely to impede him.
The police car circles and departs.
Now …
But
'Paul, I want that stack-unit back down here where it belongs, now.'

What do you do?
'I'm a creator' sez the lorry-film-hobo
who was a colonel.
An' Steve is anger'd
when gear goes missing
from the place he had first telled every one there was nothing there.
Then just one trainer goes missing.
We analyse it: sabotage.
Against which only magical cans of drink effect.

At night.
Then there is Badger Man with his bolt-cutters,
Black Moth with screwdriver,
The Bat that surpasseth the window.
At fair-time
the girlfriend phones.
OK sez Paul and reassures
we don't have to stay with the others,
sure we can be on our own.

*

The fox-brown dog
is a vast companion.
My Sunday morning.
Which of the 12 starters had dropped out altogether?

Paul and Pauline sleep.
Jo is up out working.
Delvan with Brit.
I go boldly to the video.
Is this key found in the cupboard?
Skeleton.

Shim was talking of treasure in the Wandle.
There had been an Anglo-Saxon cemetery at Mitcham:
note cranial anomalies.
Some spines to two skulls.
Some with no skull.
A skull buried alone.
And a skull between the feet.
Someone has to speak.
Is the dog a good dog?

Irritated
out of his native calmness
is Paul
pours the cup of coffee
on Steve's head.
It will be painful for both of them.
The Last episode brings a violent end …

Media Studies

The spore-spreader
denies.
Asserts nothing alternative.
But everything is page after page
it is all the same prediction
and you get back every similar tag of confirmation.
The character is circular.

The money of the state
is the money of the state-guarder's friends.
Pretend it, if it helps,
prolix, merit.

The cherry-heater
certainty ploy
many make mankind
if it is a simulate
what are the wild waves of coal-rock more
likely at?
There must be a motive.

Several mugs.
A table.
A bench for the buses.
The surplus brick spaces or holidays
have been excused further function,
unpeople have unhomes.
The plans with bright gospel trees
golden paving
designer magenta tar –
takes place.

The dignity of worry
a toxic product
tanks 'n' bars 'n' military axles
will bring water to primitive countries.
The only voice of democracy a sort of contént.

To be at union.
A shadow of a duality, a head that has bifurcated and extruded
    fondle, antidotal.

At best, we balance.
The petrol bricks us in,
the rules are hand-jerked hymns,
for a little, for a very little,
everything matches.
But much.

O Mokey,
it's rich is war.
The fists drive the head into gear,
or even then he tears off one shoe,
hoys it into nowhere.
Limp-aid.

Musical Note

alright it is Finnish orchestra on the video,
so why have they all got my neighbours' faces?
Except the conductor
who looks like Dave (the stock-car guy) fra Sund'land.
Close-ups do not dispell th'impression.
Re-wind.
Right at the start some prom-clique yells out
'Big Brother Is Watching You'
but the BBC commentator feigns incomprehension.
But how they shot the magic amazes me.
Becos if you watched it, I bet you'd see all your neighbours too.

Ride

Ride the
it is a risk
start it
ride it
the dolphin driver

how subtle it is
reins radio
he is sweet
tack-prick
her is sweet
tits of cashew pip

why figure it
fold it
thank it
sez no plea
heart of the
beaten and corroded sea
side by side

now the rider
is an arch, a dip
a fin,
hockless diver
there is a swather of water
a room

Thirteen Thoughts as though Woken in Caravan Town at Dawn by 150 Policemen in Riot Gear With Helicopter and Film Back-Up at Saltersgate Near Tow Law In Co. Durham On The Sixth of March 1996

1.

a street-horse
the guest of the box
rainy-bone
the miscal tunnel of nose
an eggy arch
all work out
a puzzle
by protestant enhousement

jee-ye, jee-ye
happy horse of head of tappets
this the icy unwanted land
we bed in,
dog-injuns thistly, warm

2.

we are not so near the soil
as some

there is
not much love in
plazzy stars of the empyrean
some black-white lino
each is in his bed
and banging like stone

some it fevered purbeck tissue
of limestone
or unidimensional map-flat glow to yellow, and
blue slate, red sand,

the smokey-spreckled white ash and fancy-fecund grit
chicken-bright
that are

pin the disk
and stain the glass
eely letters
and lead-motor

the liquor-tranq
a trice or two
serves to ex-quick environs

how many breakings of legs
now many series of eggs
is easter?

so many dead centres
so many live photos
in excitery

we are several zoos
the lion-cage overlaps the banks of otters
the tinsel lips of the snake
and the lucky arse-shoe

some bits are blank
or
stink
a skunk
but all point east

3.

sclick!
the scarab
double of symbol
endeavouring living

upstairs and downstairs is dirt
aces of ash
choke (like a crash!) echo
sock-serpents pile up.

the TV is oats and X's
devoted and art-lucky
a high priesthood enhoaxed in clitoral glassy cam'ras
in the swirls and pixels
to trap
but any catapults act on.

4.

under the shepherd a policeman
under the grant-body is the hunter
these are but lips 'n' skins
the commonwealth's hat 'n' coat

I sorta shook as the police ran up an' grabbed
I dorsent try an' run
at the holt's end the chal
turn my back
then they
stood my ground
an' stamp earth's sheets
the van was searched an' sacked, strong
they wanted everyone out
stick mood
to line up in the snow
I am na protest,
hoof at the rich king
seeing
some lass cuff'd an' pulled away …
picked out
by ghost-scent
made show of
we haven't to fight back
how pikies are to be tret

as all say

5.

Beélzebubbed
by instructions,
agonal initiative goes slack

I get a smack.

and seeing things as you are,
a star.

Riddle me what the red robin has gecked
to get his chest

As awful as us?

Empty things full because full things have fulled them
And the very moon-colour magics us.

It is time to steal.
Stealing is not accepting.

Thru my ears you sing Alleluia
So I smash the door.

6.

In the hit-n-quit torture of the daily world
puppet ghouls
slick tracers if tricks
come 'n' knock regular
(tack-tack)
on the lock

But I'd part with my heart for a sov'rin season ticket to get an' live
where humans

ripple in sequel
across the sky-screen
slimly connected to something airy of a script

Meanwhile minus:
sans hubris
sans hand-light
sloganeers
move in for the take
looting any penny of precious edge of view
slack at the poet-pocket

what I see
a blank blue strip
'n' jungle guns
ova vietcong movie
shooting behind roots 'n'
winking chords
frond over zealous group-men
and endless

the only answer of
rabble of riches
bursts
into total nightshine

7.

the helicopter that was going to rescue capitalism
has to pull out becos of snipers.
Snipers are small gunsters
with booby-slip ink antennae
ticketting out counter-imperial cling-gas info
thru radiating pipes.

Ev'ry page printed
is another bubble attack.
Tin quins of rhythms are a merciless beat
on the bald taxer.

Sun-lip & hair-flames to lap all the demands
for totems, for sprite-solids.

Here will be set no god-alls
masks for guidance of nature
of my nature.

8.

spurious
data, desiderata
pluming
of a centricity
expressing things that need to be
for the equations to be in balance.
As if there is no limit to our receptivity.

9.

You, you will be a rhubarb
Or a molehill
As the provider of decisions sez,
his game on the landing.
It is go on: unguessable destinations
also ample time to test or prove
are you viable.
Sweet day! see …
the rules and root. A
Coercion:
        transfer
            you
                to chance.

10.

We have babies 'n' births
sometimes secessions; burials; communities are moved,

demolition eases the feral-search for ground for housing
the kings of the dock-weed be warned.
and the opulent win the shadow-box,
choose the puppets on show for hands with legs 'n' wages
we are subliminated into tokens 'n' riddle-stanzas
or left a road-march

11.

Listen to the wolf on the railway-line
she is one with the wheels all homeless dotted lines
innings and turnings
invisible diagrams like
a dry industry

12.

the trellised hairs of the house-arms
retract
unwelcome
as are our coat of action
the massive core of the counties
do ill / do well
there is no assignation of any estimate of account
after all

13.

I envisage grave rustic patterns of day
equal efforts
damp routines for rodents
quick
clips
sweepings sossing in ten-jewel cups
they live in egypt-towns / truck-counties

lo! dull tablets and little coal blanks range up

spheritend cocoa-blinks
see-thru pastilles
helical gem-light
bickers
turns
squitches
fiery Grand Basin animals
they horse and rove
blow heaven-houses

Brittle ship and canny tank
blind and fume
million-mort
a belly-rusted tilth for awks to be peopled of
pods
and tickle up of life
in sequin lenses
tilt-sway-sing bits
'I do not imagine that this is a systematic destructive campaign
for that would imply intelligence.'

[Untitled]

In the brick middle ovens
we set closures, elusions, as texts
turquoise glazes
and virulent red
is transport
along transform
gleams white field
showery bird-words love and enamel
a product of Etruria.
Tyran is deity of wallpaper
Aplu of moved lives
Charun hammers down the heart,
crack in the fire

slip on the floor
as oaty letters are crumb-rolls,
sprouts and stanzas
that crack out
consumed to be
(of the glossy paint)
inky
a colony.
The grey girl prodding at ash
in tufa and cones and tombs of
clayey sunny grooves sparkle rhyme-mixed
motors
twinkly paraglosses on the rim
the bone-dust admixture is
gold-rounded eyes
that is hottest wrestlers'
a unwinning complex establishments
you can exchange
good times to be born.
To become
simple ornate people to unform to
being finite.

The Durham Coal-Field

The lion 'n the lizard
man the pit-head
that is a little soil 'n a little stone
an' naught but earthish
wiv a few lime-flowers
'n head-bowls
for now the (helmet) white mine-rule's finished

The guild of the cold coal-mangle
the bishop's minerality
these no longer worth a slot

they fill no denes guard no cliff
sit under trains hardly not
there is no more god-landscape
what tho' everything the white man plays at forms fact.

Ho heckles of the ocean dragon's fist
have sprawled arc
be
the
painless pale sand
no more house-high brick-head strata can establish
make a step-world to purple

Notes

General abbreviations and bibliography:

BSC: A Book of Spilt Cities. Buckfastleigh: Etruscan Books, 1999.
CEP: Collected Earlier Poems (1966-80), ed. Alan Halsey & Ken Edwards. Hastings: Reality Street, 2010.
Disc: BG collected poems compiled & issued electronically, 1991, rev. 1996.
EE: Essay on Entity. Seaham: Amra Imprint, 1993.
Files: the many digital files left by BG on his computer at the time of his death.
LMO: The Lion Man & Others. London: Veer Books, 2008.
MF: The Mud Fort. Cambridge: Salt Publishing, 2004.
NS: Nomad Sense. London: Talus Editions, 1998.
S&S: Skemmies an' Stanes: two poems in dialect. Seaham: Amra Imprint, [1993].
TF: A Tour of the Fairground. Exbourne: Etruscan Books, 2007.
WNM: Worlds of New Measure: An Anthology of five contemporary British Poets, ed. Clive Bush. London: Talus Editions, 1997.

All texts appear in *Disc* unless noted as e.g. '*Q* only'.
Year of publication for undated items supplied by the bibliography compiled by Doug Jones and published in *The Salt Companion to Bill Griffiths*, ed. Will Rowe (Cambridge: Salt Publishing, 2007).

Calendar Contents

First edition, an A4 pamphlet, 16pp printed rectos only, published as *Spanner* 31, Hereford 1992.
'St Cecilia's Day.' *Disc* adds '(classical)' at end of penultimate line.
'All Saints: MFV Golden Arrow.' Reprinted in *MF* as 'MFV Golden Arrow.'
'Palm Sunday.' Reprinted in *MF* as 'Hand Complex.'
'Sandwiches.' *Disc* note: 'the title implies a three-segment stanza.'

The Great North Forest

First edition, an A5 pamphlet, 16pp, published by Amra Imprint, Seaham 1992.
Extracts reprinted in *WNM* (first and last sections) and *MF* ('Xmas 2' & 'In the Great North Forest').

Mid North Sea High

First edition, an A5 pamphlet, 16pp, published by Amra Imprint, Seaham 1992.

Quotidiana [Q]

First edition, an A5 pamphlet, 16pp, published by Amra Imprint, Seaham [1992]. The poems were untitled and presented as a continuous sequence divided by asterisks. Some poems were given later titles as noted; those designated 'Untitled' appear in *Q* only.

'On the Sun'. Reprinted in *MF*.

'Kurt in Context.' In *Disc* the hero's name is Carl.

'The Haswell Change-Over.' Text follows the few revisions in *LMO*. Previously reprinted in *WNM*.

'Starting Up with Doves.' Text follows the revisions to the dialect in *S&S* & *MF*.

Review of Brian Greenaway / Notes from Delvan MacIntosh.

First edition, an A5 landscape pamphlet, 32pp, published by Amra Imprint, Seaham [1992]. In the title of this edition 'Delvan' is misspelt 'Delvin', corrected in later references.

The first section of the Amra text of 'Review' was reprinted in *WNM*. Our text follows the revised version collected in *TF*. 'Notes' has not previously been reprinted and does not appear in *Disc* or *Files*, perhaps because BG re-used some of the material elsewhere.

In the Amra edition both texts were set in centred capital letters throughout. BG abandoned this setting for *TF* but it is retained here for 'Notes' in the absence of an authorial revision.

The Amra text of 'Review' shows the following significant variants:

Section 1, stanza 14: the final lines read 'but small, enpotted, / stays low. / And lastly, leafless, / it cannot even feed. / First bud, then root and leaf, I try / make mine or nothing, / correcting or kill – / I sour every virgin thing / into its own smashed blood / to be tied forever.'

Stanza 16, first lines: 'And his Son / saved him. Jesus / calmed me / to listen to Him.'

Section 2, an extra stanza following stanza 3: 'A man who called like a crow / cawing blue laugh sang called / like making me of, some jibe / black-eye high-voice'.

Final line reads 'Some ladyless life.'

Section 3, two extra stanzas after stanza 2: 'Where are the wives? / What happened to the home, the child, / the income – / were they never born? // Hero? The screen's gone dead.'

Section 6: single-line stanza following stanza 4: 'This was got out?'

Scaffold Hill

First edition, an A5 pamphlet, 16pp, published by Amra Imprint, Seaham [1992]. The Amra text is radically rearranged here, following *Files*. In *Disc* four sections appear under the title 'Birthday Poems' but for the title 'Scaffold Hill' there is only the note 'my error for Shadon's Hill in Sidney Webb *The Story of the Durham Miners*, 1921, p.43, re meeting of 40,000 men to oppose continuance of yearly bonds …' The second section appears as 'Birthday Poem' in *MF*.

Dialect Poems

Title, text and order as *Disc*. The first eight poems, in variant order, comprised *The Cuddy Anthem: a mini dialect anthology*, 20pp printed rectos only, published by Amra Imprint, Seaham [1993], with the preface:

'In mid 1993, with the up-coming creation of a new centralised Co. Durham and the appointment of a new Bishop predicted, it seemed just the time for people to get together and create a new County Anthem for St Cuthbert's Land. A competition was launched among the inmates of Duck Yard, but, sad to say, the level of entries was not very high and the adjudicator decided, on the closure of the competition last week, that the prize could not be awarded. (He then ate the rice cake himself.)

'To save something from this luckless fiasco, Amra Imprint has decided to publish a selection of the entries, and after some forthright and energetic exchanges of views, our editor agreed not to identify the competitors by name. My, it did take a time to disentangle him from the computer!

'On the plus side, anonymous works get to qualify as authentic folk material, which is always worth a few pence. So tidy up a text (or rewrite it), balance a tune underneath, and you could have a winner! Or need a nose job.

'Gan lucky, Bill'.

'The Tilcon Quarry' also appeared in *S&S*, and 'On the Tyne' in *Poetry Marathon '93 Charity Anthology* (B.J.Allen's Press, 1993).

Delvan's Book

First edition, an A5 pamphlet, 24pp, published by Amra Imprint, Seaham [1993]. The collection also included the much earlier sequence '4 Debates', reprinted in *CEP*, pp.220-223.

'Account.' Last line added in *Disc*.

'Reverie.' Line 16, 'topple off': *Disc* correction for 'tipple off'.

'Wandsworth.' Reprinted in *WNM*.

'Conan in Trouble.' Reprinted in *MF*.

'Medical Report.' Reprinted in *BSC* & *MF*.

'Hanuman.' Reprinted in *MF*. *Disc* supplies note: 'Hanuman is the monkey-god of Hindu and Buddhist legend; and patron of boxing.'

Satires

First edition, an A5 pamphlet, 24pp, published by Amra Imprint, Seaham [1993]. The collection also included section ten of *Mid North Sea High* (lines beginning 'black / white' under the title 'Model Poem').

'Winchester.' Stanza beginning 'The mingiest cells' supplied by *Disc*. The italicised stanza quotes in its entirety the earlier poem 'Alf and Thor – *Winchester*' (*CEP*, p.53).

'The Tories.' Following slight revisions in *Disc*.

'Settling Accounts.' *Disc*'s stanza breaks replace the ellipses in published stanzaless version.

Star Fish Jail

Published in four editions by Amra Imprint, Seaham. Text follows the 4th edition, A5 landscape, 28pp printed rectos only, issued in October 1994 with preface signed 'BG':

'The 1st edition, in 40 limited copies, was brought out around Easter 1993, to raise funds for the prisoner whose story the poem represents. The second edition came out at the end of the summer 1993, the material being considerably expanded and reorganised at that stage; that revised format was followed in the 3rd edition (March 1994) and this 4th, in both cases with some changes of detail.

'I issued the poem in my name, in the first instance because a prisoner is liable to punishment if he gets work printed while serving a sentence (so much for creative writing therapy); and even though that is now no longer relevant, it still seems prudent that any responsibility for the issue of this piece should remain with me. It is though a two-author work, growing from conversational and oral material, to reach focus in my own theory.

'Which is that prisons have a sacrificial role; and survive (like the majority of contemporary literature?) solely to support the myth of middle class privileged existence by creating a sector of population that can be abused, confined and dehumanised. The ratio is probably something like one lyric sonnet to every 3-day sentence in solitary confinement.

'Prisons and prisoners in some sense need each other: it is a symbiosis where the controlling class can play at doing good while doing whatever it likes, and the victim class can invent a reciprocal myth of resistance that makes more sense than anything available in the "real" world. This cycle of credence can only be tackled from outside, and I consider it urgent that it should be, before conditions degenerate further.'

Disc supplies note: 'this long poem was written for Delvan Ricardo MacIntosh, when Magistrates at Wimbledon sentenced him to prison for alleged crimes to which a confession was obtained by applying drugs in a strip cell in Wandsworth, and further continued previous fines, so that on completion of the sentence he would be automatically returned to Wandsworth, where a regime of assault by staff on non-white prisoners is seemingly part of the policy of the prison.'

Extracts from the poem were included in *WNM* (stanza beginning 'When I got out' to end) and *MF* (second stanza with three lines added from later passage).

Liam's Song

First published as *RWC Issue 23*, an A4 pamphlet, 9pp printed rectos only, Caversham [1994]. There are three distinct versions of this sequence: as published in 1994; a radical rearrangement with occasional word-changes in *Disc*, followed here; revised excerpts blended with additional and later material in the third part of *BSC*, 'The University'. 'Liam's Song (extracts)' in *MF* is a different work consisting of extracts from *The Alien* (see below).

Disc notes 'the Liam referred to is Liam Killigree from Morden in SW London, jailed for hitting a plain clothes policeman with a plastic milk-crate.' A note in *BSC* adds 'In 1998 I was finally introduced to Liam Killigrew, but he was content with a new freedom and unlikely to contribute further to this work.'

The quotation beginning 'No / I'm not going' is from Stephen King's filmscript *The Graveyard Shift*.

The Secret Commonwealth

First edition, an A5 pamphlet, 16pp, published by Oasis Books, London 1994. Reprinted in *TF* with the revised stanza breaks adopted here.

The Alien

Text follows the first of two *Disc* versions in arranging these poems as a 3-part sequence. They have not previously been published as such but this was clearly BG's intention at the time *Disc* was compiled. Part One was published as 'The Alien' in *The Invisible Reader*, ed. Bridget Penney & Paul Holman, Invisible Books, London 1995. Text follows this published version, as does the second *Disc* version – the first is considerably abridged. Parts Two & Three were published as 'Work World' & 'Pharmacopoeia' in *WNM* and dated 1997, erroneously since *Disc* was compiled in 1996.

The poems were not reprinted in intact form and BG appears to have abandoned the sequence as such by the time he compiled *MF* in which four fragments are collected under the title 'Liam's Song (*extracts*)' – confusingly, since they appear in neither the 1994 *Liam's Song* nor its rearrangement in *BSC*. 'Liam's Song (*extracts*)' consists of *The Alien* Part One sections beginning 'The room …', 'Like concentrating', 'Once …' and the first section of Part Three.

The Coal World: Murton Tales Reworked as Dialect Verse

First edition, a quarto pamphlet, published by Amra Imprint, Seaham 1995 'for 111th Durham Miners Gala', with preface by BG:

'These songs are based on episodes from F. N. Platt's book, *The Canny Man*, written in the 1970s about a Murton family, and especially Tim Platts who was born in the middle of the 19th century.

'The publication was issued when the author had already left the area, and affords no contact address of any kind. I have therefore to hope that no one will mind much about my adaptations, which I have tried to keep within the spirit of the original text (restoring a dialect context and providing a rough rhythmical format, compatible with song or chant.

'These episodes of life and inset stories seem far too good to let be forgotten in the manner most little press efforts get overlooked. I thought I would try to give them a new start …'

'The Box-Eggs' was collected in *MF*, omitting the final stanza.

The Lion Man or Four Poems in One

First edition, a quarto pamphlet, 29pp printed rectos only, published by Amra Imprint, Seaham 1995. Part Three as far as 'Ditto and ditto' was reprinted as 'The Lion Man' in *LMO* with two word-changes adopted here. Four sections of Part Three and one of Part Four were reprinted as 'Shopping' in *MF*. Some sections were also included in the *Disc* version of *Rousseau and the Wicked* (see below).

BG notes in the Amra edition:

'Part One: "For fire is a thief" – a quotation from the Anglo-Saxon Laws; kroang-ruangs – eastern boxing charms worn on the arm; Kamandi material from comic script by Jack Kirby; "Juvenes vestri visiones videbunt" – "your young men will see visions" (Latin of Joel 2.28).

'Part Three: "The evident God" – Keats, *Hyperion* Bk. 1; Sneffels – reference to Jules Verne *Voyage to the Centre of the Earth*.

'Part Four: "some sort of theistic hysteria" – from film script of *Inner Space*; Beveridge i.e.

his *Social Insurance and Allied Services* (1942); holo-anti-makariate – very unholy; drungars – commanders; oklo-biázamine – crowd trouble; paidiot – childish.'

Amra Pamphlets 1996

Single-poem pamphlets published in limited print-runs. 'On the Abuse of Drugs' was reprinted in *LMO*; sections 2, 3 & 6 renumbered 1-3 appeared as 'Medical Histories' in *MF*. 'The Genesis of Iron' was reprinted in *NS* & *MF*; text follows *MF* in removing stanza breaks. 'Hungary' was reprinted in *NS* & *MF* with slight variants – text follows *MF*. 'The Labyrinth' was reprinted in *MF*. 'On the Platform at Stockton' was reprinted in *BSC* & *MF*, where it accidentally continues with an unconnected and later poem, 'On The Trawler'.

Baldur's Lacrimosa

First edition, an A5 pamphlet, 24pp, published by Writers Forum, London 1996. Text follows *Disc*'s minor revisions, mainly to punctuation.

Rousseau and the Wicked

First edition published by Invisible Books, London 1996, 64pp. [*RW*]

Our text follows the *RW* version. In *Disc* the title is given to a sequence of 113 poems with BG's headnote 'published by Invisible Books as a selection from the below. Unneeded material shaped to form The Lion Man.' In our text the poems diverted to 'The Lion Man' have been returned to that sequence. BG diverted other 'unneeded material' to 'Quad' (p.491), 'The Fire' (p.494) and 'Paul's Survival Tips' (p.495). Four unpublished poems from the *Disc* version are gathered in the appendix.

RW includes the following notes by BG:

1: Quotation is from Sir Gavin de Beer's *Jean-Jacques Rousseau and the World* (London, 1972) p.89. Wootton is a country house in Derbyshire.

2: The allusion is to Jane Austen's *Northanger Abbey*.

4: The quotation is from the introduction to the *British National Formulary* (1982).

5 & 6 include extracts from letters written me from HMP Wandsworth.

9: The allusion is to the work of George Herbert.

10: wairsh: insipidness; bellant: lead poisoning.

11: The allusion is to *Hamlet*.

12: The quotation is an Income Support formula.

13: imago: final butterfly stage. The quotations are from Arthur R. Thompson's *Nature by Night* (London, 1949) ch. 11.

14: cracky: gossipy.

15: lickerty: at a fast pace.

17: The fossil block in question was raised from the pit just prior to closure and is believed by some to be a Coal-Age tree trunk. The quotation is from W. Appleby's introduction to J. Granger's *General View of the Agriculture of the County of Durham* (London, 1794). lowper: something that leaps.

30: The Tin Islands or 'Cassiterides' was the Ancient Greek name for Britain (or part of it).

38: speed: go fast or succeed.

43: six footed refinement: hexameter compatibility.

45: Silver fur is the attribute of Hanuman.

46: A reworking of an Egyptian text in K. Sethe's *Dramatische Texte zu altegyptischen Mysterienspiele* (Leipzig, 1928).

49: On the curious status of *Oreopithecus* see Vernon Reynolds' *The Apes* (London, 1968) p.102.

50: graval: as if from grave (noun).

52: The allusion is to the work of John Donne. netty: toilet.

55: The allusion is to the work of Arthur Hugh Clough. couthed: recognised; baff week: non-pay week.

Four poems were reprinted in *MF*: 13 ('Evolving'), 19 ('Self-Analysis'), 42 ('Back Garden') and 47 ('Toy World'). 7, with some revision, is incorporated in 'Reveries' 9 (p.485).

Other Poems

'On the Bridge.' *Disc* note 'concerns esp. the designs of Sunderland pottery.'

'Marquisisms.' *Disc* note 'the statue of the 3rd Marquis in Durham Market Place appears to point at the Cathedral itself.'

'The Ace & Other Scenes.' Published in *Active in Airtime* 1 (Colchester, 1992).

'In Rufinum (after Claudian).' The passage '"Flectite signa ..." to '... varii dracones' appears as 'Claudian on Dragons' in *MF*; text follows a few revisions in *Disc*.

'At the Nevsky Promenade.' Collected in 'Newcastle from a Van Window', *Tyne Txts* (with Tom Pickard), Amra Imprint in association with Morden Poets (Newcastle upon Tyne, 2004).

'Rat to Boat-Master.' Published in *Angel Exhaust* 8 (Southend 1992).

'Petimusque Damusque.' Published in *Horace Whom I Hated So*, ed. Harry Gilonis, Five Eyes of Wiwaxia (London, 1992). Not in *Disc* or *Files*.

'Found Potato Poem.' Collected in *MF*.

'Dragons.' Published as 'On Dragons' in *EE*. Text follows the revised version in *LMO* supported by *Disc*.

'Gang Poem.' Published in *EE*.

'Introduction to a Library.' Collected in *MF*.

'Contribution to Kelvin's Project.' Published in *Short Attention Span*, ed. Kelvin Corcoran, Between Meetings (Cheltenham, 1995).

'The City of Egypt.' Published in *Motley for Mottram: Tributes to Eric Mottram on his 70th Birthday*, ed. Bill Griffiths & Bob Cobbing, Amra Imprint & Writers Forum (Seaham & London, 1994).

'On Show.' *Disc* note to quoted passage: 're Westminster Abbey, 1643.'

'Jingle.' Collected in *MF*.

'Claudian on Transport.' *Disc* note: 'uses various Latin texts of the author, esp. De Lucasta (on the lobster).'

'Birds & Wind' & 'On the Beach.' Published in *Object Permanence* 2 (Glasgow, 1994).

'Detective Notes.' Collected in *WNM*.

'Anti-Sound Poems.' *Disc* notes 'published in And for Bob's birthday' (item untraced and not recorded in the Jones bibliography).

'How Highpoint is Better than Wandsworth.' Collected in *MF* & *TF*. Variants in *TF* are adopted here as BG's later revision. *Disc* includes a few slightly variant sections as 'Appendix'; one which is entirely new is inserted here as the penultimate section. *TF* text ends at 'single sleepers it dreams'. Some sections, alongside letters from Delvan MacIntosh and some BG replies, appear in *Seventy-Six Day Wanno, Mississippi and Highpoint Journal*, Amra Imprint (Seaham [1993]). Luke Roberts has identified two states of this pamphlet, in one of which (possibly the earlier) additional letters appear instead of the poems.

'The Best Jigsaw.' Collected in *MF*.

'Two Poems for Bob Cobbing in One Style.' Published in *And* 9 (London, 1995). The first poem was collected in *MF* as 'Bob Cobbing in London'.

'Reveries.' Published in *Conductors of Chaos*, ed. Iain Sinclair, Picador (London, 1996). Poems 6 & 9 collected in *MF*.

'Umbro.' Published by Short Run (Cheltenham, 1995). Appendix supplied by *Disc*.

'Quad.' Collected in *MF* & *LMO*. All except the last of these poems were included in the *Disc* version of 'Rousseau and the Wicked'.

'The Fire.' All except the second stanza included in the *Disc* version of 'Rousseau and the Wicked'.

'Paul's Survival Tips.' Published in *Talus* 9-10 (London, 1997). The first poem was included in the *Disc* version of 'Rousseau and the Wicked'.

'Media Studies.' Collected in *NS*.

'Musical Note.' Published in *Talus* 9-10 (London, 1997).

'Thirteen Thoughts …' Published in *WNM*.

'[Untitled].' Published in *Etruscan Jetty: Anthology of the Six Towns Poetry Festival Nov 1st, 2nd, 3rd 1996*, Etruscan Books (Newcastle under Lyme, 1996). Footnote states 'Commissioned by *6tpf* to launch etruscan books.' Not in *Disc* or *Files*.

'The Durham Coal-Field.' Published in *Talisman: A Journal of Contemporary Poetry and Poetics* 16 (Jersey City, 1996). Not in *Disc* or *Files*.

Alphabetical List of Titles

Account, 151
The Ace & Other Scenes, 393
The Alien, 230
All Saints: MFV Golden Arrow, 21
Alliterations, 411
Alphabet of Tories, 183
Amra Pamphlets 1996, 305
Anti-Sound Poems, 463
At the Nevsky Promenade, 405
Baldur's Lacrimosa, 325
Birds & Wind, 458
The Best Jigsaw,, 472
The Borrowers Aloft, 457
The Box-Eggs, 268
Calendar Contents, 13
Carol, 22
The City of Egypt, 437
Claudian on Transport, 455
The Coal World: Murton Tales Reworked as Dialect Verse, 263
The Coggly, 140
Conan in Trouble, 159
Contribution to Kelvin's Project, 437
Delvan in the SW London Magistrates Court, 153
Delvan's Book, 149
Detective Notes, 461
Dialect Poems incorporating The Cuddy Anthem: a mini dialect anthology, 121
'Did 'oo heer that hinney?', 142
'Dragons', 420
The Durham Coal-Field, 509
Elements, 15
The Emergency, 125
The Fire, 494
Fish, 454
Found Potato Poem, 419
Gang Poem, 427
The Genesis of Iron, 311
The Great North Forest, 31
Hanuman, 161

Harley, 396
The Haswell Change-Over, 75
Histories, 313
The Hog, 456
Hoo the Rabbits Wor Horribly Thret, 270
How Highpoint is Better than Wandsworth, 465
Hungary, 316
'If yi dinna pay yor poll-tax ower', 124
In Church, 447
In Rufinum (after Claudian), 399
In the Neet, 141
Introduction to a Library, 435
'It'z a puzzle OK', 123
Jetty Song, 138
Jingle, 454
Kurt in Context, 70
The Labyrinth, 320
The Lion Man or Four Poems in One, 275
Letter (1), 157
Letter (2), 158
Liam's Song, 211
'Lookanaw! Aa dreamt this g'eat mammy-church', 133
'Looksthanaw', 130
Marquisisms, 390
Maxims for St Swithin's Day, 28
Media Studies, 498
Medical Report, 160
Mid North Sea High, 49
Moon-Time (2), 19
Moon-Time, 18
More Bike (Perpetual Motion), 397
The Move, 267
Musical Note, 499
Name, 412
New Year, 448
Night-Rings, 24
Notes, 390

'Nows in the g'eat hwelve', 123
On Christianity, 176
On Show, 451
On St Benet's Day, 21
On the Abuse of Drugs, 307
On the Beach, 460
On the Bridge, 389
On the Platform at Stockton, 322
On the Sun, 69
On the Tyne, 139
On TV, 173
On Vane Tempest Provisionally Shut, 23 October, in the Afternoon, 1992, 144
Other Poems, 387
The Owl, 442
Paladin Try To Get Payment To Me Split Into Two Cheques, 188
Palm Sunday (2), 29
Palm Sunday, 26
The Parlous Chyase (after Lewis Carroll), 137
Paul's Survival Tips, 495
Perpetuum Mobile, 441
'Petimusque Damusque', 417
Picture, 392
Poem ('Lazarus'), 418
Poem ('The force that thru …'), 419
Poem ('this / is work to'), 435
Quad, 491
Quest, 410
Quotidiana, 67
Quotidians, 27
Rain-Time (2), 17
Rain-Time, 16
Rat to Boat-Master, 413
Retraction, 416
Reverie, 152
Reveries, 478
Review of Brian Greenaway & Notes from Delvan MacIntosh, 85

Ride
Rousseau and the Wicked, 341
Sandwiches, 29
Satires, 167
Scaffold Hill, 105
The Secret Commonwealth, 221
Settling Accounts, 189
Sextet, 408
Spare Stanzas, 415
St Cecilia's Day, 19
St Valentine's Day (2), 24
Star Fish Jail, 190
Starting the Fight, 445
Starting Up With Doves, 79
The Strike, 272
Sunday, 25
Terzetto, 153
'There sartenly is some canny mysteries', 128
Thirteen Thoughts as though Woken in Caravan Town …, 501
The Tilcon Quarry, 134
Tom, 266
The Tories, 174
The Trapper Boy Starts Work, 265
Two Poems for Bob Cobbing in One Style, 475
Umbro, 489
[Untitled] 'Chucking the / carpet in the tip', 71
[Untitled] 'House-breakers …', 73
[Untitled] 'In the brick middle ovens', 508
[Untitled] 'It's Sylvester's Day', 83
[Untitled] 'Quiz-miss', 72
[Untitled] 'Sanger the showman worked like this', 74
[Untitled] 'Shit! / A pub-full of myrmidons', 72
[Untitled] 'What does the Gym do?', 82
Valentine's Day, 17

Vampire, 412
Verses in Awe, 405
Wandsworth, 156
'We are upaheet, upaheet, upaheet', 127
Wimbledon Court, 452
Winchester, 169
Work-Song (2), 23
Work-Song, 17
Work, 398
'Ye can keep Pensher', 132

REALITY STREET titles in print

Poetry series

Kelvin Corcoran: *Lyric Lyric* (1993)
Maggie O'Sullivan: *In the House of the Shaman* (1993)
Allen Fisher: *Dispossession and Cure* (1994)
Fanny Howe: *O'Clock* (1995)
Maggie O'Sullivan (ed.): *Out of Everywhere* (1996)
Cris Cheek/Sianed Jones: *Songs From Navigation* (1997)
Lisa Robertson: *Debbie: An Epic* (1997)
Maurice Scully: *Steps* (1997)
Denise Riley: *Selected Poems* (2000)
Lisa Robertson: *The Weather* (2001)
Lawrence Upton *Wire Sculptures* (2003)
Ken Edwards: *eight + six* (2003)
Redell Olsen: *Secure Portable Space* (2004)
Peter Riley: *Excavations* (2004)
Allen Fisher: *Place* (2005)
Tony Baker: *In Transit* (2005)
Jeff Hilson: *stretchers* (2006)
Maurice Scully: *Sonata* (2006)
Maggie O'Sullivan: *Body of Work* (2006)
Sarah Riggs: *chain of minuscule decisions in the form of a feeling* (2007)
Carol Watts: *Wrack* (2007)
Jeff Hilson (ed.): *The Reality Street Book of Sonnets* (2008)
Peter Jaeger: *Rapid Eye Movement* (2009)
Wendy Mulford: *The Land Between* (2009)
Allan K Horwitz/Ken Edwards (ed.): *Botsotso* (2009)
Bill Griffiths: *Collected Earlier Poems* (2010)
Fanny Howe: *Emergence* (2010)
Jim Goar: *Seoul Bus Poems* (2010)
James Davies: *Plants* (2011)
Carol Watts: *Occasionals* (2011)
Paul Brown: *A Cabin in the Mountains* (2012)
Maggie O'Sullivan: *Waterfalls* (2012)
Peter Hughes: *Allotment Architecture* (2013)
Andrea Brady: *Cut From the Rushes* (2013)
Bill Griffiths: *Collected Poems & Sequences* (2014)
Peter Hughes: *Quite Frankly* (2015)
Emily Critchley (ed.): *Out of Everywhere 2* (2015)

Narrative series

Ken Edwards: *Futures* (1998, reprinted 2010)
John Hall: *Apricot Pages* (2005)
David Miller: *The Dorothy and Benno Stories* (2005)
Douglas Oliver: *Whisper 'Louise'* (2005)
Paul Griffiths: *let me tell you* (2008)
John Gilmore: *Head of a Man* (2011)
Richard Makin: *Dwelling* (2011)
Leopold Haas: *The Raft* (2011)
Johan de Wit: *Gero Nimo* (2011)
David Miller (ed.): *The Alchemist's Mind* (2012)
Sean Pemberton: *White* (2012)
Ken Edwards: *Down With Beauty* (2013)
Philip Terry: *tapestry* (2013)
Lou Rowan: *Alphabet of Love Serial* (2015)

For updates on titles in print, a listing of out-of-print titles, and to order Reality Street books, please go to www.realitystreet.co.uk. *For any other enquiries, email* info@realitystreet.co.uk *or write to the address on the reverse of the title page.*

REALITY STREET depends for its continuing existence on the Reality Street Supporters scheme. For details of how to become a Reality Street Supporter, or to be put on the mailing list for news of forthcoming publications, write to the address on the reverse of the title page, or email **info@realitystreet.co.uk**

Visit our website at: **www.realitystreet.co.uk/supporter-scheme.php**

Reality Street Supporters who have sponsored this book:

Joanne Ashcroft
Alan Baker
Tony Baker
Peter Bamfield
Tina Bass
Fred Beake
Chris Beckett
Charles Bernstein
John Bloomberg-Rissman
Jasper Brinton
Manuel Brito
Peter Brown
Clive Bush
Duncan Campbell
John Cayley
Cris Cheek
Stephen Clews
Simon Collings
Clare Connors
Ian Davidson
David Dowker
Laurie Duggan
Carrie Etter
Allen Fisher
Jim Goar & Sang-yeon Lee
Paul Griffiths
Chris Gutkind
Catherine Hales
John Hall
Jeff Hilson
Peter Hodgkiss
Rob Holloway
Peter Hughes
Michael Hunt
Keith Jebb

Nicholas Johnson
Pierre Joris
Linda Kemp
Lisa Kiew
Joshua Kotin
Steve Lake
Tom Leonard
Chris Lord
Michael Mann
JCC Mays
James McDonald
Ian Mcewen
Maggie O'Sullivan
Richard Parker
Gareth Prior
Tom Quale
Josh Robinson
Samuel Rogers
Lou Rowan
Robert Sheppard
Iain Sinclair
Jason Skeet
Valerie Soar
Andrew Taylor
Philip Terry
Scott Thurston
Keith Tuma
Lawrence Upton
Stephen Want
Sam Ward
Carol Watts
John Wilkinson
Tyrone Williams
Lissa Wolsak
Anonymous x 1